JEAN RHYS
WOMAN IN PASSAGE

JEAN RHYS
WOMAN IN PASSAGE
A Critical Study
of the Novels of Jean Rhys

HELEN NEBEKER

EDEN PRESS
WOMEN'S PUBLICATIONS
Montréal Canada

JEAN RHYS: WOMAN IN PASSAGE
A Critical Study of the Novels of Jean Rhys
Helen Nebeker

Credits: Permission to quote copyrighted passages in Jean Rhys, *Quartet, After Leaving Mr. Mackenzie, Voyage in the Dark, Good Morning Midnight, Wide Sargasso Sea,* and *Smile, Please,* given by Andre Deutsch Limited, London, U.K., Harper & Row, Publishers, Incorporated, New York, and W. W. Norton & Company, Incorporated, New York. Back cover photo of Jean Rhys © Vogue Studio, Norman Eales, courtesy of Longmans Group, Ltd. Typesetting and Production: Vicky Bach and Molly Pulver. Front cover drawing by Linda Fulford. Cover design by J.W. Stewart.

ISBN: 0-920792-04-9
First Edition

Printed in Canada at John Deyell Company
Dépôt légal — deuxième trimestre 1981
Bibliothèque nationale du Québec

To

Sabrina Paige . .

My Little Princess

Sabrina fair,
　　Listen where thou art sitting
Under the glassie, cool, translucent wave,
　　In twisted braids of lillies knitting
　　The loose train of thy amber-dropping hair;
　　Listen for dear honor's sake,
Goddess of the silver lake,
　　Listen and save!

John Milton
(From *Comus*)

TABLE OF CONTENTS

PREFACE

The emergence of Jean Rhys as a major literary discovery of the twentieth century, after years of obscurity, is now almost common academic knowledge. Although she had published five books—four novels and a collection of short stories[1]—between 1927 and 1939, it was not until the publication of *Wide Sargasso Sea,* in 1966, that the prominence predicted forty years earlier by Ford Madox Ford in a preface to her collection of short stories, *The Left Bank,* was realized. Previously, her novels had achieved some critical acclaim by reviewers and reading public alike, but for various reasons Rhys disappeared from public view after the publication of *Good Morning, Midnight* in 1939, and her five books subsequently went out of print. Then, in 1958, the BBC revived interest in her works with a dramatization of *Good Morning, Midnight* and the outcome is literary history. Her latest novel, *Wide Sargasso Sea,* is a triumph; her other works have been reissued; she is being read throughout the world.

Born August 24, 1894, in the Windward Islands of the West Indies, her mother Creole and her father a Welsh doctor, Jean Rhys (rēs) was brought to England at sixteen to live with an aunt at Cambridge and to attend the Royal Academy of Dramatic Arts. At seventeen, however, her father, William Rhys Williams, died and she began a bohemian life as a chorus girl, touring provincial theatres until, after the first World War, she married a Dutch poet with whom she lived a vagabond existence in the demimonde of Paris and other Continental cities. Her experiences during these years form the framework for at least her first four novels.

Unfortunately, awareness of her biographical emphasis has often led critics either to dismiss Rhys's writings with veiled condescension or to praise it effusively as they assess only superficially her literary contribution. This condescension reveals itself in reviews such as this from the *New York Times* concerning Rhys's second novel, *After*

i

Leavng Mr. Mackenzie. The critic writes:

> The author has no interest in achieving anything except a portrait of a certain woman. . . . Miss Rhys's novel is the latest addition to the vast body of fiction which hails Flaubert as master. It offers no new note in treatment. . . .Miss Rhys's study, slight and certainly over-simplified as it is, contains many of the merits of its species. It succeeds in bringing the reader a small segment of life which is in turn an infinitesimal fragment of life.
>
> *New York Times Book Review*
> (June 28, 1931, p. 6)

Another later critic, Elgin Mellown,[2] addressing himself to the same novel, dismisses it summarily:

> . . . Rhys's point of view is so patently that of the main female character and so biased in her favor that the abrupt shifts into the thoughts of another character . . . destroy the continuity of the narrative and weaken its psychological verisimilitude. (p. 470)

This "main female character," this "portrait of a certain woman," becomes, ambivalently, either woman who lives by exploiting man or, as Mellown describes her, "woman, the victim of love who is destined to suffer in an environment hostile to her."[3] Thus, Rhys's critics reduce the female protagonists of her novels to a single character—a portrait of Rhys herself—who changes only in name and minor details of background. Concomitantly, working from the vantage point of biographical interpretation, they attribute ostensible defects of style and characterization—responsible, they believe, for her early obscurity—to failure to separate personal experience from aesthetic creation. This failure, they say, results in limited thematic impact. They further insist that it is only as she achieves objective distance from herself that she realizes her potential and finally creates that character whose "abasement and destruction"—as Martin Levin describes it—linger in the mind.

Ironically, even as they have written of Rhys's inability to separate fact from fiction, many critics—essentially male—fall into that very trap, imposing upon Rhys's characters and themes their peculiar subjective experience. In the process they veer sharply from the aesthetic reality. One sees this, for example, in an article such as Mellown's where, in order to prove his thesis that Rhys develops only one character, one psychological type in the body of her work, he avoids the publication sequence of the first four novels, arranging them, rather, according to their internal chronology. By so doing, he can show each succeeding protagonist becoming an older version of the former—young Anna (*Voyage in the Dark*, 1935) becoming a less innocent Marya (*Quartet*, 1928) who becomes a more desperate, abused Julia (*After Leaving Mr. Mackenzie*, 1931) who emerges as the disillusioned, suicidal Sasha of *Good Morning, Midnight* (1939). This approach, while offering a convenient evasion of many complexities and ambiguities in the novels, is, nevertheless, a major distortion. Such distortion not only permits perversion of Rhys's thematic progression but forces Mellown, quite logically, to separate Miss Rhys's last—and most powerful—novel from the mainstream of her art. Antoinette, that Creole heroine of *Wide Sargasso Sea* who marries Edward Rochester of Bronte's *Jane Eyre*, simply will not fit into the sequence.

That this wrenching disturbs him, at least subliminally, shows in his attempt, confused and abstract, to somehow integrate the novel—and Antoinette—into the current of Rhys's previous works:

> Here, then, spelled out clearer than in any of the previous novels, are the details of the life of the now familiar Rhys heroine: a happy childhood in a tropical state of nature, growth into adolescence without the presence of a father, a complete submission to physical love, the inevitable loss of that love, and the consequent misery. In one sense, then, . . . Antoinette Cosway *is* the embodiment of Marya, Julia, Anna, and Sasha. On the other hand, however, her character lies in a somewhat different sphere from theirs. They are shadows of an archetypal figure. . . . Antoinette, while a manifestation of the same archetypal figure, is however a positive character who is not to be confused with anyone else. She may be representative of nineteenth-century Creole girls at the mercy of fortune-hunting younger sons, and she may even be an example of tropical hot blood reacting to the icy restraint of the north, but she is not, like the other Rhys heroines, Woman with a capital W.

> Interestingly enough, Rochester does not share this individuality. Rhys's men all have basically the same

psychology; they are creatures with physical desires who have the power of simple, logical thinking. A man's heart, according to Rhys, is never much involved with his physical desires. (p. 472)

Without intending either scorn or undue harshness, passages such as this exemplify how critics have distorted and overlooked in their generalities Rhys's art and consequent thematic impact. Certainly anyone having more than a passing acquaintance with Rhys's works must take issue with the confusion and misinterpretation evident here. For example, how can a careful, thoughtful reading of Rhys's novel sustain the viewpoint that Rhys writes of "a happy childhood," of a "complete submission to physical love"? How can a questioning mind accept Antoinette as at one and the same time an embodiment of four other women, a "manifestation of the same archetypal figure" and yet antithetically "a character not to be confused with anyone else," not "like the other Rhys heroines, Woman with a capital W"? How can even the most literal reader dismiss Rhys's men as simple physical creatures, possessing no individuality, yet, paradoxically, having "the power of simple, logical thinking"?

Furthermore, in addition to this typical glossing over of particularities in favor of generalities concerning her characters and themes, critics have never substantively faced the basic critical question of Miss Rhys's undeniable power. If the body of her work consists of five extremely short novels—really scarcely more than novelettes (the short stories are not at issue here); if they are limited in their scope to the creation of a single character—and that character a prostitute whose experiences are confined to the limited existence of the demimonde of London and Paris; if even that dominant characterization is flawed in its development and hence its impact, how, then, does one account for the enthusiastic revival accorded Rhys's work? Is this acclaim a product primarily of the new emphasis on uncovering and reviving works of women authors, a direct result of the new feminist consciousness? Must the praise of Miss Rhys's stylistic power be suspect—in the light of her ostensible technical deficiencies—as at best specious, at worst effusively false? Can the almost dichotomous public reaction to her novels—either a puzzled indifference, a rejection of character and theme or an acclaim suspiciously excessive in terms of her limited output—be explained by any valid critical criteria? The attempt to answer and resolve these issues has been the genesis of this book.

II

My task as a critic has been three-fold. One, to free myself from the preconception that Rhys's plots and characters, overtly autobiographical in detail and experience, can offer the reader little but a limited view of life. Second, to resist the influence on the intellect arising from two sources: (1) previous critical pronouncements (2) the author's own international fame. Finally, to address myself to the unexplored complexities—technical and thematic—of the novels, first individually and then as an *oeuvre*, a thematically unified totality.

This has not been an easy undertaking. The final product presupposes on the part of the reader some acquaintance with Rhys's work and a willingness to suspend judgment: himself to go through the three-fold process explained above. This material will sometimes seem difficult; there is no easy way to unravel the consummate artistry and complexity of such deceptively simple work. To abstract and generalize would be convenient and probably preclude some criticism of both my method and style. But such an approach would be a refutation of my critical integrity and an insult to Miss Rhys's technical artistry and intellectual perception. Since this study stands as a pioneer, hopefully opening the door for other in-depth evaluation, I have chosen for method the only valid approach: a study of each novel as an entity, in chronological order as Rhys published them. Only in such controlled analysis will we be able to ascertain her growth as an artist and as a woman searching for her own answers to the complexities of life. This method (undoubtedly tedious to some) requires much of the reader: a retentive mind and a commitment to respect an intellect grappling with a world of ideas both old and new, through the medium of her art.

III

Rhys begins this grappling tentatively, uneasily, in her first novel, *Quartet* (1928), where, through characters caught in sordid circumstances of life closely paralleling her own, she attempts to sort out the moral and intellectual framework of her world. That she does this emotionally and unevenly should not be surprising in a young artist. That, despite the uncontrolled emotion and consequent unevenness, she should so clearly evoke the stifling ghost of her Victorian heritage attests to the clarity of her artistic perception, conscious or otherwise.

Building upon premises she establishes tenuously for herself in *Quartet,* Rhys moves into greater complexities with her second novel, *After Leaving Mr. Mackenzie* (1931). Here she complicates our critical task as she continues probing for a controlling metaphor or myth through which she can convey her emerging vision. The evolution of this metaphor will lead Rhys—and me—through shadowy mazes of Freudian symbols and into the Jungian world of mythic archetype. At this point, I must acknowledge my awareness of the dangerous paths I tread. I know that this critical approach will be anathema to some, that archetypal interpretation in particular is bound to raise the hackles of many critics. Foes of psychological interpretation—Freudian or Jungian—will insist with some validity that such criticism is ''imposition'' upon what may not have been authorial intention and that such intention must be the decisive factor in any interpretation. While I appreciate the premises from which they operate, the fact remains that these antagonists flail at a body of work of reputable and acknowledged mythologists, psychoanalysts, religionists, anthropologists, philosophers and critical theorists too numerous to list, let alone discuss. To rule out their ideas, ideas which have become a part of the collective knowledge of the liberally educated, is to dismiss out of hand a vast critical discussion, a discussion embracing ancient myth, Judeo scripture, Greek classics, Roman epic, Shakespearean tragedy, Miltonic Christianity, not to mention a whole *oeuvre* of more modern literature.

Therefore, while acknowledging the right of any individual critic to reject psychological or archetypal interpretation as a personal bias, I nevertheless rest my case for such an interpretation upon two factors: (1) the groundwork already laid—and generally assimilated—by reputable scholars; (2) the critical demands placed upon me by Rhys's work itself.

This second point returns us to the issue of authorial intent as the decisive factor in valid interpretation. I suggest—as have many others —that conscious intent *cannot* be the primary consideration, that the conscious awareness of an artist is always at the mercy of the unconscious. But, of course, with this declaration we have come full circle to arrive at an impasse, an impasse rooted in acceptance or rejection of so-called Freudian-Jungian theory. Miss Rhys herself, in a personal comment to me written in the last months of her life, points up this dilemma:

I do feel that [you read] into my books a lot that I didn't

mean, except there is 'I know but I know not how I know.' As a matter of fact, Freud, Adler and so on are just names to me and I know little about Jean-Paul Sartre and the Existentialists. Also I'm not, strictly speaking, a feminist at all. However, as I say, it is impossible to be quite certain of what is underneath what one writes, perhaps unconsciously. Or indeed, what is underneath anything. . . .

Diana Athill, Rhys's editor at Andre Deutsch, reinforces this controversy of conscious versus unconscious intent when she writes me in a letter dated September 1, 1978:

Jean's own often, often, often repeated account of herself as a writer is that she starts from fact, the compulsion being to *get it right,* to get it down exactly as it really was; then, because *shape* is tremendously important, she has to leave out this or enlarge that—the book itself, taking shape under her hands, dictates what is left out or changed or enlarged. It 'takes over'. And that is that. Well—that myths get themselves expressed through such an almost mediumistic procedure is one explanation—one interpretation—of what goes on. . . .

Then, admitting that "none of us here are Jungians—none of us really believe it," she nevertheless concludes, "Having known Jean for years I am convinced that she is much more an 'instinct' than an 'intellect'—her power coming from her mysterious (and of course mystery is there) *need* to be exact—to get as near as she can to the truth of an experience." Finally, in a marvelous postscript, Athill writes: "She [Jean] once said to me 'There are times when I feel as though I were a pen in someone else's hand.' It was when she was telling how she never *intended* to write a book and really rather resented the fact that she kept on having to. At other times, tho', she has made it clear that if she stops having something to write she will be dead - or desperate to be so, supposing it doesn't happen automatically."

Thus, admitting the unresolvable dilemma, I return to my assertion that the author's intent is less significant than the artistic creation. The validity of an interpretation must be tested not by what one imagines was—or was not—the author's original intent but by what emerges in the finished product.

And so, in *After Leaving Mr. Mackenzie,* we can see Rhys reflecting the chaos of her world, consciously and unconsciously, in the ideological currency of her time—the currency of psychoanalysis, socialism, existentialism, etc. She was a sensitive artist living among other artists and intellectuals. The world they inhabited was falling apart around them, even as it was rising Phoenix-like in new social and philosophic forms. Rhys would have needed no formal knowledge of Freud, Jung, socialism, existentialism in order to respond to these currents in the Zeitgeist. Jean-Paul Sartre and existentialism are only words; the sense of "nothingness" is real and universal. Freud, Jung, Adler and their probings are clinical and academic; the urgings of the inner self are immediate and uncontrollable. Against this background of social and personal stirrings, in psychological and archetypal motifs, Rhys fleshes out women and men whose frustrations will torment us and whose pain will tear our eyes. Deftly sketching all the circumscription of their lives, she will link and merge peoples and times until the lives of all women and men in all times and places are meshed inextricably in a symphony of exquisite pain. And chillingly underneath runs the eternal current: the theme of "nothingness" that haunts the human race and the realization that the one clear truth of existence is the fact of "nothing."

From this theme of "nothingness," the existential reality, Rhys moves onward in her third published novel to the *Voyage in the Dark* (1935), a journey into psychic shadows through which she will take the reader who is disciplined to her demands. Moving surely now into her metaphor—and toward ultimate mythopoesis—Rhys employs one of the most common Jungian archetypes, the journey or pilgrimage in search of the lost Eden. This journey is, of course, the search for SELF. As Anna Morgan, the narrator-protagonist, takes her journey into the unconscious memories and fears that manipulate her life, so the reader makes a journey into personal awareness, hopefully emerging—reborn, as it were—into the light of self-acceptance.

But in Anna's symbolic death and rebirth, her personal journey into the dark, Rhys will open to our vision yet another level of complexity. This final complexity—fusing every detail of every novel and culminating in the fire and brilliance of that great novel *Wide Sargasso Sea*—will take us into a dark, almost forgotten racial memory of a prehistoric time when the *Female Principle* dominated. This was before the Judaic-Christian patriarchal myth had subdued the god-goddess worship of Graeco-Olympian mythology, a mythology which itself had absorbed—though not quite destroyed—the more ancient Celtic religions of prehistoric goddess-worship. Understanding this, we will see how, in increasingly focused and controlled mythopoesis, Rhys has turned from the restrictive male-centered vision of *Quartet* and *After Leaving Mr. Mackenzie* and has reconstructed the dim outlines of a female-centered myth (long lost in the mists of time) in which woman had dignity and function and was accorded worship and love because of her unique female nature.

Unfortunately, however, in Rhys's myth, this ancient reality has long been dead, leaving woman estranged—probably forever—from her archetypal SELF. And though Rhys permits Anna to make her journey of discovery and to profit perhaps therefrom, for Rhys, herself, the journey seems to have brought not life but death.

This theme of the living dead is developed in the person of Sasha, the narrator-protagonist of *Good Morning, Midnight* (1939), the last of the four novels which critics have designated autobiographical. Rhys, using a superbly controlled, first-person narrative focus, permits Sasha to reveal her appalling awareness of herself and the world she inhabits. For Sasha, there is no hope, no illusion. She has "no pride, no name, no face, no country." Fat, middle-aged, a former prostitute by necessity and choice, Sasha attempts to drink herself to death, living on a small inheritance which obviates any further dependence upon the largesse of men. But, in Paris, on a holiday financed by a woman friend, Sasha—perhaps surrogate for Rhys—finally acknowledges *and accepts* the terrible "blackness" or "nothingness" which is life—or death! Sasha's ultimate abjuration of fear, her willingness to face symbolic death—in essence the archetypal rite of initiation which Rhys has indicated in earlier works—is the whole process of *Good Morning, Midnight*.

Sadly, despite their praise for the novel and what has been called its "unnerving dénouement," critics have consistently ignored Rhys's careful insistence on detail, thereby missing not only the thematic intent of *Good Morning, Midnight* but also the thematic progression of Rhys's works as a body. As they avoid coming to grips with the paradoxes inherent in the title, as they fail to examine the significance of Rhys's use of Emily Dickinson's brief poem as epigram to the work, critics indicate clearly their innocence of her supreme artistic control. Obviously such points must be examined carefully in the body of this work.

My critical task culminates in an examination of *Wide Sargasso Sea*, first as an entity and then in its relation to Charlotte Bronte's *Jane Eyre*. Although critics generally see this last novel as essentially outside the mainstream of Rhys's preceding works (in other words, it is no longer autobiographical), such is not the case. For it is in this final, brilliant novel that Rhys redefines for herself and her readers all the themes she has previously explored, that she completes her myth of woman's reality and that she postulates the only viable solution to the problems inherent in that reality.

Choosing to synthesize her myth of woman in the person of the mad Bertha Mason Rochester, shadowy, beastlike creature of *Jane Eyre*, Rhys creates from Bronte's original character the compelling and fiery Antoinette Cosway, the young Jamaican Creole heiress who had married the youthful Rochester. Imprisoned in the cold, dark chamber at Thornfield Hall, Antoinette (now Bertha), in moments of apparent lucidity, views in retrospect the debacle of her life. Rhys's choice of Bronte's minor character, Bertha, for her protagonist, Antoinette, is no happenstance, no product of mere sympathy for the under-dog, as has been suggested. By careful contrivance or brilliant intuition, Rhys uses this masterpiece of a nineteenth-century authoress to illustrate and deepen a major theme toward which she has been working. For nineteenth-century Charlotte Bronte, a victim of Victorian middle-class bigotry, prudery and repression, had found escape, perhaps even sanity, by creating from the window of her personal experience the character of Jane Eyre, a woman crushed as Bronte herself had been by the weight of the Victorian ethic. Thus Bronte, in both her person and her artistic creation, is the predecessor of twentieth-century Rhys who, trapped in essentially the same Victorian ethic as Charlotte and Jane, has also sought escape, personally and artistically. *Jane Eyre*, then, when we understand fully what Rhys is about, provides added dimension for *Wide Sargasso Sea*, which, in turn, contributes such overtones to Bronte's nineteenth-century work that it can never again be read innocently. In fact, *Jane Eyre*, read in the light of *Wide Sargasso Sea*, emerges as a new work and provides further comprehension of the unconscious forces which perhaps shaped the mind and art of Bronte.

This interpretation, however, is so complicated, so interwoven with all that Rhys has previously developed, that it cannot be delineated in a brief preface. Suffice it to say that *Wide Sargasso Sea* emerges as a crescendo of pain for all poor mad creatures, buffeted as they are by the "wild blast" of the gods of the universe even as they struggle with the devils of their own tortured souls. This pain will devolve, as we re-read *Jane Eyre*, into an overwhelming sense of pity and horror—tragedy in its truly classic sense—as we are forced to the inescapable truth of Rhys's myth. There is, we realize, no triumph, no ultimate hope for woman *or* man. The cycle of life-death continues endlessly. There is no way back to the Garden of Eden.

Thus, finally, we will arrive at full awareness of Rhys's power as an artist. Seeking in the blackness of the prison of her female existence a light of hope, searching for some dignity in her personal female identity, Rhys discovers—and finally accepts—what is for her, truth. In so doing, she speaks to men and women alike, as they take tortuously their own dark voyages into the secret realm of knowledge, only to discover the implacability of the eternal cycle.

This discovery is the end of our critical search.

Chapter 1

QUARTET [4]

THE GENESIS OF MYTH

> . . .Beware
> Of good Samaritans—walk to the right
> Or hide thee by the roadside out of sight
> Or greet them with the smile that villains wear.
>
> R.C. Dunning

In Jean Rhys's earliest novel, *Quartet,* originally published in 1928 under the title *Postures* and almost off-handedly dismissed as sentimentally autobiographical, melodramatic, aesthetically unconvincing, we get our first glimpse of Rhys's complexity and latent genius. Inexplicably, critics seem unaware that in this supposedly slight work Rhys begins an intellectual exploration which will culminate only with the writing of *Wide Sargasso Sea,* some forty years later. For, in fact, in the story of Marya Zelli, Rhys develops far more than a stereotyped portrait of "woman fallen into prostitution because she is the victim of her own unassuageable desires"—the synthesized protagonist which Rhys's critics have created from their own subjective responses. (See Preface discussion.) Far from being so simplistic, Rhys carefully sketches the complexity of four human beings caught in biological, emotional, social and linguistic constructs. In so doing, she lays bare the bones of the social-intellectual-philosophic heritage bequeathed the twentieth century by the Victorian age. This skeleton in the closet of Anglo-Saxon culture has only recently been acknowledged and its insidious impact increasingly examined. It is against an unconsciously sensed but not yet delineated Victorian framework that Rhys reveals the economic helplessness and the emotional sterility of woman, trapped as she is in a world controlled exclusively by the materialistic Anglo-Saxon male.

Ingeniously, however, out of what might have resulted in only a mish-mash of intellectual and social clichés, Rhys transforms platitude into art. Transcending her seeming homiletic on the plight of woman in a world corrupted by men, she moves into an examination of the chains which bind not only women but men. In so doing, she reveals clearly and compassionately that man, too, is victimized, circumscribed by forces which he cannot recognize and by women who use the myth of their frailty and childishness as weapons against the men they ambivalently exploit and despise. Thus, even in her first, perhaps most imperfect novel, Rhys clearly reveals that she is a woman many years ahead of her time. She also refutes unquestionably the charge that she writes only from a restricted female view about only "a certain kind of woman."

II

The plot of *Quartet,* told from a shifting, seemingly uncontrolled narrative focus, concerns the plight of twenty-eight-year-old Marya Zelli, who accepts the friendship and protection of a British couple, Lois and Hugh (H.J.) Heidler, when Stephan, her thirty-six-year-old husband, is arrested in Paris for theft or larceny. Heidler, with his wife's connivance, soon entices Marya into an affair, at first a *ménage à trois* and then, because of Lois's animosity, a separate arrangement. A year later, with Stephan released from prison and facing immediate deportation, Marya temporarily returns to him out of loyalty, Heidler having indignantly broken off their affair because, as he says, "I've never shared a woman in my life, not knowingly anyhow, and I'm not going to start now." Marya attempts to tell Stephan of the demoralizing year she has endured: the affair with Heidler, the scorn of Lois, her final terrible emptiness. However, instead of the pity and consolation she hopes for, Stephan hears her confession with contempt, manifests hatred for her weakness and, finally, in theatrical rage, threatens vengeance against Heidler. Marya turns on him violently, screaming out her love for Heidler, whereupon Stephan walks out, only to be immediately picked up by a prostitute of brief acquaintance.

On the surface, the superficiality of this plot, the defect of narrative focus, the lack of motivation and function in minor characters, the almost undisguised autobiography, the melodrama of the ending seem sufficient to cancel any aesthetic impact or thematic significance. Unbelievably though, the impact is there! One puts down the novel—less than two hundred brief pages—disturbed, impressed, only to read again, hoping to discover what has been missed. Suddenly recognition overwhelms. For beneath the surface facts of Rhys's personal experience as a Marya Zelli unfolds the Victorian framework already discussed: the Zeitgeist, the world-view of Marya *née* Jean, shaped as it is by the philosophy of the time and reinforced by its literature and language. It is this undercurrent to which Rhys's contemporary readers responded and which more innocent readers rejected, unable to understand it consciously or to acknowledge it unconsciously.

Once this underlying historical-philosophical framework is discovered, the alleged technical[5] and intellectual defects of the novel emerge in a different light. That is, enmeshed in social and intellectual concepts tacitly accepted but largely unexamined, circumscribed by conventions of language and vision not even suspected by most of her generation, Rhys has attempted in *Quartet* to give some semblance of coherence to the truths she ''feels'' but cannot verbalize. Thus, the defects of the novel are inherent in the incoherence of the world she views. The narrative focus cannot be stabilized because too many possibilities for exploration exist. Minor characters invade the plot to mouth intellectual views more or less tenable but not yet tested and accepted by either Rhys or her protagonist. The dénouement must be melodramatic because for the Maryas of the world there is no order, no hope—only rejection by the men to whom they cling and self-hatred and fear within themselves. But out of this mélange, Rhys begins to mould a body of truth which will metamorphose into mythopoesis within the context of her next four novels.

III

To understand the genesis of Rhys's myth-making process, we must look beneath the abstraction of plot to particularities. *Quartet* opens in Paris of 1922, where Marya, British expatriate, has gone hoping to escape the ugliness, the coldness and sterility she associates with London. Here in Paris, with a profligate, lying husband, Marya,

"reckless, lazy, a vagabond by nature," is "for the first time in her life
. . .very near to being happy." Drawn to the "sordid streets," the
"gay" restaurants, the "wild gaieties" of her "very gentle and expert
lover" husband, who is paradoxically a "stranger and alien" and a
"bad lot," Marya consciously rejects her previous Anglo-Saxon world
of repression, bourgeois prejudice, poverty and brutality. Ambivalently, however, she associates respectability, intelligence, solidity,
masculine strength with all that is English. Similarly, even though she
embraces that which is French or foreign (Stephan is a Pole with
implications of Jewishness) as earthy, vital, warm, even "life, itself,"
Marya realizes that this world of gaiety is fantasy, illusion, never solid,
real. The English, she knows, " 'touch life with gloves on. . .pretending
about something all the time. . .quite nice and decent things of course.
But still. . .' ". The French, however, seemingly so different, " 'pre-
tend every bit as much, only about different things and not so obviously. . .' " (p. 7). Thus Marya clearly realizes that, ultimately, nothing is
what it seems. It is this "unreality of everything" that overwhelms
Marya, probably a surrogate for Rhys, herself twenty-eight in 1922.

Almost certainly self-projection accounts in part for certain technical deficiencies of *Quartet*. Too close to the reality of the Maryas of
the early twentieth century to objectify and poetize, Rhys has not yet
discovered the metaphor which will enable her to do so and thus find
her theme. At this point in her development, both as person and
author, she can only concoct a kind of *pot au feu* of personal and social
commentary. Life, she says, through her character, Marya, is a tawdry
"game" wherein the rich exploit and the poor suffer. Men, she suggests, are beasts; they exploit the weak and defenseless women who
depend upon them and they, in turn, exploit and humiliate each other
because of the economic realities of their lives. Ultimately, used and
rejected, the artistic woman adrift in this alien world has no hope, no
resource except to throw herelf upon the mercy of another man who
will, by the very nature of things, use her sexually and again betray
her.

Many of Rhys's ideas are, of course, reaction to the Victorian
Zeitgeist which was her reality. The turbulent history of social reform in
late Victorian and Edwardian England—particularly the evolution of
the socialist and women's rights movements—is common knowledge
thanks to much recent scholarship. But the Victorian-derived assump-
tions which still bound the minds of those oblivious to the changing
reality is less widely comprehended. Briefly then, and generally, what

4

would have been the "reality" of turn-of-the-century Anglo-Saxons—the milieu in which a Jean Rhys would have matured? [6]

Essentially, it was Victorian in concept: male dominated, Anglo-Saxon, materialistic. Therefore, in *Quartet*, Heidler, the protector and subsequent exploiter, is English of German descent and obviously free from economic concern. Epitomizing the late-Victorian stereotype, he is a "tall, fair man of perhaps forty-five. . .shoulders tremendous. . .eyes . . .light blue and intelligent. . .with an underlying. . .brutality. . .kind, peaceful and exceedingly healthy." (pp. 10, 13). Because the economic facts of the time so dictated, such men were woman's only life-line—males who would protect, cherish, harbor (hopefully in the sacred bonds of matrimony) from the harsh realities of a cruel world.

Furthermore, in this culture which Rhys would have inherited, woman lived in an Aristotelian oriented world of either-or, black-white. Thus, either a woman was a "respectable lady" or she was not. With husband and money, this status was assured. Without these safeguards, the way to respectability might be more difficult but must be found. With luck, the less-than-affluent spinster could find refuge within the original family circle of a father or brother. Denied this, she might become a servant, knowing her "place" and thereby remaining a "lady." Or she might, given property by inheritance, keep a "decent" boarding house or become a governess or seamstress or seek employment in a shop or factory. Any of these alternatives, however, promised only the barest existence—dullness, poverty, abasement. Eventually, too old or too frail to work, the unfortunate unprotected woman might face either the work-house or the degradation of prostitution. "Decent" Christian people would, of course, reserve judgment on the lower-class victims of circumstance. But women of "respectable," though poor, background who had broken from the established pattern of marriage, family or the drabness of the servant's life to become "fallen women," were extended no mercy. Needless to say, in spite of such middle-class morality, the lure of greater material comfort and more exciting life beckoned increasingly to the "genteel" working girl of the late nineteenth and early twentieth century.

It is these pressures felt by middle-class girls of her generation which Rhys illustrates through the character of Marya. She, having turned her back, at the age of nineteen, on her "respectable," "presentable," even "quite good" but poverty-stricken background to pursue the "glittering" life of a show girl, has learned the truths of such life. Men are "dreary swine" and life is "a vague procession of towns. . .a vague procession of men. . .exactly alike." At twenty-four, unemployed, fearing the loss of all-important youth, she meets Stephan Zelli, non-Anglo-Saxon, non-materialist. With him, she leaves her "hard, monotonous," degrading English life for a reality promising more happiness. With him, the "gentle and expert lover," she is "the petted, cherished child, the desired mistress, the worshipped, perfumed goddess." In other words, through Marya, Rhys—consciously or unconsciously—reveals the dream of Victorian woman as well as the desire of Victorian man: to see woman as pet, child, mistress, goddess, but never as competent, functioning, secure human who just happens to be female. Those protesting that these ideas are nineteenth century, not twentieth, should realize that these attitudes still prevail and are only recently undergoing an examination engendered by the feminist movement.

At any rate, Rhys shows Marya, who has had the courage to reject Victorian middle-class morality and respectable poverty, becoming chorus girl, then prostitute—a fact which Stephan quickly assesses and accepts before he marries her. Despite her unconventionality, Marya is still dominated by the dictum that woman's only hope, dim though it may be, lies in marriage. Her marriage to Stephan, however, is doomed since it has no economic basis, a prerequisite in the Victorian vision. Stephan, one of the "down-trodden of the earth" in the cliché of rising socialism, is sent to prison. Subsequently, Marya, alone and without money, must accept the protection promised by the Victorian myth: Heidler, the Anglo-Saxon gentleman, the aloof father-image so "majestic and paternal in a dressing gown" that "it seemed natural she should wait on him." Obviously, Rhys presents in Heidler only a superficially disguised God-the-Father image, an image central not only to the Victorian patriarchal order particularly but to western civilization generally.

Additionally, in Heidler, evoking the ghost of Ford Madox Ford from her own past,[7] Rhys creates an image of Victorian-male-perversion personified and, through him, offers appalling insight into less generally known aspects of the Victorian Zeitgeist. Respected, married to a younger and obviously attractive "woman of the earth," who is "strong, dark" with a mouth "large and thick lipped, but not insensitive," H.J., this "rock of a man with his big shoulders and quiet voice," not only seduces Marya, a married woman, but humiliates both her and his wife, Lois, in the process. That he has indulged in such action many times in the past, with men as well as women, is suggested

6

by the never-defined nuances of rumor surrounding the Heidlers. In these details, Rhys bows to the Victorian concept of masculine sexuality which cannot find fulfillment within the bonds of marriage, even though the implicit earthiness and perversion of Lois herself suggest interesting possibilities of eroticism.

Man, says Rhys, reflecting again the unconsciously accepted ideas of her Zeitgeist, is highly flammable. Thus Heidler must be "tortured by desire." "Don't you know," he says to Marya, "I wanted you the first time I saw you?" Moreover, both Heidler and Rhys know that when men desire, women succumb, particularly those who have already "fallen." Sex is the reality in this male world; love is woman's illusion.

Heidler flaunts this truth to Marya: " 'I've been watching you tonight and now I know that somebody else will get you if I don't. You're that sort. . .I've got every right to take advantage of it if I want to. That's the truth, and all the rest is sob stuff.' " (p. 72).

Marya hates him, and men generally, for this masculine contempt: " 'Sob stuff, sex stuff. That's the way men talk. And they look at you with hard, greedy eyes. I hate them with their greedy eyes.' She felt despair and a kind of hard rage. 'It's all wrong,' she thought. 'Everything's wrong.' " (p. 72). Nevertheless, subsequently, despite her hatred and despair, when Heidler touches her, Marya feels "warm and secure, then weak and so desolate that tears came into her eyes." (p. 73).

In the light of these details and contradictions, it becomes evident that the "Rhys woman" is not a "victim of love. . .at the mercy of her uncontrollable desires" as Mellown (p. 464) would have us believe. Rather she is a victim in a distorted world where man's only view of woman is sexual and woman's only hope, submission.

Marya is herself aware of this victimization:

> [Marya] remembered her tears and her submissions and the long hours she had spent walking between two rows of street lamps, solitary, possessed by pity, as by a devil. 'I've been wasting my life,' she thought. How have I stood it for so long?
>
> And her longing for joy, for any joy, for any pleasure was a mad thing in her heart. It was sharp like pain and she clenched her teeth. It was like some splendid caged animal roused and fighting to get out. It was an unborn child jumping, leaping, kicking at her side. (p. 74)

However, for Marya, and woman in general, there is no joy, no understanding of her woman's pain. Attempting to convey her agony to Heidler, Marya says, " 'I don't want to be hurt anymore. . .If I am hurt again, I shall go mad. You don't know. . .How can you know? I can't stand any more, I won't stand it.' " (p. 77). But Heidler, rejecting her meaning and her emotions, murmurs "tenderly," " 'Rubbish!. . . Rubbish!' " That Rhys means us to understand that this is woman's experience, not Marya's alone, is clear. For Lois, Heidler's wife who is financially and socially secure and represents a different level of society, echoes Marya's despair, her voice trembling and tears in her eyes:" '. . .H.J., I love him so terribly. . .and he isn't always awfully nice to me.' They sat side by side on the divan and wept together. Marya wondered how she could ever have thought Lois hard. This soft creature, this fellow-woman, hurt and bewildered by life even as she was." (p. 53).

Clearly, both Marya and Lois unconsciously mask their dependence and sexual abasement under the name of "love," preserving their self-respect which is more important to them than the opinions of others concerning their "fallen" state. It is this need for respectability and self-respect that causes Marya—fallen into desperate ways in her youth because of the circumstances of her show-girl existence and the necessity to exist—eventually to marry Stephan and in the name of love, to be, in her fashion, loyal to him. "I love you," she tells him in prison, even though the reader has already recognized that gratitude for emotional and economic survival governs her feelings for him. This truth is reinforced when only shortly after her declaration of wifely love, Marya thinks, as Heidler takes her in his arms: " 'How gentle he is, I was lost before I knew him. All my life before I knew him was like being lost on a cold, dark night.' She shivered. Then she smiled and shut her eyes again. He whispered: 'I love you, I love you. What did you say?' 'That you don't understand.' " (p. 83).

This need for love, Rhys implies, is woman's eternal delusion. Woman forever convinces herself that "the man, the male, the important person, the only person who matters," (p. 81) will assuage the fear that haunts all women. This fear is "some vague dimly-apprehended catastrophe" that cannot be explained: "It was a vague and shadowy fear of something cruel and stupid that had caught her and would never let her go. She had always known that it was there—hidden under the more or less pleasant surface of things. Always. *Ever since she was a child.* You could argue about hunger or cold or loneliness, but with that

8

fear you couldn't argue. It went too deep. You were too mysteriously sure of its terror.'' (p. 33. Emphasis added.)

Only Stephan, non-Anglo in his perception of women and their reality, can see the fallacy of this delusion. He voices the truth to Marya when she runs to him for help after Heidler has rejected her. Confessing her ''love'' for Heidler, despite his callous treatment, Marya pleads with Stephan, '' 'I'm so unhappy that I think I'm going to die of it. My heart is broken. . .Help me!' '' (p. 182). Unsympathetically Stephan laughs: '' *'You must think I'm Jesus Christ. . .How can I help you? What fools women are! It isn't only that they're beasts and traitors, but they're above all such fools. Of course, that's how they get caught. Unhappy! Of course you're unhappy.'* '' (p. 182. Emphasis added.)

With Stephan's reference to Jesus Christ, Rhys turns from the god-father image suggested in the person of Heidler to the archetypal saviour-hero figure. In so doing, she offers interesting insight not only into her personally evolving concepts but into the changing world which she experiences. That is, the stern, punishing, patriarchal image of the old order—whether in terms of god *or* man—of necessity must give way to new visions offering more hope. Thus, in one line, Rhys evokes her magic. For not only does she summarize here the changing mind-set of the crumbling Victorian world, she indicates personal movement away from need-dependency upon the vengeful-loving-father image and introduces a motif which will increasingly dominate her later work as she takes her long journey into myth-making.

As though this were not sufficient genius, Rhys takes us one step further into myth and theme in the ensuing scene between Marya and Stephan. For Stephan, feeling compassion, offers his '' 'poor Mado' '' the only comfort he can conceive, trying to take her in his arms. But Marya rejects him: '' 'No, don't touch me,' she said. 'Don't kiss me. That isn't what I want.' '' (p. 182).

At this point, Marya's—and perhaps Rhys's—ambivalence concerning love and money exerts itself. For even as she ''screams'' of Heidler—who has offered her money in payment for their liaison—'' 'I love him! I love him!' '' she berates Stephan:

> 'You left me all alone without any money,' she said. 'And you didn't care a bit what happened to me. Not really, not deep down, you didn't. And now you say beastly things to me. *I hate you.*'
>   . . .Suddenly he had become the symbol of everything

that all her life had baffled and tortured her. Her only idea was to find words that would hurt him—*vile words to scream at him*. (p. 184. Emphasis added.)

And in this last line, Rhys returns to a familiar, haunting refrain expressed repeatedly in the phrases: "You don't understand." "How can you understand?" "They wouldn't understand." Where, Rhys is asking, and how, does woman find the words to communicate her fear, her rage, her repressed sexual desires, her scorn for a world so perverted? Where are the "vile words," so available and permissible to men in their male-structured world, to "spit out all the butt-ends" of her days and ways? There are no words for woman, she concludes. Woman may cry, grovel at the feet of men, use the myth of frailty and childishness as weapons against the world and men: "She was quivering and abject in his arms, like some unfortunate dog abasing itself before its master. . .he felt tender towards her. . ." (p. 130). But if she asserts herself, if she tries to "talk again," she becomes "a bore," "quite incoherent."

Woman's dilemma, Rhys senses, is rooted in the problem of language. In a male-structured world, where the "rational" is masculine and the "emotional" is feminine, how does a woman describe experience that is specific to her as woman, without having it rejected by man as neurotic, female "rubbish"? How does she scream out, "I think, I feel, I fear"?

And with this awareness of woman's inability to express herself in ways to which man will give credence, Rhys has finally chanced upon the key by which she will unlock the door of her female prison and find her way to light. Woman, she has vaguely begun to understand, must find a language, a metaphor through which she can express *her* pain, *her* grief, *her* longing, in *terms acceptable to man*. Only then can she bring order out of chaos, coherence out of madness. This, then, is the genesis of Rhys's ultimate myth-making.

IV

From *Quartet*, however, derives only the bare framework from which that final myth will emerge. This framework encompasses basic premises which Rhys has painfully developed in her story of Marya. Synthesized, they reflect the essence of Rhys's intellectual probings and her emotional responses. From her experiences she has learned: (1) the Anglo-Saxon world is cold, male-dominated, economically threatening and woman's only hope lies in masculine protection. (2) The cold, rational Anglo-Saxon male, secure in his sexual role, his economic superiority, will care for woman financially if she acts the parts in which he has cast her; he will even play the "game of love" as long as it does not interfere with the "logic" (Hugh, Heidler's first name, means "mind," "intelligence") of his life. (3) Warm, feeling, liberated woman may prefer the care-free world of the Stephan Zellis, the sordidness and excitement of Paris to the coldness of England and all it stands for, but this sense of life and freedom is at best a transitory "illusion," "fantasy." (4) Woman senses that there are possibilities for friendship, even succor, from her own sex,[8] but the very nature of sexual competition for masculine protection precludes such empathy. (5) Money is essentially the *sine qua non* for both men and women; the have-nots are doomed.

Ingeniously, in developing these premises, Rhys has transcended her subject, creating vividly and sympathetically, not "marionettes," posturing and mouthing her themes, but four human beings, at once individual and type. (Perhaps for this reason Rhys preferred the American title *Quartet* to the British *Postures*.) Functioning as both individualized character and generalized type, Marya ("Maria Hughes" translates to "bitter mind") is the disillusioned young woman of bitter experience seeking some means of enduring life. Hating-loving man, immersed in self-pity and self-loathing, drawn to but rejecting women, unaware of sexual needs which reveal themselves in unconscious Freudian symbols, Marya is doomed to unhappiness and desertion. Stripped, she is the symbol of the neurotic, sick, tortured, emotional "fallen" woman of Victorian creation.

Lois Heidler is antagonist to Marya—even her name indicating "battle-maiden." Secure in the protective relationship of marriage, perverted though her husband may be, she represents woman as adjunct to man. Unhappy as her lot is, she accepts the role of her Victorian heritage: ". . .Obviously of the species wife. There she was: formidable, very formidable, an instrument made, exactly shaped and sharpened for one purpose. She didn't analyse; she didn't react violently; she didn't go in for absurd generosities or pities. Her motto was: 'I don't think women ought to make nuisances of themselves. I don't make a nuisance of myself; I grin and bear it, and I think that other women ought to grin and bear it, too.' " (p. 97). Lois does not believe in fate; she mocks Marya's philosophy of " '. . .fate and terror. The weak creature doomed and all that—such nonsense' " (p. 87), and she and Marya stare "coldly" at each other.

Heidler, of course, is the logical consequence of the Victorian ideas of masculinity. With his wife, Lois, he becomes for Marya, evil personified, "the cruellest devil in the world," against whom she hadn't a chance, "naive sinner that she was." But cruel devil though he is, Rhys shows that he abides by his code, which is, of course, Victorian. He is a gentleman: he is discreet in his perversions; he will not dishonor himself by sharing a woman—though his women must share him; he will provide a cast-off paramour a decent amount of money—if she throws herself on his mercy—until she can get on her feet. Rhys will be a long time freeing herself from the dominance of this "decent" Anglo-Saxon masculine image.

Stephan Zelli is foil for all that is Victorian and English. Freed from that perverting stricture, he seems at once gay-exciting-free and pitiable-boyish-frightened. He offers Marya escape—in the traditional English way of marriage (Stephan, meaning "crown" or "garland," is quite literally the Victorian crown of approval for "decent" women)[9]— only to plunge her more deeply into the desperation of life. Ironically, Stephan is the only one who sees clearly. He knows the truth of women, "fools," "beasts," "poor things," and ultimately he rejects them. But unlike Heidler, he has the capacity to feel. He is truly concerned for the welfare of Marya while he is in prison; he is willing to attack Heidler to preserve either his or Marya's honor; he, like Marya, is weak, frightened, desiring protection and love. In contrast, Rhys indicates that Marya has neither the capacity nor sensitivity to understand or to be concerned in any real way with her husband's needs. Her economic needs transcend all. Ultimately, at the novel's conclusion, it is Stephan with whom we sympathize. Having freed himself from Marya, we see him trapped once again by parasitic woman: " *'Encore une grue,'* he was thinking. At that moment women seemed to him loathsome, horrible—soft and disgusting weights suspended round the necks of men, dragging them downwards. At the same time he longed to lay his head on Mademoiselle Chardin's shoulder and weep his life away." (p. 186).

In this final revelation of man's despair, of woman as man's economic, if not moral and spiritual, albatross, Rhys transcends her time, suggesting that much of man's real dislike of woman—perhaps even his sexual exploitation of her—is rooted in his unconscious sense of perpetual economic obligation. Since the obligation exists, perhaps he exploits it to the fullest. Conversely, as woman rails against man's sexual exploitation, berating him for assuaging his guilt with money, she nevertheless feeds and lives upon him like some parasitic vine.

At any rate, as Stephan departs with Mademoiselle Chardin, Rhys brings her characters full circle in a curious version of the seasonal myth. Beginning in October and ending in September, the novel's focus has shifted from Marya's depression and isolation to Stephan's sense of oppression and melancholy. Thus Rhys's transcendence of her seeming homiletic on the plight of woman in a world corrupted by men. For though Marya lies in her room "crumpled and still" and Stephan is free to move out into the world, clearly Rhys says that freedom is only another illusion. Man, too, is circumscribed. Outside the room, another stronger siren waits to entrap. It is night. It is autumn, the archetypal season of death and sacrifice and tragedy. For everyone in Rhys-land, winter is always just around the corner.

Chapter 2

AFTER LEAVING MR. MACKENZIE [10]

THE EMERGING VISION

Rhys continues probing for her controlling metaphor or myth in her second novel, *After Leaving Mr. Mackenzie,* (1931; hereafter abbreviated *ALMM*). This work is so complex it almost defies discussion and perhaps for this reason critics have oversimplified and misconstrued its impact. Like *Quartet,* the plot is at once deceivingly simple in thrust and complicated in detail. The setting is April in Paris, the heroine Julia Martin, seemingly an older and darker Marya Zelli. Although the year is never definitely indicated, the story opens some ten years after the war while Julia is living in a cheap room recovering from psychic wounds incurred six months earlier when Mr. Mackenzie had ended their affair. "Decent Englishman" that he is, he has sent her a regular weekly allowance of three hundred francs, but now in April, with a final severance check of fifteen hundred francs, he has abjured further responsibility. Julia, in a rage, seeks him out in a near-by restaurant and during an embarrassing public scene returns the check in a melodramatic gesture. Later the same evening she meets George Horsfield, a young Englishman, from whom she accepts—during the course of a platonic evening—fifteen hundred francs. George sympathetically encourages Julia to return to London where she has hopes her first lover, W. Neil James, will aid her financially. The rest of the plot concerns Julia's ten-day sojourn in London where she visits James and her family—a sister, a paternal uncle, and an invalid mother who dies during the visit. On the night of the funeral, after having buried her mother and quarreled with her sister and uncle, Julia sleeps with George for the first and last time. Then, having received twenty pounds as a brush-off from the ex-lover, James, Julia returns to Paris. Ten days later, rousing from a lethargy of despair because of ten pounds sent by George and planning the new wardrobe she will buy with it, Julia goes out into the evening where she encounters Mackenzie, borrowing from him, on the spur of the moment, one hundred francs.

The meager plot belies the complexity of this novel. The major difficulty—and perhaps defect—lies in understanding Rhys's diffuse thematic purpose. In *Quartet,* the conscious emphasis was primarily on the plight of woman in a capitalistic, male-structured, essentially Victorian Zeitgeist. But in this second novel, Rhys's intellectual comprehension has broadened. Her thematic confusion reflects her personal struggle to construct a viable philosophy within the changing Zeitgeist of her time. Actually, once sorted out, one sees that Rhys presents an almost panoramic view of changing twentieth-century philosophy, a view which she had perhaps unconsciously chanced upon in *Quartet.* This changing philosophy is revealed from three different but merging perspectives. The most obvious perspective is focused in the various characterizations, the second in the shifting thematic emphasis, and the third—a synthesis of the other two—in a controlling mythic pattern. These aspects constantly merge and overlap, making a sequential rather than a subject-focused discussion mandatory.

II

Of the three emphases, the mythic implications are the first to strike the reader in the opening description of Julia's Paris hotel room:

> Her room on the second floor was large and high-ceilinged, but it had a sombre and one-eyed aspect because the solitary window was very much to one side.
>
> The room had individuality. Its gloom was touched with a fantasy accentuated by the pattern of the wallpaper. A large bird, sitting on the branch of a tree, faced, with open beak, a strange, wingless creature, half-bird, half-lizard, which also had its beak open and its neck stretched in a belligerent attitude. The branch on which they were perched sprouted fungus and queerly shaped leaves and fruit. (p. 10)

In two paragraphs, through archetypal symbols [11] now generally understood, if not always accepted, Rhys synthesizes—consciously or un-consciously—the truths she arrived at in *Quartet,* alerting the reader to the purpose of her story. From the "room" of her private thoughts, she will communicate through her "window"—off-sided though it may be —her vision of the strange wingless creature (woman) undergoing metamorphosis, who is threatened by a large bird (a symbol of tran-scendence) with open beak, symbolizing man in his dominating capac-ity. Perched on the same phallic branch (a tree is symbolic of life) which sprouts only fungus and distorted fruits and leaves (all sex symbols), the wingless creature faces the menace with belligerent open beak, driven by the instinct for survival.

The reader, aware of the symbolic implications of the wallpaper as Julia is not, learns that for Julia, "The effect of all this was, odd-ly enough, not sinister but cheerful and rather stimulating. Besides, Julia was tired of striped papers." (p. 10). Thus Rhys suggests that Julia—and perhaps she, herself—is unconsciously ready to reject the traditional "striped wallpaper" of the past and to at least contemplate that which is different. As Rhys continues her description, further symbolic images emerge:

> The bed was large and comfortable. . .There was a wardrobe
> . . .a red plush sofa and—opposite the bed and reflecting it—
> a very spotted mirror in a gilt frame. . .At the farther end of
> it stood an unframed oil-painting of a half empty bottle of red
> wine, a knife, and a piece of Gruyere cheese. . . .Every object
> in the picture was slightly distorted and full of obscure mean-
> ing. . . .But she really hated the picture. . . .The picture and
> the sofa were linked in her mind. *The picture was the more*
> *alarming in its perversion and the sofa the more dismal. The*
> *picture stood for the idea, the spirit, and the sofa stood for*
> *the act.* (p. 10. Emphasis added.)

By now, the reader can almost guess the philosophical conclusion which Rhys will reach by the end of her novel. The bed and all it stands for, while a reality of Julia's life, is reflected in a gilt-framed, less-than-true mirror. The oil painting of red wine and good cheese and a knife symbolizes the concerns of woman—food, drink (perhaps sacramental in its overtones) and the phallic blade. But this reality is strangely dis-torted. Thus Julia, though she symbolically links the "economics" of life with the "spirit" or "essence" and knows that they are achieved by the act (everything associated with the sofa), nevertheless sees the distortion and hates it—though in the end she will be unable to reject it.

The archetypal images continue unfolding in the details of Julia's life. Financially secure, physically unexploited during the six months of Mackenzie's support, Julia is not "altogether unhappy." "Locked in her room," she feels safe. But sometimes she is confused and frightened by her thoughts:

> . . .consumed with hatred of the world and everybody in it—and especially of Mr. Mackenzie. . .
> Then she would feel horribly fatigued and would lie on the bed for a long time without moving. The rumble of the life outside was like the sound of the sea which was rising gradually around her. . . .Her mind was a confusion of memory and imagination. It was always places that she though of, not people. . .dark shadows of houses in a street white with sunshine; or of trees with slender black branches and young green leaves. . .or a dark-purple sea. . . . (p. 12)

Here, in muted strokes, Rhys offers a vision of the primal consciousness, the collective unconscious with its archetypal images of sea and shadow and tree and sunshine. This feeling within Julia is not simply an unconscious sexual urge in the limited Freudian sense, but a primal urge toward a realization of Self. The images evoke the Jungian process of "individuation" in which the consciousness begins to come to terms with the inner center or Self, seeking "totality" through a merging of the conscious with the unconscious, the female principle with the male. The next lines support this deeper analysis: "Nowadays, something had happened to her; she was tired. She hardly ever thought of *men,* or of *love.*" (p. 12. Emphasis added.) This tiredness which Julia feels arises from the struggle going on within her and is the unconscious surrender of will or conscious struggle, without which psychic illumination cannot occur. In the detail of that last sentence quoted above Rhys leaves no doubt that deeper forces than thoughts of men or the illusion of love are possessing her protagonist.

Following a brief description of Julia—thin, finely marked eyebrows; thick dark hair with red highlights; long, slender foreign hands; her nationality and social background "rubbed off" by her hard life—Rhys continues mythic emphasis as Julia makes up for the evening, "elaborately and carefully," as a "substitute for the mask she would

17

have liked to wear." In Jungian interpretation, the mask, of course, denotes the means whereby the wearer "transcends" his "persona" or his conscious role to become archetype. Hence the reader feels the underlying irony and pathos of woman, unconsciously yearning for identity but able to find it only in terms of make-up, physical attractiveness, and clothes. Julia's concern over her old coat and her fatness, her constant powdering of her face, her insatiable desire for new clothes reinforce this idea of woman's need to find Selfhood, even though it must be in distorted terms.

Such archetypal symbols continue to permeate and control the second chapter of *After Leaving Mr. Mackenzie*. Standing before a shop window, Julia looks at a picture of a male figure encircled by a huge corkscrew which bears the inscription: *'La vie est un spiral, flottant dans l'espace, que les hommes grimpent et redescendent très, très très sérieusement.'* Since the "spiral" is a form of the "mandala"—a symbol of the unified SELF—and since in itself the spiral represents creative force which evolves new, more advanced forms out of existing patterns or orders, Rhys records in this brief episode her observation that the male may evolve toward integrated Selfhood from patterns already familiar to him. This comprehension pains when, juxtaposed with the potential for male fulfillment, we see Julia, wearing her old coat, her too-short dress, her "mask" of make-up, walk on, feeling ". . .complete in herself, detached, independent of the rest of humanity." (p. 17). Ironically, awaiting her at the hotel is Mackenzie's note with the fifteen hundred francs, payment for services rendered!

Julia's response to this final communication from her lover also has symbolic overtones. So recently "complete. . .independent of. . . humanity" in her illusory economic freedom, Julia feels a momentary bewilderment and then excitedly begins to plan her future on the basis of the fifteen hundred francs. Oblivious to the necessity for frugality, staring at herself in the looking-glass—a distorted reflection of her reality—she tells herself: " 'I must get some new clothes. That's the first thing to do. . . .I don't look so bad, do I? I've still got something to fight the world with, haven't I?' " (p. 19). Sadly, we realize that the room, originally so full of potential revelation, "already had a different aspect," as she leaves it.

At this point, the symbolic suggestions of Julia's name become clear. (By this time Rhys's probably unconscious preoccupation with naming—onomastics—has itself become archetypal.) Julia (Greek for "youthful") Martin (Latin for "warrior") is an aging but immature warrior against life as she sees it. She goes forth to battle the world sexually, though no longer possessed of youth and beauty, the prerequisites for victory. But, as she sits in a cafe drinking Pernod and planning her "new clothes with passion and voluptuousness," the vision of Mackenzie's "cool and derisory smile" fills her with "dreary and abject humiliation" and she longs "to sob aloud."

III

At this point, Rhys shifts from her archetypal motif and turns to developing the character of Mackenzie, thus introducing the second perspective through which she will reveal her changing philosophy. It is tempting and easy for the critic to dismiss Mackenzie as simply the object of Julia's bitter hate and fear, the symbol "of organized society against which she had not a dog's chance" (p. 22). But Mackenzie functions as far more than the last in a long line of betrayers who are responsible for Julia's "degradation." He is, as was Heidler in *Quartet*, representative of the economically secure, upper-middle-class Victorian male. Rhys, however, fills out his type, as she does not with Heidler, making him no longer "devil"—or "god"—personified, but a man caught in the framework of his society. His mind may be "tight and tidy"; "adapted to the social system"; he may live by a "certain code of morals and manners from which he seldom departs"; but he has published in his youth a book of poems; he is drawn to "strangeness and recklessness; he feels haunted by "ungenerous action"; and he pities Julia, even though he rejects her irresponsibility and her lack of self-control.

In these more human qualities, Rhys indicates the changing role accorded man in a world where he obviously controls less and less. Thus Rhys suggests, as she has done previously in the person of Stephan (*Quartet*), that man, too, is vulnerable. Furthermore, at a symbolic level, Mackenzie has climbed the "spiral" from Heidler— although both are rooted in the older Victorian code—and emerges closer to completion. Thus Rhys makes Mackenzie a more humanized, responsible product of his social system than was Heidler. Certainly Rhys's vision concerning that which she consciously hated has at once softened and sharpened.

Emphasizing this increased awareness and compassion is Rhys's return to a theme raised in *Quartet:* man's innate animosity for the woman he, himself, has created. Mackenzie, thinking of his relationship with Julia, remembers that ". . .After seeing him two or three times she had spent the night with him at a tawdry hotel. Perhaps that was the reason why, when he came to think of it, he had never really liked her." But that he is aware of his own hypocrisy is immediately revealed as he thinks: " 'I hate hypocrites.' She had said that once. Quite casually. . . ." Nevertheless, his negative thoughts of Julia continue: ". . .She was the soft sort. Anybody could tell that. Afraid of life. Had to screw herself up to it all the time. He had liked that at first. Then it had become a bit of a bore." (p. 25).

Implicit in these details is Rhys's comment that the role the Victorian male has assigned woman has begun to oppress even him. That this role is rooted in her sexual function is revealed in Mackenzie's unconscious choice of language. The fullness of his animosity emerges as he continues in a brutal denunciation:

> . . .After all that time she had not saved a penny. . .she was a female without the instinct of self-preservation. . .She began to depress him. . . .something which rose from the bottom of Mr. Mackenzie's soul objected to giving her a lump sum of money, which of course she would immediately spend. Then, however much she might now protest to the contrary, she would come back for more.
>
> He had abruptly refused, adding some scathing but truthful remarks. (pp. 26-7)

Once again, as she has done in *Quartet,* Rhys reveals that the seeds of man's hatred and fear of woman lie in her financial and emotional demands. Compassionately she permits Mackenzie's resentment, frustration, even helplessness to emerge in a scene with Julia who berates him with: " 'Tell me, do you really like life? Do you think it's fair?' " (p. 30). And he thinks: " 'No, of course life isn't fair. It's damned unfair, really. . .but what does she expect me to do about it. *I'm not God Almighty.* ' " (p. 30. Emphasis added.)

So Rhys returns us to the archetypal motif of God the Father, an image of responsibility rejected by Mackenzie, the heir of the dying Victorian era. Then we remember Stephan Zelli, in *Quartet,* saying to Marya, "You must think I'm Jesus Christ!" and we realize that Rhys knows, as do her maturing masculine antagonists, that women cannot expect men to play the roles of God the Father or Christ the Saviour in their lives.

In the end, abjuring responsibility for her situation but unable to free himself from guilt, Mackenzie remains antagonistic toward the emotional and financial threat which Julia represents. "He had no pity for her; she was a dangerous person." Only after she leaves, and he has eaten hot food and drunk good wine, secure in his unthreatened world, is he again able to pity her. " 'Poor devil,' he thought. 'She's got damn all.' " Mackenzie's words, "Poor devil," anticipate the myth of woman as devil which Rhys will develop in her next published novel, *Voyage in the Dark*.

IV

One theme of *Quartet* which is strikingly missing from Rhys's second novel is that of woman's inability to communicate her feelings to others. Julia does not say, repeatedly, as did Marya, "How can you understand? What can you know?" The reason for this, I believe, is that in finding the archetypal metaphor, Rhys has found the means of voicing the formerly inexpressible. In addition, her shifting narrative focus—criticized by many as a disturbing defect—suggests that communication is a many-leveled process. Thus, though Julia reveals to Mackenzie tawdry facts of her life—marriage, the child that died, divorce (though perhaps she had never really been married at all, as Mackenzie thinks to himself)—the truth of these details is suspect. Julia recites the script she thinks Mackenzie might expect from her "sort of woman" who, he knows, "would be certain to tell you lies anyhow." Typically, she mistakes her script for tragedy while Mackenzie sees only comedy: "Surely [he thinks] even she must see that she was trying to make a tragedy out of a situation that was fundamentally comical. The discarded mistress—the faithful lawyer defending the honour of the client. . ." (p. 31).

With youthful George Horsfield, however, Julia can play her role with different impact, because George's personality and experience permit it. So, through her deliberate shifts of focus, Rhys tells us that women assume identities, not from within themselves but from the ideas of men who cross their lives. Furthermore, the seemingly uncontrolled narrative voice becomes an effective device for showing that men, as well as women, play predetermined roles which in turn condition their response to others. For this reason, Horsfield achieves importance at three levels: (1) as individual character; (2) in terms of his implications for Julia's characterization; (3) as vehicle for the development of Rhys's over-all mythic pattern.

Working at these three levels, in sharp, brilliant strokes, Rhys quickly draws a contrast between Mackenzie and George. Although both men are English, Mackenzie is of medium height and colouring, whereas George is "the dark young man." While Mackenzie is the stock "capitalist," wealthy and retired at the age of forty-eight, George seems to have inherited only a temporary financial windfall which has permitted him to spend six months kicking up his heels. Unlike Mackenzie, George is romantically sensitive, feeling the "sweet sadness" of life in Paris, drawn by the women who flaunt "their legs and breasts," pitying a woman like Julia whose scene in the restaurant he has witnessed. George senses—as did Marya of *Quartet*—that much of life is fantastic, dreamlike, distorted, as in a poor looking-glass, the same image rendered Julia in the opening scene of the novel. Furthermore, Horsfield is tolerant, echoing Rhys's changing concept of the Anglo-Saxon, who becomes, as Julia thinks, not the "cold hypocrite" of the cliché, but merely "cautious, ponderous, childish," at root genuine. Having himself known disillusionment, perhaps poverty, George can sympathize with Julia as Mackenzie cannot. Therefore, because of his vision of life, Julia can confide details of her own life—real or imagined—that she could not voice to Mackenzie.

Furthermore, with George, Julia can play to the hilt her stereotype of impotent, suffering womanhood. To him she reveals her wanderings with men, her experience with an older woman, her youthful desire for adventure such as she imagines a boy has when he wants to run away to sea—only in her adventure, "men were mixed up, because they had to be." And hearing all these details of her life, "Mr. Horsfield was filled with a glow of warm humanity. He thought: 'Hang it all, one can't leave this unfortunate creature alone to go and drink herself dotty.' " (p. 54).

In the same way, he had felt "powerful and dominant" when he had given Julia fifteen hundred francs earlier, though he was "jarred" when she accepted the money as her due without protest or surprise. George is drawn by pity and a sense of protectiveness. But he does not want to make love to her, because her crying and sniffling over a dated, sentimental film they have seen together offend him. This film is Rhys's comment on Julia's sentimental, romantic vision, her archaic quality: "On the screen a strange, slim youth with a long, white face and mad eyes wooed a beautiful lady the width of whose hips gave an archaic but magnificent air to the whole proceeding. . .a woman behind them told the world at large that everybody in the film seemed to be *dingo*. . .'' (p. 44).

Later, listening to Julia's rambling, sentimental story, George, himself a sentimentalist, "imagines" her life and her family: "No money. No bloody money. . . .members of the vast crowd. . .And this one had rebelled. Not intelligently, but violently and instinctively. He saw the whole thing." (p. 54). In spite of his sympathy, however, he is irritated by her vagueness concerning her role: ''. . .She spoke as if she were trying to recall a book she had read or a story she had heard and Mr. Horsfield felt irritated by her vagueness, 'because,' he thought, 'your life is your life, and you must be pretty definite about it. Or if it's a story you are making up, you ought at least to have it pat.' '' (p. 50). Ironically, at the end of their evening together, though he has given her his address so that she may look him up if she comes to London, George's last thoughts of Julia are in terms of a bawdy song: "Roll me over on my right side, Roll me over slow; Roll me over on my right side, 'Cause my left side hurts me so.'' (p. 56). Thus, through Horsfield, Rhys reveals a sympathetic but certainly sharp perception of Julia. She gets kicked around like a dog, but she keeps asking for it.

V

Functioning at still another level, Horsfield reveals further the intricate nuances in Rhys's developing mythos. For Horsfield illustrates the next level on the spiral, the move toward perfection or self-realization discussed earlier. As Mackenzie has surpassed Heidler in that development, so George is a more perfected Mackenzie. Younger, darker (Rhys progressively stresses the darker complexioned racial strains as being more earthy, vital, closer to "essence"),[12] George is more sensitively attuned to those things archetypally associated with the "female principle." Even his name archetypally supports this interpretation. For "George" is Greek, meaning "tiller of the field"—a masculine *and* feminine image—and "Horsfield" breaks down into two archetypes: the horse, representing the instinctive drives of the unconscious; the field, an archetype of the "mother." Thus, through George, once again Rhys returns us to her theme of the Search-for-Self, revealing symbolically that this wholeness depends upon the acceptance and merging of the male and female principles that are a part of every man and woman!

Unfortunately, George, though he has a larger vision than Heidler or Mackenzie, cannot fully transcend the hold of the past, and again, even as Julia unfolds the details of her life, we are left unsure of the truth. Because of the narrative focus, everything Julia reveals must be filtered through the mirror of George's reality, flawed as it is by the myths which work upon him as a male.

Therefore, in an effort to more truly reveal Julia's reality—and flesh out her own forming myth—Rhys introduces Julia's older female friend, Ruth, a sculptress. Through Ruth ("a beautiful friend"), Rhys can symbolically suggest that the "female perception" can be understood only by one prepared by nature to understand it—never a man, only another sensitive, artistic female. Thus Julia seeks communion with another woman—an archetype of the unconscious—in a symbolic attempt to discover SELF. The sculptress is introduced as Julia tells George of her attraction to the older woman and how she (Julia) had tried to tell her the truth about herself:

> 'Only she was all shut up. . . .And she thought that every-
> thing outside was stupid. . . .And then. . . .I was telling her
> everything else too. . .
>
> . . .all the time I was talking I had the feeling I was
> explaining things not only to Ruth. . .but I was explaining
> them to myself too. . .It was as if I were before a judge, and I
> were explaining that everything I had done had always been
> the only possible thing to do. . .
>
> I wanted her to understand. I felt that it was awfully
> important that some human being should know what I had
> done and why I had done it. . .
>
> But I knew when she spoke that she didn't believe a
> word. . . .I might have known she would be like that.'
> (pp. 51-2)

Although overtly Rhys may seem to echo here a conclusion drawn in *Quartet* through the person of Lois—that ironically, woman cannot hope for any real rapport with other women, antagonists that they are—at a symbolic level, she is revealing that ultimately one cannot fool the unconscious with conscious rationalization. The validity of this interpretation becomes clear in Julia's subsequent admissions: " 'It was a beastly feeling I got—that I didn't quite believe myself, either. . . .And

I felt as if all my life and all myself were floating away from me like smoke and there was nothing to lay hold of—nothing. And it was a beastly feeling, a foul feeling, like looking over the edge of the world. It was more frightening than I can ever tell you. It made me sick in my stomach.' '' (p. 53).

Now here is power! This is truth—frightening, sickening, gut-level truth! To an expanding consciousness, a new vision is often so threatening, so like the darkness of unexplored space where all is floating, without fixed referent, that it can be conveyed only symbolically. So Rhys attempts to communicate through her imagery the overwhelming pain and fear of women as they strive to know and become what they "really are," to emerge from "strange, wingless creatures, half-bird, half-lizard."

Julia voices this sense of cosmic void further, telling George of her futile effort to communicate with one who should have understood her:

'I wanted to say to Ruth: "Yes, of course you're right. I never did all that. But who am I then? Will you tell me that? Who am I, and how did I get here?" . . .When I got home I pulled out all the photographs. . .my marriage-book and my passport. And the papers about my baby who died and was buried in Hamburg.

'But it had all gone, as if it had never been. And I was there, like a ghost. And then I was frightened, and *yet I knew that if I could get to the end of what I was feeling it would be the truth about myself and about the world and about everything that one puzzles and pains about all the time.*' (pp. 53-4. Emphasis added.)

In that last sentence, Rhys summarizes the ultimate experience—the theme—to which all five novels will lead us: the truth about Rhys, her heroines, all women, possibly some men, even the world in general, reeling from pain. But Rhys has far to go before she can synthesize all this. At this point, she can only show the truth symbolically as Julia remembers a picture on the wall of Ruth's studio: ". . .a woman lying on a couch, . . .a lovely, lovely body. . .proud, like an utterly lovely proud animal. And a face like a mask, a long, dark face, and very big eyes. The eyes were blank, like a mask, but when you looked. . .a real woman, a live woman." (p. 52).

Lying in wait behind the mask-like, long, dark face with its blank eyes and the lovely body (woman deadened by the suppressions of her life) lies archetypal woman, real, live woman! Rhys's ability to use the mask at both the literal and mythic level to open new vistas of exploration illustrates her growing aesthetic and technical power.

VI

Before Julia can penetrate the mystery of the mask, she must make the archetypal "journey of discovery" from Paris to London. As she has done before, Rhys prepares us in advance for the ultimate results of that experience. Archetypally, the usual "journey into awareness" is a night sea journey from west to east (a symbolic journey from death to life). But Julia's journey is from east to west and Rhys emphasizes the train journey, avoiding completely the sea crossing. In essence, she is foreshadowing Julia's inability to effect change in her life—or, borrowing from a "seasonal myth" image implicit in the April setting, to yield summer fruit. If such conclusions seem strained at this point, subsequent discussion will, I think, validate my interpretation.

As prelude to her abortive trip, Julia has an experience through which Rhys indicates again that, though Julia borders on self-discovery, she is still victim of her past and present. The evening before she departs for London, Julia is accosted in the dark by a man who mutters proposals in a "low slithery voice." Wanting to "hit him," "possessed by rage," wanting to "fly at him and strike him," she tells him that he is "ignoble." But the man replies: " 'Not at all,' . . .I have some money and am willing to give it to you. Why do you say that I am ignoble?' " (p. 59). And again, given the reality of Julia's life, this is truth. In spite of her rage, presumably they then go to the hotel together and there, "her forebodings about the future were changed into a feeling of exultation. She looked at herself in the glass and thought: 'After all, I'm not finished. . . I'm not finished at all.' " (p. 59). Thus once more Julia settles for a flawed reflection of reality—a reflection that asserts her identity is secure and certain as long as she is attractive to men who will pay.

Then Julia makes her journey to London.

Julia's return to her old haunts in London, while suggesting details of her former life, primarily involves her meetings with five significant people. The first we examine, a former lover, W. Neal James, quickly falls into the pattern of the Victorian male stereotype, his name reinforcing this significance. That is, if the initial "W." stands for Walter (the name given the first lover in *Voyage in the Dark*, which is the earliest novel according to internal chronology), then the name translates: Walter—Teutonic "mighty warrior"; Neal—Celtic "champion"; James—Hebrew "the supplanter". Thus W. Neal James is the powerful champion who has taken the place of—husband? independence? personal responsibility? (The deeper significance of this will be discussed in the light of later novels.) James, now nearing sixty (referring again to chronology in *Voyage*), had evidently been the first lover, the seducer, of nineteen-year-old Julia. Preparing for her meeting with him, Julia remembers that when he ended the affair, James had been "eternally grateful" for her "sweetness and generosity." Subsequently, he had "lent" her a "good deal of money." Now, years later, he responds "almost at once" to the letter Julia has sent him upon her arrival in London. He is, she thinks, "so kind, so cautious, so perfectly certain that all is for the best" and he is "respectable and secure."

But when she actually meets him, after some seventeen years, Julia knows the truth! "Because he has money he's a kind of God. Because I have none I'm a kind of worm. A worm because I've failed and I have no money. A worm because I'm not even sure if I hate [him]." (p. 112). For Julia, James represents the system which corrupts and the sex which exploits, the male "capitalist" who has created her reality, who controls her vision of herself. With him, there can be no communication, no playing the role of impotent, suffering womanhood, no sentimentalizing of her dead little son—real or imagined— [13] "lying in a hospital with a card tied round his wrist." His only response would be—and this is perhaps, as Rhys structures it, Julia's dialogue with herself—"Look here, I don't believe that; you're making it up." James echoes Heidler (*Quartet*), when he says, as Julia recites her tale of woe, "My dear, don't harrow me. I don't want to hear." Julia knows what she will admit to Horsfield later: " 'I was for sleeping with—not for talking to. And quite right, too, I suppose.' " (p. 173). In the face of her knowledge, Julia plays another role, the role in which James has cast her, good sport, corruptible woman: ". . .She drank the whiskey.

27

Gaiety spread through her. . . .She said: 'Look here, why talk about harrowing? Harrowing doesn't come into it. I've had good times—lots of good times.' " (p. 114).

But in the midst of the lie, Rhys has Julia offer an insight about herself that has the ring of truth, a revelation that she has chosen for herself the direction of her life: "She thought: 'I had a shot at the life I wanted. And I failed. . . .All right! I might have succeeded, and if I had, people would have licked my boots for me.' " (p. 114). And then she falls back into her role of helpless, fatalistic woman: "She said: 'Anyhow, I don't know how I could have done differently. . . .Do you think I could have done differently?' " (p. 114).

Surprisingly, James, by implication a believer in the Victorian view that working women are naturally corruptible, that they inevitably seek out their own fate as surely as good women control their destiny, replies: " 'Don't ask me. I'm not the person to ask that sort of thing, am I? I don't know. Probably you couldn't." (p. 114). Then we find that the war has changed James, given him the perspective to understand that some "really decent guys" don't "get on," simply because of "bad luck": " '. . .some women too. Though mind you. . women are a different thing altogether. Because it's all nonsense; *the life of a man and the life of a woman can't be compared.* They're up against entirely different things the whole time. What's the use of talking nonsense about it?' " (pp. 116-17. Emphasis added.) Which shows that James understands everything and understands nothing!

That James is a predecessor of Mackenzie is obvious in his age, his attitudes, his affluence which is seemingly not rooted in the competitive capitalistic system. In the same way, Uncle Griffiths, older than James—sixty-five, though he looks much younger—completes the "spiral" of life sequence, representing, as he does, an older, patriarchal order from which James, Mackenzie, and George derive. Almost Norse in description, broad, short, unwrinkled, red complexioned (Griffith means "red-haired" and Julia's hair has "too red lights"), "solid and powerful," he represents to Julia and her family "the large and powerful male." Because he is practical, self-concerned, Julia feels contempt for him, perhaps unjustly. For Julia has violated the order in which he is rooted—the patriarchal family. In his objective, rational view, Julia has made her bed and must now lie in it. Rhys does not condemn Uncle Griffiths, as does Julia, for being unfeeling, hard. She permits him a sense of humor, love for his wife, whom he married impulsively, without subsequent regret. She emphasizes that he provides for himself and his wife, a burden upon no one, and would help Norah, Julia's sister, if he could. Furthermore, he knows a truth of life: " 'Of course, everybody has to sit on their own bottoms. I've found that out all my life. You mustn't grumble if you find it out too.' " (p. 84).

But wise though he appears, Uncle Griffiths is at best a benevolent despot whose reality cannot be penetrated. After the funeral of Julia's mother, comfortable, well-fed, surrounded by his "audience of females": ". . .He talked and talked. He talked about life, about literature, about Dostoevsky. He said: 'Why see the world through the eyes of an epileptic?' " (p. 113). Or of a "woman" he might just as easily have substituted. And when Julia mechanically says, " 'But he might see things very clearly, mightn't he? At moments.' " (p. 133), Griffiths can only reply: "Clearly? Why clearly? How do you mean clearly?" To which, of course, there is no answer!

Patriarchal Uncle Griffiths can, however, understand and approve of Julia's younger sister, Norah, who has chosen to stay within the family framework, to measure up to the responsibility of caring for her invalid mother, "making do" as best she can, while expecting no better life. Cliché though her type might be, Norah[14] emerges in the capable hands of Rhys as a sympathetic character for whom we are able to have compassion and even hope. Since Norah represents that which Rhys rejected in her own life, one must admire both her artistic control and her intellectual maturity in developing the character.

Norah, dark like her sister Julia, is tall, strongly built, straight-backed. Her face wears an expression of endurance and her voice is sweet "with a warm and tender quality," although Julia sees her face "cold as though warmth and tenderness were dead in her." She is, in Julia's eyes, plainly labelled "middle class, no money": ". . .scrupulously, fiercely clean, but with all the daintiness and prettiness perforce cut out. Everything about her betrayed the woman. . .brought up to certain tastes, then left without the money to gratify them. . .[forbidden] even the relief of rebellion against her lot. . ." (p. 74). Norah is similarly shocked by Julia, "indisputably changed for the worse" during the last three years. She thinks, " 'She doesn't even look like a lady now.' "

At the meeting of the sisters in the home of the dying mother the pull between compassion and hatred is masterful. Julia's visible emotion for her sister touches us: ". . .her sister seemed to her like a character in a tremendous tragedy moving, dark, tranquil, and beautiful, across a background of yellowish snow.'' (p. 102). Her gentleness with Norah—now on the defensive about the sordidness of her own life —is in sharp contrast with Norah's desire to see Julia hurt and humiliated. But the reader understands Norah's need to strike out when the starkness of her life unfolds. As she reads from a book: ''The slave had no hope, and knew of no change. . .no other world, no other life. She had no wish, no hope, no love. . .The absence of pain and hunger was her happiness, and when she felt unhappy she was tired, more than usual after the day's labour. . .'' (p. 103), we realize that this is the truth of Norah's existence. But when Rhys forces upon us the recognition that this is also the reality of Julia who has sought to escape the fate of her sister, we feel a stab of sympathy for the pain of woman's lot.

Norah, however, has no room for compassion and understanding. She only knows that she is ''tall and straight and slim and young—well, fairly young,'' and that her life is ''like being buried alive.'' ''It isn't fair, it isn't fair,'' she sobs. Julia's return home has forced Norah to realize that in the nine years of caring for her mother, sustained by ''unvarying admiration—the feeling that one was doing what one ought to do, the approval of God and man. . .[feeling] protected and safe,'' (p. 104), her youth has vanished, her soft heart grown hard and bitter and that the voices of approval are those of ''beasts and devils,'' the same ''beasts and devils'' that torture Julia in her different life.

But at least, for Norah, there will be recompense for her years of duty: ''. . .Aunt Sophie's will, and the will her mother had made. . .at long last she would have some money of her own and be able to do what she liked.'' (p. 105). Financially secure—*the sine qua non* of both men and women in Rhys's view—Norah, at the death of her mother, can begin her own quest for fulfillment. She will leave London with her middle-aged, mannish companion, Wyatt, to seek what life offers. But not before she and Julia have a fight in which all the animosities of both their lives unleash themselves in verbal violence. In that scene, which follows the funeral, Rhys reveals again the irony of women able to see each other only in those stereotypes *created by men*. Hence, women cannot reach out in sisterhood, understanding the pain and frustration they all endure as women. Rather, they must seize arms, do battle against each other, engaged as they are in the battle for economic survival. ''Good'' Norah (Greek for ''light''), once without financial hope for herself, must triumph over penniless Julia (a symbolic ''youth''), provoking her to anger and incoherence, even though inwardly both sisters desire communication. "Bad" Julia must hate and rage against her sister who symbolizes for her the "mean beasts," "the good, respectable people" whom she at once envies and hates.

Lashing out at Norah: " '. . .What do you know about me, or care? Not a damn thing. . . .I cried about you. Have you ever cried one tear for me? You've never looked at me as if you cared whether I lived or died. . . .It's because you're jealous. . .You're jealous of me, jealous, jealous, jealous. Eaten up with it.' " (p. 136), Julia is at once oblivious and perceptive. What does either girl really know about the other? Or, as Rhys will suggest time and again, anyone about anyone? As she wallows in self-pity over her sister's indifference, Julia totally ignores the fact that for years her sister has borne the burden of their mother and poverty while she, at least, has had the opportunity to search for something better. But she speaks truth when she says that the Norahs are jealous of their seemingly more free, perhaps more glamorous sisters. Because, of course, they do not know the other reality.

That Rhys senses that women's animosities are rooted not in their own natures—as man even today would have women believe—but in male constructs is indicated by a subtle detail. At the moment Julia is shouting to her sobbing sister, "I didn't start it. I didn't start it," Uncle Griffiths appears at the door of the sitting room and says, "Will you stop making that noise? It's disgraceful; it's unheard of." And Julia replies, "You're an abominable old man."

The scene of rage and weeping ends with Wyatt, Norah's companion, gently pushing Julia out the door because of the harm done Norah. Wyatt then returns to comfort Norah, now weeping over the plight of her sister.

There are interesting symbolic overtones in this minor character, Wyatt. Rhys seems in her to have introduced an animus image to further her feminine myth. The "wise old man," a familiar archetype which often serves as a guide into the secrets of the unconscious, seems to have metamorphosed into a mannish, middle-aged woman who rolls her own cigarettes, has lived in Paris, and now will guide Norah in search for identity permitted by her recent financial windfall. "Wyatt," a French derivative, means "guide." Thus Rhys's growing myth once more suggests that woman (the intuitive, unconscious force) must be the guide in any search for SELF, even though she retains a mannish façade.

In similar manner, Rhys, the woman author, guides her reader in the search for greater understanding of Woman's SELF. In this search, Julia's mother assumes importance far beyond her relatively minor role in the plot. Without her, Rhys cannot extend our vision and her other themes fail. Ostensibly, Julia's mother provides the foreign heritage of Julia, necessary in Rhys's growing myth because of her inability to envision anything warm and vital coming from the cold Anglo-Saxon world. Julia's mother is Brazilian born, "transplanted" from a warm world of "orange trees" to the "cold, grey country" of England, not a "country to be really happy in," but a place where one "sickens for the sun." Julia, sitting beside her dark-skinned, high-cheek-boned, dying mother—"still beautiful as an animal would be in old age"—remembers when "her mother had been the warm centre of the world. . .the sweet, warm centre of the world. . ." (p. 107). And then she had changed to become "a dark, austere, rather plump woman. . .worried," unreasonable, whom Julia had grown to fear, dislike, ignore, tolerate, and finally to sentimentalize as her mother.

But this ancient woman is a fighter, struggling for every tortured breath, though impotent and paralyzed. Only once does she recognize her daughter. Julia sees ". . .her mother's black eyes open again and stare back into hers with recognition and surprise and anger. They said: 'Is this why you have come back? Have you come to laugh at me?' " (p. 100). And the mother begins to whimper and howl like a dog. Norah, keeper of fire and hearth, moves in to comfort as she has done so many years. Julia leaves, not to see her mother again until moments before her death when "something in the poise of her body and in her serene face was old, old, old." Julia's last view of her comes after the nurse has prepared the dead body: ". . . Julia thought her mother's sunken face, bound with white linen, looked frightening—horribly frightening, like a mask. Always masks had frightened and fascinated her." (p. 124).

With the reference to "masks," all of the overtones previously suggested coalesce. This "beautiful" woman—"more beautiful than either of us," as Julia has said to Norah—emerges as a mother archetype, Earth-Mother, bearer of life and source of love, the female principle personified. But though she is "old, old, old" and has fought long after her body is paralysed and useless, she is dead. And her only offspring are Norah—symbol of a kind of light or virtue—who has done the best for her mother that she could; and Julia, at whom she has look-ed with "recognition and surprise and anger." These two "realities"—the one rooted in a kind of depressing "duty" and deprivation (the results of the pressures of the superego or the Zeitgeist), the other in egocentrism and an alien, distorted vision (the manifestation of the ego)—will never measure up to the progenitor, the great archetypal woman. As Norah has said: "We're soft, or lazy, or something." But Rhys knows the problem is deeper than that. The old reality, long since an anachronism (just as is Uncle Griffiths), is dead. There is no return to the security of that "sweet, warm centre." As men must face the precariousness of life, *"un spiral, flottant dans l'espace,"* woman must, if there is any way at all for her, throw off her paralysis and face life, void though it may seem.

But Julia, on the verge of recognizing the truths synthesized in the person of her mother, is ultimately frightened by the "mask" and all that it entails. Her final gesture of unconscious understanding is the bouquet of roses she buys for her mother's funeral with her last ten shillings. Not a gesture of disdain for money and "her sister's and uncle's absolute disapproval of her," as Mellown suggests (p. 465), but a last token of love for that which is beautiful but like the roses, fragile and transitory. From this point on, Julia can only grapple with the "nothingness" that is for her the truth of existence.

IX

Moving into this theme of nothingness, Rhys at once reveals her growing technical skill and her awareness of the post-war "existential" philosophy. Just as she had been attuned to the Zeitgeist of the English socialist revolution and the furor of the women's rights movements, so she understands and contemplates for her own mythology the possibil-ities of the existential "nothing," merging them with Freudian symbols in a carefully controlled technique.

This synthesis begins with the dream-like state Julia experiences as she walks the "strangely empty. . .streets of a grey dream" before her mother's death. The dream motif intensifies during the funeral when, "she was obsessed with the feeling that she was so close to seeing the thing that was behind all this talking and posturing and that the talking and posturing were there to prevent her from seeing it." (p. 130). The funeral, with its prayers and kneelings and promises of future life, is the posturing that keeps her from seeing the "nothingness": ". . .her brain was making a huge effort to grapple with nothingness. And the effort hurt; yet it was almost successful. In another minute she would know. And then a dam inside her head burst, and she leant her head on her arms and sobbed." (p. 130).

Pitying Julia, suddenly the reader realizes that Rhys has so manipulated her structure that this sense of "dream" and "nothingness," overtly attributed to Julia's neurasthenic perception alone, has somehow merged into practical Norah's vision. The demarcation between characters simply cannot be textually clarified. Furthermore, Uncle Griffiths is "frightened" and self-sacrificing Norah tries "to pray and cannot." Julia abandons herself completely to crying and remorse; then, curiously, she becomes, "a defiant flame shooting upward not to plead but to threaten. Then the flame sank down again, useless, having reached *nothing.*" (p. 131. Emphasis added.) Beyond the prayers and the penitence, this is the threat, the fear that haunts all the human race —*nothingness.* But Julia knows that when you are childish, "you could be comforted quite childishly. 'Of course,' she thought, 'Heaven. Naturally. I daresay all this is a lot of fuss about *nothing.*' " (p. 131. Emphasis added.)

The haunting fear repressed, the family returns home to eat and laugh and talk. "Life is sweet and truly a pleasant thing." Then Julia and Norah fight. Julia, "calm and indifferent," feeling "nothing," goes into the night "peaceful and purified." Because "she could not imagine a future, time stood still." Here is existentialism summarized. Knowing the *absolute* of "nothingness," Julia "accepts" and in that acceptance gives "life" (a nothing) "meaning" (a nothing). Without a "future" in which youth and beauty are necessary, "time" has no meaning, holds no threat of aging, a fear which has previously dominated Julia's thoughts. Thus the negatives of nothingness yield the positive results of serenity and confidence. Illustrating this, on her homeward trip, when a prosperous man attempts an acquaintance, Julia uncharacteristically refuses his offer of dinner, letting his card fall from her lap as she leaves the train. Julia has reversed her pattern of action, not because she sees hope of something better but because she knows there is nothing. [15]

But for the Julias of the world the peace of nothingness can be only temporary; the void must be quickly filled. So that same evening, after dinner and dancing with Horsfield in a macabre cafe among macabre characters, Julia begs him to spend the night, hoping to cancel out the darkness with "love"—that which passes for life.

After her evening with Horsfield, Julia awakens, feeling "well and rested, not unhappy." But her mind seems "strangely empty. . .an empty room through which memories stalk. . ." And looking at herself in a small mirror—again the symbolic overtones of reflection as opposed to reality—Julia remembers her childhood when the natural world seemed friendly, though she was always afraid of people. She remembers how quickly the world cancels out the child's natural innocence and ". . .suddenly something happens and you stop being yourself. You become what others force you to be. You lose your wisdom and your soul." (p. 159). Then the theme returns to "nothingness," with Rhys doing curious things as she forces language into reverses of meaning. For this happy childhood is not really happy at all; it is a time when you were: ". . .happy about nothing. . . .When you were happy about nothing you had to jump up and down. . .You ran as if you were flying. . .And all the time you ran, you were thinking, *with a tight feeling in your throat:* 'I'm happy—happy—happy. . . .' " (p. 159. Emphasis added.) In other words, beneath the words of happiness, even in youth, there is a constriction in the throat and a feverish, conscious assertion of happiness, in the face of "nothing." And then you could remember the "first time you were afraid," when "You were walking along a long path, shadowed for some distance with trees. But at the end of the path was an open space and the glare of white sunlight. . ." (p. 159). And you caught butterflies and you killed and mutilated them. And "if the idiot broke its own wings that wasn't your fault, and the only thing to do was to chuck it away and try again. If people didn't understand that, you couldn't help it." (p. 160).

There is terrible irony in this childish cruelty, of course, in the light of Julia's own fate, but in the next paragraph, Rhys forces the reader to understand that the fear has nothing to do with the battered, bruised butterflies but with the realization of "nothingness." And that realization is tied to the "glare of sunlight":

> That was the first time you were afraid of *nothing*—that day when you were catching butterflies—when you had reached the *patch of sunlight. You were not afraid in the shadow, but you were afraid in the sun.*
>
> The sunlight was still, desolate, and arid. And you knew that something huge was just behind you. You ran. You fell and cut your knee. You got up and ran again, panting, your

heart thumping, much too frightened to cry.

But when you got home you cried. You cried for a long time; and you never told anybody why.

The last time you were happy about *nothing;* the first time you were afraid about *nothing.* Which came first? (p. 160. Emphasis added.)

This sense of "nothingness" haunts Julia throughout the evening with Horsfield and, in the ensuing fiasco when the landlady catches Horsfield sneaking up to her room, finally overwhelms her. She sends him away, wanting "nothing but to be left alone and to sleep." Alone, relaxed, she thinks: " 'Nothing matters. Nothing can be worse than how I feel now, nothing.' It was like a clock ticking in her head, 'Nothing matters, nothing matters. . . .' " (p. 166).

Again Rhys forces complicated reversals: "*nothing* matters" becomes "nothing *matters!*" And this is the canker in man's soul as every existentialist will attest.

But, in the midst of Julia's agony—an agony we all understand—Rhys swings attention to George Horsfield, in much the same way as she has done with Zelli at the conclusion of *Quartet.* Julia lies on her bed, cold and hostile, hating George. But Rhys lets us know that George is not the enemy. An enlightened male, he understands Julia's misery; he hates the people and the system which control both their lives; he yearns to be free: he will "sell the business," "get something out of life" before he is "too old to feel." Nevertheless, returning to his "pleasant, peaceful, spacious" book-lined room after leaving Julia at the hotel, he sees with startling clarity what the reader must also see if he is to avoid a grievous oversimplification of Rhys's art: ". . .'I don't see how I can bring her here exactly. . . .I can't bring her here.' Suddenly he saw Julia not as a representative of the insulted and injured, but as a solid human being. . .she must have a bed to sleep in, food, clothes, companionship—or she would be lonely; understanding of her own peculiar point of view—or she would be aggrieved." (p. 168).

Horsfield knows, as does Rhys, at least unconsciously, that woman cannot be transported into a world of peace and order simply because one pities her, as we have seen George pity his cat. She is not a pathetic abstraction; she is an individual, a human being who wants the same things George wants (and what the women's rights movements have all been about): economic security, friendship (not sexual exploitation), and understanding of her "reality" as valid.

But just as Rhys will not present George as the villain, neither will she let him play the role of Saviour. Though he symbolizes enlightened, evolving man, and though he sympathizes with Julia's plight, it is "in a cold and theoretical way." Seeing all that he has with "great clarity," he is nevertheless "appalled" and ultimately will not "be rushed into anything." Rhys seems to tell us that man's own need for survival precludes involvement beyond a sentimental pity and a gratuitous handout. From this point, Rhys never again takes up the "spiral" of man's evolution in her novels.

X

The final section of *After Leaving Mr. Mackenzie* is anticlimactic. Rhys has said it all and now hammers it home. Julia returns from her journey having changed not at all. She still sees woman as prisoner, confined to her bedroom. As she contemplates placing an advertisement seeking employment as governess or companion, for which she has no references and is in no way prepared, a letter arrives from George with ten pounds and another brush-off. She leaves her confining room to walk the streets thinking of new clothes, of "love," denying "age." Later she sees a "slim woman with full soft breasts" to whom she longs to talk—again the symbolic urge to communicate with the unconscious. Later still, she thinks, "After all, what have I done? I haven't done anything," which is, for the true existentialist, the only sin. All of this we have heard before.

Then Rhys makes a final mythic statement, in the episode between Julia and a young man who follows her on the street—a scene reminiscent of the experience preceding her trip to London. Though Julia wants to tell the "boy" to leave, she cannot and they "walk on side by side—tense like two animals." In the light she sees that he is a ". . .boy —wearing a cap, very pale and with very small, dark eyes set deeply in his head. He gave her a rapid glance, 'Oh, la la,' he said. 'Ah, non alors.' He turned about and walked away. 'Well,' said Julia aloud, 'that's funny. The joke's on me this time,' " (p. 187). She walks on seeing nothing but the "young man's little eyes, which had looked at her with such deadly and impartial criticism. She thought again: 'That was really funny. The joke was on me that time.' " (p. 188).

Patently this scene has more significance than just a rejection by a "boy" walking the streets looking for a pick-up (particularly in view of the brief scene which follows where Julia gazes "indifferent and cold, like a stone," on a poor, drooping skeleton of a man). This "boy" is at once Julia's "animus"— masculine half of the soul image—and, more importantly, the archetypal "trickster," who though dominated by physical appetite often evolves to become a guide, an initiator into the unconscious. Julia, however, is not yet ready for initiation into even limited truth and the "boy" must reject her, his eyes "deadly and impartial" in their perception. Julia will continue to believe that woman is victimized by man's sexual demands, unable to see that it is woman who seeks sexual attention; that it is woman who seeks both sexual abasement and economic support, even as she protests, "That is not what I meant at all, that is not it at all. YOU BEASTS!"

Rhys concludes this statement in Julia's final scene with MacKenzie where she takes him for another hundred francs and goes into the streets at "the hour between dog and wolf, as they say."[16]

To summarize these ideas further is literally impossible because the complexity of Rhys's vision is not yet fully controlled either intellectually or technically. But the power is there; each detail works to purpose; her myth is assuming outline. The later novels will refine and process the wheat from the chaff.

Chapter 3

VOYAGE IN THE DARK [17]

APOLOGIA

It is in my understanding and interpretation of Rhys's third novel, first published in 1935, that I anticipate reader resistance or, at least, reservation. The reasons for this are two-fold. First of all, *Voyage in the Dark* has received almost no earnest critical attention. Its main importance to critics has been the internal chronology which places it first in the sequence of what are called the autobiographical novels. Thus this novel supposedly reveals, in the person of nineteen-year-old Anna, the genesis of what Mellown called Rhys's "portrait of degraded womanhood," chronicling "Anna's never-ceasing descent on the scale of personal and social values." Furthermore, it is from *Voyage* that critics have derived their concept of the peaceful security of Anna's (and by extension, Rhys's) innocent childhood, a childhood spent happily in the warm clime of the West Indies before adulthood left her shivering and afraid in the cold northern world of an alien England. Those happy youthful days, so summarizes Mellown (p. 463), forever lead Anna to seek "that warmth and security which she knew in childhood in the game of sexual love with a partner old enough to be her father." Having disposed thus neatly of Rhys's novel, critics have not felt compelled to examine it more closely as a work of art. Such an examination, therefore, cannot fail to evoke some response.

A second reason for resistance or reservation is more complex and has been alluded to in the Preface of this work. That is, since the exploration of Rhys's art in this novel involves me in ever deepening and widening whirlpools of archetypal motif and myth, critical hackles already rising at previous suggestion of symbol and archetype may well bristle belligerently as I attempt to unravel the mythopoeic detail of this third novel. Particularly, I anticipate the question of authorial intent, especially with reference to the emphasis on name interpretation, a matter I have briefly touched on in discussions of *Quartet* and *After Leaving Mr. Mackenzie*. Therefore, perhaps at this point, further clarification concerning "onomastics" is required.

II

Let me begin by stating that the study of the origin, history and meaning of proper names (onomastics) is a reputable area of investigation which extends into various fields of philology, linguistics, anthropology, mythology and literary criticism. Possibly, for many skeptics, the conclusive test of authenticity may rest on the fact that the *Publication of the Modern Language Association* lists "onomastics" as a separate category in its Subject Index.

In further support of the integrity of an onomastic approach, I suggest that most readers know that in nearly every culture studied by anthropologists, linguists, mythologists, there is well-documented evidence of the awe associated with the naming process. A well-known instance, for example, is the primitives' belief in the power inherent in knowing the name of an enemy. Hence the practice of giving, at birth, a real or secret name, known only to a few, as opposed to a generally-known name, whose use entails no threat of control or possession. This bit of lore is easily grasped in the Western fairy tale of Rumpelstiltzkin, the little dwarf who, his name discovered, was forced literally to tear himself in half, a mythic self-destruct.

Similar awe for the power of name is reflected in innumerable religious conventions, Eastern and Western. In the Hebrew traditions, for example, Jahveh, sacred name for Deity, was sacrosanct, not to be pronounced except in the substitute form of Adonai-Lord. In the creation story, Adam, placed in Eden and granted dominion over fish and fowl, "gave *names* to all cattle and to the fowl of the air and to every beast of the field" (by implication thus gaining control), and "whatsoever Adam called every living creature, that was the name thereof." And Adam called his wife "Eve" *meaning* "mother of all living." Continuing to exemplify the importance and significance of names in the Judaic myth, Abram becomes Abraham; Sarai, his wife, becomes, by order of God, Sarah. Jacob, having wrestled with the angel, becomes Israel. And so it goes.

The motif of name-giving continues in the *New Testament*. The "Gospel of John" opens with: "In the beginning was the *Word* and the *Word* was with God, and the *Word* was God." The final book of the *New Testament,* "Revelations," records: ". . .the Spirit. . .will give him a white stone, and in the stone a *new name* written, *which no man knoweth* saving he that receiveth it." (*King James Bible,* "Revelations" 2:17. Emphasis added.) And in between these two books are numerous significant references to the importance of name.

Such delineation could continue almost endlessly, in theogony after theogony. But that is not the purpose here. Hopefully these few examples will suffice to cajole skeptical critics to at least a tentative acceptance of the possible archetypal significance of names. This will permit me to proceed to the vital matter of author intention.

III

In answering the question as to whether Jean Rhys, the author, knowingly and deliberately chose names which would effect a theme which she had consciously, deliberately, intellectually predetermined, the answer is unequivocally NO! In a letter to me dated October 24, 1978 (nearly half a century after publication of *Voyage in the Dark*), Diana Athill quotes Rhys's comment concerning my onomastic interpretations: "I don't know anything about what names are supposed to mean." Aha, some critics will say, surely that settles the issue! But, stubbornly, let me reiterate—and hopefully validate—a contention developed earlier in the Preface of this work (cf. pp. vi-viii). That is, that the author's conscious intent is less significant than the emergent artistic creation and that the validity of an interpretation is best tested in the context of the finished product, not in what one imagines was—or was not—the author's conscious intention.

Working from this basic critical premise, my personal belief, borne out in the texts of the various novels—and in *Voyage in the Dark* in particular—is that Jean Rhys, consciously or unconsciously, was attuned not only to the overtones of names but also to the underlying mythic motifs associated therewith. First, and perhaps only circumstantially, she chose for her *nom de plume* her father's middle name, the Welsh Rhys (not Rees as recorded in *Who's Who 1978* London: Adam & Charles Black, p. 2056). Rhys is itself a famous Celtic name and the name of one of the great 19th-20th century scholars of Celtic

Britain: Professor John Rhys, whose *Hibbert Lectures for 1886* and *Studies in the Arthurian Legend,* Oxford, 1901, are considered even today as definitive studies of Celtic mythology. Significantly, Celtic mythology itself is replete with examples of archetypal name magic.

Acknowledging that these facts may only be happenstance, I nevertheless must infer that Rhys had been given some knowledge of her Welsh heritage by that father she so obviously loved. I base this not only upon Rhys's deliberate introduction of the myth motif (see subsequent discussions) but upon her familiarity with the Welsh language. This is evidenced—as is her love for her father—in this passage from *Voyage in the Dark* wherein Anna (the voice for Rhys's own memories) thinks of her father:

> He had a red moustache, my father. And Hester was always saying, 'Poor Gerald, poor Gerald.' But if you'd seen him walking up Market Street, swinging his arms and with his brown shoes flashing in the sun, you wouldn't have been sorry for him. That time when he said, 'The Welsh word for grief is hiraeth.' Hiraeth. And that time when I was crying about nothing and I thought he'd be wild, but he hugged me up and he didn't say anything. . . . He hugged me up and then he said, 'I believe you're going to be like me, you poor little devil.' (pp. 94-5)

Add to this the fact that in four out of the five novels, protagonists undergo some kind of name change: Marya of *Quartet* has changed her name—or at least the spelling—from the more common Maria, the name of the namesake aunt; Anna in *Voyage* insists that Anna Morgan is not her real name; Sasha of *Good Morning Midnight* has changed her name from Sophia to Sasha, in an attempt to change her luck; Antoinette, the fiery Creole, is forced to subdue her identity in the Anglican Bertha Rochester. Certainly these details suggest at least *unconscious* recognition of the importance of name by Rhys and permit some gropings on my part.

Especially are these gropings permissible if they can pass the simplest of tests: do my interpretations of names work in the context of the other details of interpretation? That is, for example, could all that is associated with the name Ethel Matthews be switched and associated with the character Anna Morgan? Could a Walter Jeffries become a Carl Redman? Furthermore, do the interpretatons distort meaning or

do they open up comprehension, clarifying and sustaining other significant aspects? In this way, the validity of interpretation may be tested
within the context of Rhys's work of art.

IV

Admitting that my "apologia" may seem to some at best specious
and "authorial intention" still remain their primary criterion for validity, I turn finally—and again—to that intention. And in so doing, I must
re-evoke the dilemma discussed in the Preface: i.e., does even the
author ever really know what has been at the soul of an undeniable
work of art? To answer that question, let Rhys speak for herself:

> It's hard to explain how, when and where a fact becomes a
> book. I start to write about something that has happened or
> is happening to me, but somehow other things start chang-
> ing. *It's as if the book had taken possession.* Sometimes a
> character will run away from me, like Grace Poole, the nurse
> in *Wide Sargasso Sea,* and get more important than I in-
> tended. It *happened beyond my will.* But the feelings. . .the
> feelings are always mine. . .
> . . .I feel more and more as if we're fated. It seems as if I
> was fated to write, which is a horrible fate. . . . I never meant
> to be a writer. Something had happened which made me sad,
> so I started writing about it.[18] (Emphasis added.)

Certainly there can be no doubt, from these words of the artist herself, that writing for her was not only an act of the conscious will but of
unconscious forces working within her. Forces that were almost posses-
sions! This sense of unconscious possession is also reflected in Diana
Athill's letter to me (cf. Preface, pp. vi-viii) where she quotes Rhys:
"She once said to me, 'There are times when I feel as though I were a
pen in someone else's hand.' It was when she was telling how she never
intended to write a book and really rather resented the fact that she
kept on having to. . . ."

That the work she kept on having to write was in all probability
Voyage in the Dark seems almost certain to me. For *Voyage,* though the
third of Rhys's novels to be published, was actually "written long
before anything else she wrote." I discovered this quite by accident and

after the work here published had been completed. Somehow, I was not surprised at the disclosure because my feeling all along had been that *Voyage* was seminal to Rhys's other works, even though the aesthetic sureness and the psychological insight mandated that it follow *Quartet* and *After Leaving Mr. Mackenzie*. The seeming contradiction however is easily explained from facts contained in a letter to me from Diana Athill, dated September 20, 1978:

> I am not sure whether you know that *Voyage in the Dark* was written long before anything else she wrote. She carried it round in her suitcase, never taking it out and 'feeling sick' whenever she saw it, for seven years—I think it was seven, but it was some time ago that she told me about it. (I can tell you this because if she is able to finish what she is at present working on, the story will be there). I think she worked on it a good deal when she at last decided to get it published; but the fact remains that it is a profounder book than *Quartet*, not because she wrote it with gained experience but because it came from a different level of consciousness—your interpretation is in no way weakened by the chronology of it, which is irrelevant, but I think if an awareness of the chronology were shown, it would strengthen your book or at least do away with the possibility of critics saying 'that's all very well, but. . . .'

> I base my 'from a different level of consciousness' on two things said to me by her. The first, that she bought the notebook in which she wrote *Voyage* without knowing what she was going to do with it, although she sat down to write in it that very evening. She described the process as a sort of therapeutic 'possession' (she didn't use the word 'possession') and saw it as something which miraculously disposed of the unhappiness which she had been suffering from. The second thing was that she started *Quartet* because she was very angry with Ford and wanted to pay him back—though once it got going it took shape, and ended up not quite as she had expected. Obviously on that occasion the conscious mind was the boss, to start with, anyway.

> As you will conclude from the above, I certainly don't

44

question the vital part played in the creation of a work of art by the subconscious. I just find Jungian interpretations too tidy to be convincing. But I do think nevertheless, that your apprehension of the nature of Jean's feeling for life is remarkable.

In a subsequent letter dated October 24, 1978, Athill adds the following information concerning *Voyage:*

. . . she surprised herself by writing the book; she put it into a suitcase and there it stayed for the next six or seven years, and if she happened to catch sight of it she felt sick; it came out of the suitcase when she was in dire money-trouble in Paris and had attempted to earn something by translating some short pieces written by her then husband and taking them to a woman she knew to be connected with newspapers. The woman said she couldn't use the translations but that they were well written, and had Jean ever written anything of her own? 'A sort of journal,' Jean told her; and was so desperate that when the woman said she would like to see it, she went and fetched it. The woman was impressed and offered to edit the material into a novel. She gave it some other title (I can't now remember what) and 'turned it into quite a different sort of a book, not mine at all.' So nothing came of that, except that I think it was this same woman who got Ford interested in Jean, and he encouraged her to write the sketches in *The Left Bank*. . .

In these two letters from Rhys's long-time friend and editor, then, we find conclusive evidence that the novel ultimately appearing in 1935 as *Voyage in the Dark* was actually written before *The Left Bank and Other Stories* (London:Cape) was published in 1927. Indeed we may assume that this was the work through which Rhys first met Ford Madox Ford:

While trying to help sell her husband's journalism in Paris, she encountered a Mrs. Adams, the wife of a London *Times* correspondent. Mrs. Adams asked whether Miss Rhys had herself ever written and heard that, indeed, there was a diary that Miss Rhys had kept a few years earlier. When

Mrs. Adams persisted, Miss Rhys produced the diary. Mrs. Adams typed it up, added some connecting narrative, and showed it to Ford Madox Ford. Ford, then editor of the *Transatlantic,* was equally impressed and encouraged Miss Rhys to write for publication. His urging and advice, as well as her need for money, led her to write several prose pieces based mainly on her own experience. "If you want to write the truth, you *must* write about yourself. . . . I am the only real truth I know."[19]

Furthermore, we may conclude that if Rhys had carried the manuscript around for six or seven years before bringing it reluctantly to light and another six or seven years before publishing it, then the work probably generated around 1919 when Rhys was twenty-five and before the relationship with Ford had begun.

Additionally, on the basis of Athill's letter, we are justified in claiming that *Voyage* derived from a level of consciousness—a level of truth, if you will—so threatening to the ego of the younger Jean Rhys that it could not be admitted to the light (hers or anyone else's) until the very process of psychological acceptance that I suggest in my forthcoming critique had been accomplished.

Fortunately for all of us, Rhys will reveal more truth concerning the writing of the first version of *Voyage* in an autobiography, *Smile Please,* to be published in the Spring of 1980 by Andre Deutsch, Ltd. Until that time, I rest my case and continue to delve the depths of Rhys's *Voyage in the Dark,* in terms of symbol and myth.

Postscript

Jean Rhys died on May 14, 1979, after the completion of this work. Subsequently, Andre Deutsch has published the unfinished autobiography. In a chapter entitled, "World's End and a Beginning," Rhys relates how during a period of bleak misery, when she was suffering despair because of the break-up of a love affair which had lasted nearly a year and a half, she inexplicably purchased several "black exercise books." It was that same evening, after a meager supper, "that it happened. My fingers tingled, and the palms of my hands. I pulled a chair up to the table, opened an exercise book, and wrote *This is my Diary*. But it wasn't a diary. I remembered every thing that had happened to me in the last year and a half. I remembered what he'd said, what I'd felt. I wrote on until late into the night, till I was so tired that I couldn't go on, and I fell into bed and slept.'' The chapter does not make clear how many days she wrote, possessed as it were. But, with her ''shoes off,'' remembering not ''to laugh or cry too loud,'' she filled ''three exercise books and half another, then I wrote: 'Oh, God, I'm only twenty and I'll have to go on living and living and living.' I knew then that it was finished and that there was no more to say. I put the exercise books at the bottom of my suitcase and piled my under-clothes on them. After that whenever I moved I took the exercise books but I never looked at them again for many years.'' (p. 130).

At twenty, then (which would be in 1914 if Rhys were born in 1894 as she claimed—or in 1910 if she were born in 1890 as Diana Athill indicates in the Foreword to *Smile Please*), Rhys has already framed the novel which will appear twenty to twenty-five years later as *Voyage in the Dark*, the story of Anna Morgan.

AWAKENING FROM THE DREAM

In this third novel, admittedly her favorite,[20] Rhys continues her penetration into the feminine consciousness. Having left Julia (*ALMM*) still victimized by her inability to see or to understand the messages of her unconscious, Rhys now moves more surely into her controlling metaphor, extending and deepening her archetypal motifs toward ultimate mythopoesis.

Using a common archetype, the pilgrimage in search of the lost Eden—actually the attempt to achieve integration of the SELF—Rhys begins her voyage into the dark realm of the unconscious, uncovering in the process an archetypal female SELF. The voyage in the dark of the title, then, assumes double significance. For as Anna Morgan, the narrator-protagonist, takes her journey into the experience of life—undergoing the archetypal fall from innocence to experience—the reader journeys into the unconscious memories and fears that manipu-late not only Anna, but Rhys and, by extension, woman in general. As the dark of Anna's id is penetrated, the reader becomes aware of the unconscious, accepts its impact on the conscious mind and, vicariously, achieves what Jung called the ''transcendent function of the psyche,'' or in other words, the realization and acceptance of SELF.

Initiated into awareness, realizing the conflicts of the id, ego, and superego, the reader—and perhaps Anna as well as Rhys—is freed to embrace life more maturely in her own individual terms. In the end, hopefully, woman can accept herself for what she is, no longer consumed by the self-hatred of a Marya (*Quartet*) who doesn't "give a damn for [her] idiotic body of a woman," or of a Julia (*ALMM*) who sees women "begging the world in general not to notice that they [are] women or to hold it against them," or of a Maudie (*Voyage*), Anna's friend, who feels that God hates her and her "eyes don't fit." Rhys understands, at least unconsciously, that what we *don't* know hurts us. In the agonizing process of writing out the fear and repression and ugliness of her own experience, she intuits that a knowledge and acceptance of one's nature and background, conscious and unconscious, is absolutely essential if one is to escape madness, to achieve any semblance of the peace of an integrated personality.

Additionally, in this journey of discovery, Rhys opens up another level of mythic consciousness which will fuse every detail of her novels, culminating in the consuming last novel, *Wide Sargasso Sea*.

II

The protagonist Rhys chooses for her psychic exploration is, overtly, a younger version of Marya and Julia, eighteen-year-old Anna Morgan. Born in the West Indies—fifth generation, Anna continually emphasizes—and orphaned there, Anna had been brought to England at the age of sixteen by her step-mother, Hester, to attend school in preparation for earning a living. Rejecting this pedestrian path to acceptability and excited by dreams of fame and fortune, Anna joins a touring roadshow company as a chorus girl and is earning a meager living when she meets forty-ish, well-off Walter Jeffries, beginning an affair which lasts from November until the following October, when Walter terminates the relationship. Ostensibly broken by grief, Anna drifts into open prostitution. Later, discovering she is pregnant—but not with Walter's child—she gets money for an abortion from Walter through his cousin, Vincent, and the story ends with Anna's close brush with death and her thoughts of "starting all over again. . ."

In this novel, as in those already discussed, the meagerness of the plot belies the complexity of theme, character, and technique, leading critics to over-simplify as discussed above. Representatively, Mellown sees this novel as the first in "one fairly sequential story," with the protagonist the same woman in all the novels except for superficial name changes. He also finds this novel supporting the view that the basic theme of Rhys is the contrast between woman's secure, peaceful childhood and her subsequent insecurity in the chill of England. This contrast between youth and adulthood accounts, he believes, for Anna's affair with Walter Jeffries—an "adolescent desire to find that warmth and security which she knew in childhood." He concludes that Anna "is a drifter who is shaped by the persons whom she meets. . ." (Mellown, pp. 463-467).

Superficially, these conclusions are justified. The internal chronology of *Voyage in the Dark*—October 1912 to late March or early April 1914—makes it first in a time sequence ending in 1937, in *Good Morning, Midnight*. But the fallacy of treating Rhys's novels only according to internal chronology is apparent when one realizes that, in terms of psychological penetration, this third novel must follow *After Leaving Mr. Mackenzie*. For the facts of Anna's life are similar to those truths which Julia of the earlier novel had not been able to face, thus precluding her initiation into deeper psychic awareness by the "boy"—trickster, animus, shadow—who follows and then rejects her. Only through Rhys's careful mythic and psychological preparation in the previous novel can the mature reader understand, as Anna—and Rhys—initially do not, the real significance of her childhood experiences.[21]

This understanding of Anna's early life will contradict "the happy childhood" of "peace and security" which Mellown sees as a motivating factor in her affair. Just as Marya's (*Quartet*, p. 33) "vague and shadowy fear of something cruel and stupid" had been hidden within her "ever since she was a child"; just as Julia's (*ALMM*) childhood memories of "happiness over nothing" were rooted in fear and unconscious recognition of the horror of her life, so Anna's childhood memories reveal fear, dread, even a sense of damnation. It is her repressed and coloured memories (revealed in universal mythic symbols), not the "persons whom she meets," that shape and determine Anna's character and life.

The complexity of Rhys's style and theme is apparent from the opening lines of *Voyage in the Dark*, wherein Anna, the first person narrator, introduces the dream motif of previous novels, thus compelling us to psychological probings, to journeys into the dark. The unraveling of Anna's composite existence—past and present, unconscious and conscious—continues through eighteen months of Anna's life, with flash-back and stream-of-consciousness technique moving us backward and forward in time without break or interruption. Although the time focus is clearly past-tense, we have a sense of immediacy, of being *in media res,* viewing Anna's day to day activities.

Only when we reach the last page of the novel—with Anna recovering from a post-abortion hemorrhage [22]—is the vantage point of Anna's retrospection revealed. Then we realize that Rhys has so maneuvered her structure that Anna's story really begins where it ends and ends where it begins! That is, on the final page, Anna lies in her bed, hearing the laughter of her friend, Laurie, and the machine-like doctor saying: " 'You girls are too naive to live, aren't you? . . . She'll be all right . . . Ready to start all over again in no time . . . .' " She watches the ray of light coming under the door: "I lay and watched it and thought about starting all over again. And about being new and fresh. And about morning, and misty days, when anything might happen. And about *starting all over again, all over again. . . .*" Thus, in these concluding words of the novel, we suddenly realize what the narrative structure has concealed carefully from us. That *once before* Anna had started all over again and that the whole sordid story we have just read —the plot structure of the story—has been about that new, fresh start in "misty days, *when anything might happen.* "[23] Anna, thinking of the past, freed from the past by the abortion she has just undergone, faces *again* a future of "misty days when anything might happen."

Those "misty days when anything might happen" in Anna's past, and probably in her future, were peopled by Rhys's now familiar characters, metamorphosed somewhat from the earlier novels but still reflecting the social framework which engenders the Annas and Julias and Maryas. There is Hester, the step-mother—respectable, decent, do-your-duty back-bone of English middle-class womanhood. Hester's reality is rooted in the economics of life, the "making-do" so necessary in keeping up a front. Again Rhys indulges in her name game and Hester becomes "the star" by which society steers, like Norah of *ALMM.*

Similarly, Walter Jeffries, the first man to support Anna, becomes the Victorian woman's harbor from the threatening sea of life. A composite of the males of Rhys's other novels, Walter is an upper-middle-class, affluent post-Victorian who lives by the code of all the clichés of his culture. He knows the essential corruptibility of the working girl and is willing to pay for satisfying his lusts outside the bonds of marriage. A "decent" man, Walter is rooted in the material-istic ethic of his time—the need to "get on"—even offering Anna the opportunity to study in order to improve herself and her possibilities in life. He truly cannot understand anyone not knowing what she would "really like to do." When he grows tired of her, as he has grown tired of others, his intentions are to provide for Anna until she is able to "get on." Nevertheless, in spite of his gentleness, his responsibility, his professed love, Walter knows that women are exploiters, taking man for whatever they can get, and that most of them are born "knowing their way about." Walter furthermore knows that "nice" girls are not sexually inclined and that women who are, are "rum little devils" — temptresses who serve as the devil's tool. Thus Rhys, in the character of Walter Jeffries (whose name translates into "powerful warrior" and "god's peace"), summarizes the Victorian-engendered cliché of woman's need for a male protector to insure her security and peace, illuminating, as well, the shallow, cliché-ridden intellectual and social reality of that same protector.

Walter's cousin, thirty-one-year-old Vincent Jeffries, fleshes out this masculine world as a younger, suaver, less code-ridden version of the English gentleman. Less bound by this gentleman code, he does Walter's dirty-work, acting as his go-between when the affair is ended and when money problems arise. His answer for every problem is money and because he "reads," he knows the difference between "what is real and what is just imaginary." He knows, as he writes to Anna, that "love is not everything—especially that sort of love. . .that all this rather beastly sort of love simply doesn't matter." (p. 93). As his current girl friend, Germaine, says of him, he's "the perfect specimen"—the British male with his "scorn and loathing of the female." Because of men like him, Englishmen who "don't care a damn about women," the life of the English female is bitter, sterile. Rhys uses this minor character, Germaine, as a kind of female chorus who sees the truth of men beneath their mask of love and overt sexuality. But perceptive as she may be about men, Germaine cannot see beyond her mirrored reflection (a constant Rhys motif) to the truth of her own narcissism and exploitation of men. Sexually free though she seems, she is still bound by the prudery of the time, unable to face the fact of bodily functions and in typical Victorian euphemism, "goes upstairs" to "curl her hair."

The remaining minor characters serve to fill out the cast of Anna's world and, ultimately, to extend Rhys's myth. Maudie—tall, thin, pale, with pale yellow hair and a tooth "missing on one side"—is in Anna's eyes the experienced woman of the world who has had "all sorts of things'' happen to her in her twenty-eight years. She is one of those who "are born knowing their way about," in a world where feminine survival depends upon masculine generosity as payment for sexual favors. Maudie's code of survival is summarized in a few words: " 'The thing with men is to get everything you can out of them and not care a damn. You ask any girl in London—or any girl in the whole world. . . and she'll tell you the same thing.' " Maudie, shrewdly assessing men, knows that "you've only got to . . . swank a bit, then you're all right. . . . The more you swank the better. If you don't swank a bit, nothing's any use.' " And, most importantly, Maudie knows that to be "lady-like," and to have a fur coat is to have "got on." But Maudie is vulnerable; she has the capacity for friendship; she cares about others. As her name, Maudie, implies, she is "brave in battle" in her fight to survive with a modicum of zest and gaiety in the cold, grey reality of England.

It is in Maudie's last name, Beardon, that Rhys begins to prepare her reader for the myth which will finally dominate this work. For Baird, "the minstrel" and don, "the ruler of the world," suggests ironically that the women who "sing the song" (the siren image) of sexuality, tempting and exploiting men, literally rule the world. But more than this, the minstrel is the singer of myth and the myths perpetuated in song link us with the misty past where other truths and visions prevailed—and are not yet lost. But for us the readers, this early in the story, the song is yet to be sung.

With a few deft strokes Rhys fleshes in the background of Anna's English world. Ethel Matthews, middle-aged, short, plump, cunning, is a survivor despite her sexual unattractiveness. In an effort to "get on" in the world dominated by the "men. . .devils," she sets up as a "masseuse," though she has told Anna she is a trained nurse. She rents Anna a room after the affair with Walter ends, supposedly to train her to give "manicures." She advises Anna to be nice to the men, charge whatever she can get, imply whatever she needs, and deliver nothing unless she wants to. After all, " 'Everybody's got their living to earn and if people do things thinking that they're going to get something that they don't get, what's it matter to you or me or anybody else?' " (p. 140). Clearly, though she earns her living exploiting the frailties of men (the sexual fantasies), Ethel, like other women, hates them as "brutes and idiots.''

In spite of her protestations of decency and professionalism, however, Ethel Matthews intends to exploit not only men, but her own sex as well. Her sullen hostility toward Anna's failure to bring in any "clients" disappears only when Anna begins to bring men "upstairs." Then she is able to raise her rent because " 'It's a nice flat to bring anybody to. It makes people think something of you when you bring them back to a place like this. People don't give you what you're worth . . .They give you what they think you're used to. That's where a nice flat comes in.' " (p. 157).

But Ethel, unlovely though she may be, is also vulnerable. Compassionately, Rhys reveals the fears that haunt her—economic survival, loneliness, aging—none of which nineteen-year-old Anna could relate to at the time but which twenty-year-old Anna, alone and recovering from her abortion, remembers in sharp detail. Thus once again, Rhys permits a character to reveal a fact of woman's life: the unattractive female must also survive and her way is perhaps more sordid, more pitiable than the ways offered young and more attractive women.

This theme seems to be reinforced in the character of Laurie, a former member of the touring company who pops up again in Anna's life right after she has met Ethel. Laurie Gaynor epitomizes the sexual temptress ("Lorelei" is a variation of Laurie and Gain-er is obvious) who, unlike Maudie, has won the "laurels" of her efforts. Having left the show, Laurie has become a "professional." Chic, self-assured, she is, as Ethel says, "The sort of girl I should want if I were a man." As a high-class prostitute, Laurie travels abroad, eats at the best restaurants, wears beautiful clothes and "gets along with men" because she "really likes her work" "and no kidding." Without guilt, she attempts to involve Anna in an implicitly perverted sexual activity—reminiscent of the affair with the Heidlers (*Quartet*)—flying into a rage when Anna, drunk and giddy, falls asleep in another room.

Although Laurie patently represents the milieu of success that women such as Anna and even Ethel desire, Rhys makes the episode between Laurie and Anna the ugliest in the novel. In so doing, she shows once more, as she has done in *Quartet* and *ALMM*, that the antagonism of women for women is rooted in the economics of survival and is egged on by men. As Laurie undresses drunken Anna for the sexual "performance," Joe, the American, watches: "He was like somebody sitting in the stalls, waiting for the curtain to go up. When it was all over he was ready to clap and say, 'That was well done,' or to hiss and say, 'That was badly done.' " (p. 123). Later, as the girls fight over Laurie's black dress, the only thing Anna has to wear if she is to leave the sordid scene, Joe starts to laugh. (The fact that Anna obviously senses the implications here heightens the sense of perversion.) But Joe is not a villain. He may be an amused spectator of a perverted episode engendered by his own perverted needs, but, as an American, he is not bound by the British male's view of women. He can believe in innocence, wondering why Anna runs around with Laurie who is a "tart." He does not see all women as "fair game," respecting Anna's wishes that he not sexually use her at this time. He is able to "like" Anna, to feel disturbed by her tears, to cover her with an eiderdown when she is chilled. Thus, through Joe, Rhys seems to suggest that a man's culture and blood determine his vision. It is the English climate and blood and society which crucify the soul and body of women.

III

Against this framework of individual and social constructs, the character of Anna emerges—obliquely, overtly, unconsciously—revealing at the most basic level an objective but compassionate study of the life of another "tart," Anna. Rhys reveals this as a main theme of *Voyage* in the opening scene, where Anna lies on the couch reading Emile Zola's *Nana,* feeling at once "sad, excited, frightened." Maudie, remarking that it's a dirty book says: " 'I know; it's about a tart. I think it's disgusting. I bet you a *man* writing a book about a tart *tells a lot of lies* one way and another.' " (Emphasis added.) Rhys here forecasts that she will tell us a woman's story of a tart,[24] perhaps approaching truth more closely than a man like Zola who, in the name of "realism," saw women as cruel, calculating temptresses playing on the natural, if pitiable, lusts of men. At another level, however, Rhys is building up the mythic framework—tuning the lyre, as it were, to sing *her* mythic song, as surely as the bards of old had sung their myths of the Lorelei who lured men to their deaths on the reefs.

That Rhys means to operate at the level of both the actual and the mythic is clear if one understands her use of the particular novel, *Nana,*[25] which Anna is reading. Ironically, *Nana,* a diminutive of Anna's own name, concerns the career of a mid-nineteenth-century French woman of the streets, a talentless, would-be actress, who rises to the heights of power and fame through sheer sexuality, selling her beauty and her body to man after man. Conniving, greedy, mindless, utterly evil in Zola's treatment, Nana brings destruction upon many men. In the end, however, justice triumphs: her sins are punished; she dies a horrible death from small-pox contracted from her dying son, the scrofulous son for whom she had tried to provide.

Rhys, comprehending the shallowness of Zola's sentimental, didactic prejudices, employs this male "morality play" of another time, another place to enhance the stark realism of her own emerging female truth. This truth she will ultimately evoke from nearly lost strains of mythic music deriving from the dawn of time. Initially, however, she draws us only into familiar waters, those in which the Lorelei sing and Venus-Aphrodite rises foam-born from the sea. Rhys does this easily within the facts of Zola's *Nana*. For Nana first attracts the attention of Parisian society when she appears as the Blonde Venus, in a play burlesquing the life of the Olympian gods. The fact that Anna's last name, Morgan, interprets "from the sea" reinforces the mythic overtones, if we think of Venus, rising from the sea.

Before moving fully into mythic theme, however, Rhys tells her woman's story of Anna the Tart. To tell that story and to develop her character, she plays with two contradictory yet overlapping Victorian platitudes: woman, vulnerable and fallen by nature and/or woman, the poor-seduced-innocent violated by lustful man. (These almost antithetical views illustrate, of course, man's dilemma concerning his own nature, trapped as he is between desire for a mother and for a mistress.) Mocking the cliché, Rhys presents Anna as a "nice-girl" who deliberately chooses the life of prostitution, rejecting the socially endorsed values of "being a lady," "getting ahead," "doing one's duty," etc. However, despite Anna's seemingly deliberate rejection of social values, Rhys makes us realize that at the point of choice in her life, Anna does not really *choose*. She is acted upon by too many inner and outer forces. As she rejects one cliché, she accepts another; as she breaks from a sordid life of "making-do," she automatically falls into the equally sordid life of prostitution. Always her actions are simply re-actions, impelled by forces of culture and heredity which she does not recognize and always worked upon by the literature she reads.

The problem of culture and heredity has deeply concerned Rhys in her earlier two novels. Hence she has moved from Marya in *Quartet,* who is purely British, to Julia in *After Leaving Mr. Mackenzie,* who has had the "hall-marks" rubbed off her by her career and whose Brazilian mother has diluted the sterile Anglo blood. Now, in Anna's alien heritage—West Indian for five generations on her mother's side—Rhys not only prepares her readers for an exploration into the sexuality of women (something forbidden any decent girl of Victorian background), but also finds an excellent metaphor for probing the murky secrets of the unconscious.

IV

Anna, when we are first introduced to her, is no "innocent" of life. She has been on the road for about a year; she reads *Nana,* is frightened and titillated—obviously unaware of Zola's moral implications. She has been tutored by Maudie in "all sorts of things that had happened to her" and has already learned that you've "got to swank a bit" to make it. She openly rejects being "lady-like" and when she and Maudie go out to buy a pair of stockings, letting two unknown men pick them up, Anna permits her companion of a few minutes to pay for two pairs. Taking the men, one of whom turns out to be Walter Jeffries, back to their room, Anna expects Walter to look at her "breasts or legs" as men have done before, even though she pretends to herself that she doesn't see such looks. With careful technique, Rhys shows how Anna's longing for money and warmth synthesize into the symbol of the fur coat; how her concerns over virginity and feminine curves merge into a remembrance of her island home, manifested in unconscious feminine sexual imagery: ". . .all crumpled into hills and mountains. . . rounded green hills and sharply-cut mountains." (p. 17). Clearly Anna's reality is deeply rooted in the economic and sexual, which to her at eighteen are already the same.

In November, two weeks after their initial encounter and three weeks before her stint with the show will terminate for the winter, Anna dines with Walter at his "swanky" club in London. During this encounter, her animosity for him, perhaps for men in general, is obvious. He is a Mr. "Pushmeofftheearth"; he looks as if he were "trying to size [her] up"; she feels that he doesn't believe a word of what she tells him and that he smiles "as if he were laughing" at her. "Oh, God," she thinks, "he's the sneering sort. I wish I hadn't come." Obviously, this is not a new experience for her. At eighteen she has been in other rooms with other men; and "all the time" Walter is kissing her, she remembers another man in another room who had taught her how to kiss.

Despite these intimations of experience, however, when Anna discovers the bedroom hidden behind the curtain, she seems surprised. This curious ambiguity, even ambivalence, is followed by another. For when Walter laughs at her discovery, Anna laughs too, feeling that was what she ". . .ought to do. *You can now and you can see what it's like, and why not?*" (p. 22. Emphasis Rhys's.) The italics, structurally, indicate an inner voice. But the reader does not know whether this is a voice in the present urging her to an awaited experience or a voice out of the past from an earlier experience. Nor can the reader determine whether the words refer to desire for a hitherto forbidden experience or for an experience different from those which have gone before. This ambiguity necessarily derives from Rhys's narrative technique.

The ambiguity and ambivalence continue as Anna recalls the experience: "My arms hung straight down by my sides awkwardly. He kissed me again, and his mouth was hard, and I remembered him smelling the glass of wine and I couldn't think of anything but that, and I hated him." (p. 22). Again we do not know whether Anna hates and rejects Walter's sexual advances because of her innocence or because she hates him for "testing" her, as he has tested the wine earlier in the evening before rejecting it as unfit. We only know that in hatred she pushes him away: " 'Look here, let me go,' . . .Do you think I was born yesterday, or what? . . .Damn you, let me go, damn you. Or I'll make a hell of a row.' *But as soon as he let me go I stopped hating him.*" (Emphasis added.) Walter's own ambivalence is clear to Anna as, ceasing his kisses, he says: " 'I'm very sorry. . .That was extremely stupid of me.' Looking at me with his eyes narrow and close together, as if he hated me, as if I wasn't there; and then he turned away and looked at himself in the glass." (p. 23).

Further ambiguity occurs when Walter turns from her and Anna thinks: " 'If it could go back and be just as it was before it happened and then happen differently.' " (p. 23). Go back when? Before what happened? Just her rejection of Walter, here in this room? Her first experience with a man in a room in England when she learned to mistrust? Or an experience that happened in "misty days" before she was brought to England to start "all over again"? Or "misty days" long before that? At this point, Rhys obliquely raises shadows in our minds.

Having successfully resisted Walter, Anna goes into the bedroom, obviously expecting Walter to follow. As she waits vainly for his coming, the room seems desolate, the fire and the hearth painted, the room very cold. Anna shivers, as she does constantly in this cold land among these cold people. In this reversal of Anna's expectation of sexual exploitation, Rhys shatters the myth of ravaged woman, victimized by man, hinting—as she has done with Julia at the end of *ALMM*

—that woman herself expects, even requires, sexual subjugation as her only form of identity. And Rhys permits Walter, and man in general, the last laugh. For when Anna finally gets up from the bed and goes back to rejoin Walter, he smiles, "as cool as a cucumber. 'Cheer up,' he said. 'Don't look so sad. What's the matter? Have another kummel.' " Then he sends Anna home in a taxi.

Rejected sexually,[26] Anna returns to her room obsessed with thoughts of clothes. As with Julia (*ALMM*), clothes become the identity, the only reality other than sex that woman can know. And since clothes give essence and clothes cost money, money becomes as essential for Anna as it was for Julia. Almost sadistically, having denied her sexual essence, Walter compensates by sending her twenty-five pounds—for nothing—and Anna goes off to buy a new wardrobe. In the shop of the haughty Miss Cohens, surrounded by beautiful clothes, the shop warm and smelling of fur, Anna knows: *"This is a beginning. Out of this warm room that smells of fur I'll go to all the lovely places I've ever dreamt of. This is the beginning."* (p. 28. Emphasis Rhys's.)

Thus surely and quickly—pursuing her story of a tart—Rhys has sketched one simple answer to the eternal question, "How did a nice girl like you get into the business?" The answer at the most basic level is "for money," which in turn provides essence. But Rhys knows this answer is an over-simplification. As Walter's cousin, Vincent, later admits: " 'My dear girl. . .I can't understand it. . .I simply can't understand it. Was it money? It can't have been money,' " (p. 173), and Rhys makes it clear that Walter would have provided for Anna had she not vanished without leaving a forwarding address.

If Anna does not prostitute herself for money, what then is her motivation? Rhys provides the beginning of the answer in the episode immediately following Anna's return to her room with the new clothes on which she has spent eighteen pounds. After a stormy scene with her landlady who informs her she must find herself another room because she wants "no tarts" in her house, Anna lies down on her bed, her "heart beating like hell" and the "damned room getting smaller and smaller." At this point, Rhys reintroduces the archetypal motif begun in *After Leaving Mr. Mackenzie*. The room, female archetype and symbol of private thoughts, begins to close in. Anna feels ill, unable to move. Lying in the darkness, she remembers the time in her youth when she lay ill of a fever in an unpainted room, watching a cockroach and fearful that it would fly down and touch her, sending her mad. But then black Francine had come to kill the cockroach and soothe and cool her. And oh how Anna "wanted to be black. . .always wanted to be black [because] being black is warm and gay, being white is cold and sad." (p. 31).

Through such archetypal symbols, we now understand that Anna, closer to her primal nature because of her West Indian heritage, is and has been for some time on the verge of a breakthrough into her unconscious. Her recurring spells of illness indicate the initial stage of the individuation process, which is the growth toward knowledge of SELF. The cockroach represents the dark quality within Anna that will drive her mad. And that dark quality, feared and repressed by her, is her natural, earthy sexuality. Because her society (by extension the ego and superego) forces her to deny that vital self, in the process denigrating, however subtly, the feminine essence, Anna must ambivalently desire the blackness of Francine, associated with earthiness, warmth, happiness and at the same time see herself in symbols associated with filth, threat, evil.

Francine ("free") is a kind of alter-image, the "shadow" of Anna's libido, which no "good, white, religious" girl dare admit, let alone unleash. But it is immediately made obvious that, in some way, Anna has responded to these forbidden drives. For, as she remembers Francine singing the only English song she knew, "Adieu, sweetheart, adieu," her mind jumps to:

—It was when I looked back from the boat and saw the lights of the town bobbing up and down that was the first time I really knew I was going. Uncle Bob said well you're off now and I turned my head so that nobody could see my crying—it ran down my face and splashed into the sea like the rain was splashing—Adieu sweetheart adieu—and I watched the lights heaving up and down— (p. 32)

With these lines we are returned to a consideration of Anna's previous experience with men, remembering that Anna has been brought to England to start "all over again," as the narrative structure previously discussed indicates. (cf. pp. 49-50).

Then Anna succumbs to the fever and Walter calls and straightens up the mess with the landlady and brings food and promises to send his doctor. And when he leaves, Anna's room seems "different, as if it had grown bigger." Anna has evaded the issue of her unconscious stirrings.

Following her illness, a curious "seduction" scene occurs. Anna, succumbing to the protective qualities of Walter, even as she tries to remember that at first she hadn't liked him, feels warm, alone with him in his house on Green Street (green is the archetypal color of hope). As Walter begins his overtures, putting his hand on her knee, Anna thinks, " 'Yes . . . yes . . . yes . . .' Sometimes it's like that—everything drops away except the one moment." (p. 30). Obviously Anna desires what is to come and at eighteen—and at twenty since the whole story is remembrance following her abortion—knows the ecstasy of sexual fulfillment.

Then Anna recalls that at the moment of passion, Walter "started talking about my being a virgin and it all went—the feeling of being on fire—and I was cold. 'Why did you start about that?' I said. 'What's it matter? Besides, I'm not a virgin if that's what's worrying you.' " Ambiguity again! Is Anna really a virgin and only denying her own youth and inexperience? Is she rebelling against the Victorian cliché of virginity as the prized possession of women, the crystal chalice to be desired and threatened by every male? Or is she telling us a truth about herself, either factual or as she sees it? Certainly her thoughts when she goes upstairs with Walter in no way clarify the issue: "When I got into bed there was warmth coming from him and I got close to him. *Of course you've known, always remembered, and then you forgot so utterly, except that you've always known it. Always—how long is always?*" (p. 37. Emphasis Rhys's.)

And with those last lines, Rhys forces us to the question of time and obliquely, thereby, to an extension of her mythic theme. Does Anna only know and remember experiences of her personal past life? Or is this an instinctual memory inherited from her ancient racial female consciousness? Is Rhys indicating that woman's sexuality is as innate and undeniable as man's, rooted in the timelessness of her reality? That this last interpretation is at least part of the truth seems feasible since, as she dresses, Anna indicates that this has, indeed, been her defloration: ". . . it had been just like the girls said, except that I hadn't known it would hurt so much." And when they prepare to leave the house, Anna kisses Walter's hand, Rhys so structuring the details that we cannot know whether she does so in gratitude for the experience or for the money he has slipped into her purse.

Following that night, the affair blossoms; Anna moves into better rooms and begins her life of meaningless boredom as she waits for Walter's summons. Again Rhys shows that Anna is on the verge of really breaking through to what would be to her the "darker side" of her nature. The old man, trailing along outside her window, singing hymns is probably a personification of Anna's "animus," that masculine part of the SELF urgently seeking communication with the conscious mind: " . . . Invisible men, they were. But the oldest one of all played 'The Girl I Left Behind Me' on a penny whistle." (p. 40). The room Anna now lives in is replete with female sexual symbols, almost Dionysian in their description. When Anna says, "My God, this is a funny way to live. My God, how did this happen?" her unconscious is trying to tell her, "Because you like it!" This is the motive beyond money that answers the question, "How did a nice girl like you . . .?" Rhys tells us truly that "tarts are tarts" because, like Laurie and now Anna, they "really like it. And no kidding." But Anna is not yet able to recognize this aspect of herself and immediately, in the context of the old man's singing and Anna's question of how she got into this life, Rhys shows us influences which prevent her acceptance of that natural sexuality.

V

On the lonely January Sunday that is her birthday, Anna hears the "tinny nagging sound" of church bells and remembers "heavy, melancholy" Sundays of her past. (All Rhys heroines hate the sun and Sundays.) Her thoughts revert to lost days and the truisms of her girlhood: dressing for church on Sundays with a woollen vest next to the skin because it is healthy for the body as church is healthy for the soul; wearing too-small kid gloves in the heat, because one must be ladylike; worrying about the wet patches of perspiration beneath one's arms, "a disgusting and disgraceful thing to happen to a lady." Juxtaposed with these hypocritical values—not of the English but of the whites in general—Anna remembers the heat of the earth, the smell of the stable, the coolness of the stone bath. Contrasting with the lure of the earthy, the beckoning of coolness and shadow, is the closeness of the air within the church, the hypocrisy of the Litany, during which Anna reads "bits of the marriage-service."

This theme of Anna's religious background—along with its glaring contradictions—emerges later in an evening with Walter. While Anna's thoughts center on the sexual activity to come, Walter introduces the subject of Anna's "getting on." Dismayed by his talk, she has a drink of whisky and we learn that drinking is in Anna's blood and that all her "family drink too much." Her father and her Uncle "Bo" (his real name is *Ram*sey and he and his brother have obviously spawned illegitimate children throughout the Islands) call her Hèbe and praise her for mixing a punch that is "something to warm the cockles of your heart," permitting her to drink with them. She tries to tell Walter about Constance Estate—unlike its name, decaying and crumbling in disrepair but in her memory taking on the overtones of the archetypal Eden.

She remembers the old slave-list she saw and the " '. . .names and the ages and what they did and then General Remarks.' . . . .Maillotte Boyd, aged 18, mulatto, house servant. The sins of the fathers Hester said are visited upon the children unto the third and fourth generation —don't talk such nonsense to the child Father said—a myth don't get tangled up in myths he said to me. . .'' (p. 53. Punctuation exact.)

But that, of course, is exactly what Anna—and Rhys—have done, *gotten tangled up in all kinds of myths*. Also, perhaps, in truth! For Anna's black background hinted here, strengthened by our remembrance of the nickname "hottentot" bestowed by her friends, is almost verified by Anna herself, when later in the story she says to her stepmother, Hester: " 'You're trying to make out that my mother was coloured,' . . . 'You always did try to make that out. And she wasn't.' " (p. 65). This, then, is part of Anna's unconscious trauma, her ambivalence. She desires to be black: " 'When I was a kid I wanted to be black;' " yet she simultaneously rejects that heritage, with all that it stands for in terms of her unconscious desires. In the world of decent, white people, only "rum little devils" drink and desire sex, as Walter indicates before he "mounts the stairs" with her.

This synthesis of ideas—the black world of the id opposed to the white world of the ego-superego—is demanded in light of Anna's thoughts as she lies beside Walter. She remembers the nun's teachings:

'Children, every day one should put aside a quarter of an hour for meditation on the Four Last Things. Every night before going to sleep—that's the best time—you should shut your eyes and try to think of one of the Four Last Things.' (*Question:* What are the Four Last Things? Answer: The Four Last Things are Death, Judgment, Hell and Heaven.) That was Mother St. Anthony—funny old thing she was, too.

She would say, 'Children, every night before you go to sleep you should lie straight down with your arms by your sides and your eyes shut and say: ''One day I shall be dead. One day I shall lie like this with my eyes closed and I shall be dead.'' ' ''Are you afraid of dying?' Beatrice would say. 'No, I don't believe I am. Are you?' 'Yes, I am, but I never think about it.'

Lying down with your arms by your sides and your eyes shut.

'Walter, will you put the light out? I don't like it in my eyes.' (pp. 55-6)

It is obvious from this stream of Anna's consciousness that Anna's religious heritage has taught her of sin and hell, and that her unconscious fears equate death and sex. Then, from religion, punishment and sex, Anna's thoughts automatically return to her darker heritage: *"Maillotte Boyd, aged 18. Maillotte Boyd, aged 18. . . .But I like it like this. I don't want it any other way but this."* (p. 56).

Anna's heritage, then, by choice, is the sexual—but her conflict is revealed as her thoughts turn to sadness and guilt:

That was when it was sad, when you lay awake at night and remembered things. That was when it was sad, when you stood by the bed and undressed, thinking, When he kisses me, shivers run up my back. I am hopeless, resigned, utterly happy. Is that me? I am bad, not good any longer, bad. That has no meaning, absolutely none. Just words. But something about the darkness of the streets has a meaning. (p. 57)

The confusion of Anna's conscious mind and the threat she feels coming from the dark ''street'' of her unconscious, remind us of the street where a thin, little man with ''little, sad eyes,'' is bawling out, '' 'God . . .God. . .The wrath of God. . . . . Your sins will find you out. Already the fear of death and hell is in your hearts, already the fear of God is like fire in your hearts.' '' (p. 48).

Anna's burden of conflict and guilt is not eased in her subsequent visit with Hester. In this episode, she learns that her Uncle Bo (Uncle Boozy, Hester calls him) whom she has so admired, eschews responsibility for her and will not pay her passage back to the Indies as Hester has requested. Virtuously, Hester has washed her hands of Anna for violating the code of the Victorian woman. Symbolically, then, Rhys tells us that there is no return to a lost Paradise and no refuge in a newer social system. Anna must now really find her own way. Which is, of course, what the stirrings within her have been trying to convey.

VI

Anna's thoughts, after the ugliness of her meeting with Hester, revert to Francine, black, free, laughing but always, even when she sang, sounding sad. It had been Francine who, when Anna had been "unwell for the first time," "explained" and made it seem natural and "quite all right." "All in a day's work like eating or drinking." It was white English Hester who had "jawed away" and made Anna feel that she "wanted to die." But despite Francine's solicitude, Anna knew that she ". . .disliked me too because I was white; and that I would never be able to explain to her that I hated being white. Being white and getting like Hester, and all the things you get—old and sad and everything. I kept thinking, 'no. . . .No. . . .No. . . .' *And I knew that day I'd started to grow old and nothing could stop it.*" (p. 72. Emphasis added.)

Driven by awareness of her maturing body and the urgency of fleeting time, Anna had left Francine, going up the hill to a place of big grey boulders, a place with a "hot, frowning, barren look," which was in its own way "a beautiful place." Now ambiguities begin to clarify. That is, rejecting the image of "whiteness"—propriety, age, sadness, etc.—at the time of puberty, Anna "climbs the hill" (climbing is a Freudian symbol for sexual activity and a Jungian archetype of the attempt to reach fulfillment) to a place of big, grey boulders at once fierce and beautiful. The stone in Freudian dream psychology is a male sexual symbol and in Jungian dream interpretation often symbolizes the SELF, as something that is immortal, immutable. Thus Rhys, through Anna's verbal imagery, suggests her youthful, ambivalent attempt both to escape and to find her sexual reality, and her consequent guilt over either the natural fact of menstruation (probably a result of the nuns' teachings) or some attempt at experimentation. That this first attempt was auto-erotic (as psychoanalysts indicate most early sexual experiments are) seems possible as Rhys immediately moves Anna and the reader forward in time:

I felt I was more alone than anybody had ever been in the world before and I kept thinking, 'No. . . No. . . .No. . . ' just like that. Then a cloud came in front of my eyes and seemed to blot out half of what I ought to have been able to see. It was always like that when I was going to have a headache.

I thought, 'Well, all right. This time I'll die' So I took my hat off and went and stood in the sun.

The sun at home can be terrible, like God. (p. 73)

Anna, with her religious, middle-class background,[27] her indoctrination that the body is nasty, unnatural, knows that the punishment of God awaits her—because she is a woman or because she has succumbed to temptation (the curse of Eve)—and goes out to receive it in the terrible sun. Naturally she "falls" into a fever which lasts for a long time. Her secret guilt continues to haunt her, however, and Anna feels God's wrath always awaiting her, just around the corner.[28]

These sexual overtones account for the seeming ambiguity concerning Anna's virginity. For the belief fostered among some young girls—even today—that any genitalia play is discernible and a violation of virginity would explain Anna's denial that she is a virgin despite the contradictory pain of her first night with Walter. The truth of what may seem a specious argument is validated in certain details connected with the letter Anna receives from Vincent, telling her that Walter doesn't love her any longer but that he will always be her friend and see that she is "provided for" and that she doesn't "have to worry about money (for a time at any rate)." The time is again October, and Anna has returned to her room to find the letter on her table. Not recognizing the handwriting she thinks, " 'Who on earth's that from?' " Immediately, from the unconscious depths of guilt and its concomitant expectation of punishment, Anna remembers an episode from the past. The time that she had first seen her Uncle Bo's false teeth:

. . .yellow tusks like fangs came out of his mouth and protruded down to his chin—you don't scream when you are frightened because you can't. . .I had never seen false teeth before. . .

I thought, 'But what's the matter with me? That was years and years ago, ages and ages ago. Twelve years ago or something like that. *What's this letter got to do with false teeth?*' (p. 92. Emphasis added.)

65

The answer is obvious. Unconsciously expecting punishment—which the loss of Walter will be—Anna's id supplies a memory of a specific image, *the falling out of teeth,* which in Freudian terms symbolizes castration, the punishment for onanism! This tooth imagery—interestingly, Maudie has a missing tooth—is further reinforced, when having read Vincent's letter, she immediately thinks: " . . .'What the hell's the matter with me? I must be crazy. This letter has nothing to do with false teeth.' *But I went on thinking about false teeth and then about piano-keys* and about that time *the blind man* from Martinique *came to tune the piano and then he played and we listened. . . .* (p. 94. Emphasis added.) As extracted teeth represent the punishment, the piano, Freud concluded, is a symbol of the forbidden auto-erotic or homosexual act. In Jungian framework, the blind musician is a typical personification of the SELF, attempting again to break through to Anna's conscious so that she may be freed from the grip of all the submerged and conflicting forces that cause her such devastating pain and grief.[29]

But Anna has not yet reached the point of breakthrough and sees her only hope in a reconciliation with Walter. Awaiting a taxi which will take her to him for a last futile appeal, she ". . .saw that all my life I had known that this was going to happen, and that *I'd been afraid for a long time. I'd been afraid afraid for a long time.* There's fear, of course, with everybody. But now it had grown, it had grown gigantic; *it filled me and it filled the whole world.* " (p. 92. Emphasis added.) And with this, Rhys takes us expertly from Anna's guilt concerning early sexual awareness to a more universalized consideration of the fears that seem innate in women of Anglo-Saxon cultures, where even men who say they "love" women reject them when their own selfish appetites are satisfied. This fear is what Anna wants to tell Walter about:

> 'The thing is that you don't understand. You think I want more than I do. I only want to see you sometimes, but if I never see you again I'll die. I'm dying now really, and I'm too young to die,' . . .The candles crying wax tears and the smell of stephanotis and I had to go to the funeral in a white dress and white gloves and a wreath round my head and the wreath in my hands made my gloves wet. . .they said so young to die. . . (p. 97. Punctuation exact.)

Woman's fate, Rhys implies, condemned as she is, is to know only loneliness and loss of those to whom she has given her love.

Once more, though, as she has done with Horsfield (*ALMM*), Rhys plays fair, permitting us to see that Walter does not like his role and that his hatred for Anna derives from the guilt her dependence engenders within him. Furthermore, Rhys shows us the strangling strength of "weak" women who threaten men with: " '. . .I'll hang on to your knees and make you understand and then you won't be able to, you won't be able to.' " (p. 98).

Suddenly, in the midst of her agony, Anna gives up, thinking:

'You don't know anything about me. I don't care any more.'
And I didn't care any more.

It was like letting go and falling back into water and seeing yourself grinning up through the water, your face like a mask, and seeing the bubbles coming up as if you were trying to speak from under the water. And how do you know what it's like to try to speak from under water when you're drowned? (p. 98)

So Anna sees her "mask" of helplessness mocking her, as drowning in her own fear and sexuality—not unrequited love—her unconscious tries to "speak from under the water." But sadly, as has happened before, the moment of revelation passes. Amid Walter's protestations of concern, the affair is ended. Part Two begins.

Part Two

Part Two of *Voyage in the Dark* involves the beginning of Anna's descent into the darkness of truth. Changing addresses without notifying Walter, Anna wallows for less than a month in the misery of love-rejected. Rhys makes it clear that this is a kind of playing-the-game-of-broken-heart by juxtaposing Anna's pragmatic, mundane thoughts with her protestations of love and hate. The game ends, however, as events intervene to turn Anna's thoughts from Walter to other involvements.

Having met Ethel Matthews and run into her former friend Laurie, chorus-girl-now-turned-prostitute, Anna, after the abortive and debasing evening with Joe and Laurie, moves from her cheap room in Camden Town into Ethel's more luxurious flat on *Bird* Street, implicitly hoping to improve her possibilities for making money from men. (The reader, remembering that the "bird" is a common symbol of transcendence which leads one to discovery of SELF, is alerted to the probable outcome of Anna's experience at Ethel's. The fact that "bird" is still the British slang for prostitute further enlightens the reader.) As Part Two concludes, Anna is lying in her new room thinking without seeming reason, of the past:

> . . .She'll smile and put the tray down and I'll say Francine I've had such an awful dream—it was only a dream she'll say —and on the tray the blue cup and saucer and the silver teapot so I'd know for certain that it *had started again my lovely life*—like a five-finger exercise played very slowly on the piano like a garden with a high wall round it—and every now and again thinking *I only dreamt it it never happened*. . . (p. 135. Punctuation exact. Emphasis added.)

With that last line referring to the past—"I only dreamt it it never happened"—Rhys once more suggests that previously something sinister has happened to Anna, something more than the auto-erotic experience already discussed. Anna's life has involved another time of "starting over," as this moment here in her new room is also a time of fresh start.

Part Three

The third section of *Voyage in the Dark* explores Anna's relationship with Ethel; her affair with Walter's successor, Carl Redman; her concomitant and eager embracing of prostitution as an anodyne for her fear of being left on her own again; her ludicrous yet oddly poignant relationship with Ethel; and finally, the discovery of her pregnancy and the subsequent abortion itself. Primarily, however, in this section we see Anna's increasing gropings toward psychic wholeness. On the verge of an emotional sickness-unto-death, Anna finds memories of her youth continually intruding in archetypal images of Constance Estate with its "trees, like skeletons" and "spiders" and "octopuses." Finally, after a fight with Ethel, Anna lies in bed "tired" beyond the ability to move, remembering all the "rooms" of her life. These memories coalesce in a marvelous symbolic review of all that is at the root of Anna's conflicts:

It's funny how well you can remember when you lie in the dark with your arm over your forehead. Two eyes open inside your head. The sandbox tree outside the door at home and the horse waiting with his bridle over the hook that was fixed in the tree and the sweat rolling down Joseph's face when he helped me to mount and the tear in my habit-skirt. And mounting, and then the bridge and the sound of the horse's hoofs on the wooden planks, and then the savannah. And then there is New Town, and just beyond New Town the big mango tree. It was just past there that I fell off the mule when I was a kid and it seemed such a long time before I hit the ground. The road goes along by the sea. The coconut palms lean crookedly down to the water. (Francine says that if you wash your face in fresh coconut-water every day you are always young and unwrinkled, however long you live.) You ride in a sort of dream, the saddle creaks sometimes, and you smell the sea and the good smell of the horse. And then—wait a minute. Then do you turn to the right or the left? To the left, of course. You turn to the left and the sea is at your back, and the road goes zigzag upwards. The feeling of the hills comes to you—cool and hot at the same time. Everything is green, everywhere things are growing. There is never one moment of stillness-always something buzzing. And then dark cliffs and ravines and the smell of rotten leaves and damp. That's how the road to Constance is— green, and the smell of green, and then the smell of water and dark earth and rotting leaves and damp. There's a bird called a Mountain Whistler, that calls out on one note, very high-up and sweet and piercing. You ford little rivers. . . .When you see the sea again it's far below you. . . . (pp. 150-1)

This memory would be a Jungian psychologist's dream! There is the dream metaphor itself; the smell of sea (female archetype of life, the unconscious); the lush, dark, green, rotting smell of earth and water; the good smell of the horse (symbol of the uncontrollable, instinctive drives of the unconscious). As she pounds along the road, which turn to take? The turn to the right or the left? "To the left, of course," for that is the side of the unconscious—the evil (or natural in this case) as opposed to the right which is the sphere of the conscious, the implicitly good in Anna's mind. A bird sings one to recognition, truth, and you "ford little rivers"—symbolic of a basic change in attitude or direction.

The trip

> was as long as a life sometimes. I was nearly twelve before I rode it by myself. There were bits in the road that I was afraid of. The turning where you come very suddenly out of the sun into the shadow; and the shadow was always the same shape. And the place where the woman with yaws spoke to me. I suppose she was begging but I couldn't understand because her nose and mouth were eaten away; it seemed as though she were laughing at me. I was frightened; I kept on looking backwards to see if she was following me, but when the horse came to the next ford and I saw clear water I thought I had forgotten about her. And now—there she is. (p. 152)

The shadow, of course, is the image of evil, the other side of twelve-year-old, well-brought-up, religiously-educated Anna. And the woman with yaws—her mouth and nose eaten away—is Anna's vision of her diseased, sinful self. A vision as real to her now, lying in Ethel's room, as it was at the age of twelve when she took her first journey into experience.

But once again, as Anna's unconscious is on the verge of revealing everything to her, the world intrudes when Joe and Carl, Laurie's male companions, come to call. This time Carl touches Anna, and Anna knows: "When he touched me I knew that he was quite sure I would. I thought, 'All right then, I will.' I was surprised at myself in a way and in another way I wasn't surprised. . . . 'It's always on foggy days,' I thought." (p. 154). So for Anna, the life she had had with Walter begins again, this time with Carl. The waiting, the imagining:

> . . .imagining that there was nothing I couldn't do, nothing I couldn't become. Imagining God knows what. Imagining Carl would say, 'When I leave London, I'm going to take you with me.' And imagining it although his eyes had that look—this is just for while I'm here, and I hope you get me.
>
> 'I picked up a girl in London and she. . . .Last night I slept with a girl who. . . .' That was me.

Not 'girl' perhaps. Some other word, perhaps. Never mind. (p. 157. Punctuation exact.)

Still trapped in her conventional hope for a deeper relationship with Carl, Anna nevertheless is also immersed in her own sexuality, getting "lots of practice" while he is out of town on frequent trips. Money, then, is clearly not the real motive behind her prostitution. For Anna has money to spend and to lend, giving Maudie eight pounds ten without qualm.

The bill for pleasure must be paid, however, and one evening while entertaining a "client," Anna becomes violently ill and realizes she is pregnant. Lying in bed, everything "heaving up and down," childhood memories and fears again overwhelm her and she remembers the mountains of her home and her fears of blood-sucking zombi vampires:

Obeah zombis souciants—lying in the dark frightened of the dark frightened of souciants that fly in through the window and suck your blood—they fan you to sleep with their wings and then they suck your blood—you know them in the day-time—they look like people but their eyes are red and staring and they're souciants at night—looking in the glass and thinking sometimes my eyes look like a souciant's eyes. . . (p. 163)

At this point, Anna knows that she, herself, is the blood-sucker, feeding on the ugly, frail, pitiable nature of man. And now she must be punished by bearing an illegitimate child—like poor old "Miss Jackson Colonel Jackson's illegitimate daughter."

Following the passages of memories, there are three brief, ambiguous paragraphs in which Anna obliquely counts the time of impregnation, remembers the "eternal grimaces of disapproval," the folk-lore remedies offered by friends. Then there is a break—and *Anna's actual voyage in the dark begins.*

Extremely ill from various pills which she has taken (indicated in a later discussion with Laurie), Anna dreams that she is on a ship:

. . .From the deck you could see small islands—dolls of islands—and the ship was sailing in a dolls' sea, transparent as glass.

Somebody said in my ear, 'That's your island that you talk such a lot about.'

71

And the ship was sailing very close to an island, which was home except that the trees were all wrong. These were English trees, their leaves trailing in the water. I tried to catch hold of a branch and step ashore, but the deck of the ship expanded. Sombody had fallen overboard.

And there was a sailor carrying a child's coffin. He lifted the lid, bowed and said, 'The boy bishop,' and a little dwarf with a bald head sat up in the coffin. He was wearing a priest's robes. He had a large blue ring on his third finger.

'I ought to kiss the ring,' I thought in my dream, 'and then he'll start saying "In nomine Patris, Filii. . .".'

When he stood up, the boy bishop was like a doll. His large, light eyes in a narrow, cruel face rolled like a doll's as you lean it from one side to the other. He bowed from right to left as the sailor held him up.

But I was thinking, 'What's overboard?' and I had that awful dropping of the heart.

I was still trying to walk up the deck and get ashore. I took huge, climbing, flying strides among confused figures. I was powerless and very tired, but I had to go on. And the dream rose into a climax of meaninglessness, fatigue and powerlessness, and the deck was heaving up and down, and when I woke up everything was still heaving up and down.

It was funny how, after that, I kept on dreaming about the sea. (pp. 164-5)

This dream, also, is a Jungian case-study. The ship represents, of course, Anna's archetypal voyage of discovery into the guilts and fears of her unconscious. The trauma of her pregnancy and all its consequences have finally brought Anna's conscious mind to that necessary weakened state where, involuntarily and without conscious intellectual effort, she can perhaps come to terms with her psyche. The tree images —along with the ship—are archetypes of psychic growth, a growth reflected by Anna's dream. Catholic by upbringing, attempting to abort her child conceived in prostitution, Anna will find her conflicts reflected in images of Church and of condemnation. An over-all interpretation of Anna's dream might go something like this:

The sea (symbolic of the unconscious) on which her ship sails is transparent so that Anna can see clearly. The voice—according to

Jung, a dream-voice assumes great significance and must always be trusted—says, "That's your island that you talk such a lot about." And the island seems like home, *but the trees are all wrong*. Thus the island, symbolic of Eden to Anna, cannot be achieved because the trees—a major symbol of life, at once a male and female archetype—are all wrong; they are English trees, symbolic of a masculine world, sterile, cold, grey. Anna tries to catch hold of a branch and step ashore, but somebody has fallen overboard. Significantly, pulling off a branch of a tree is a symbol of onanism; thus Anna's unconscious guilt stemming from her early adolescence demands punishment and "falling" is the punishment symbolic of death, man's fall from God.

The sailor of Anna's dream probably represents Anna herself who carries the child, perhaps now dead, in her womb as the sailor carries the child in the coffin. The child is a dwarf, misshapen, bald—as Anna later reveals she fears her unaborted child might be—but he is also a bishop, wearing priest's robes. This image offers curious overtones. The child is, of course, the one Anna is trying to abort. But the church condemns abortion and hence the religious image. However, the bald, misshapen child in priest's robes might also be Anna—the child misshapen as she sees herself—since priests' robes often symbolize the protective cover or the "mask" of the persona, already discussed extensively in the section on *ALMM*. The large blue ring (a color which much concerns Anna), which she should kiss, probably symbolizes the sterility of the inner life that Anna's upbringing endorses—the ring representing in Jungian symbology the continuity of life and the color blue associated with the intellectual, conscious life. Additionally, the priest is an hermaphroditic image. Thus Anna's dream reveals simultaneously her unconscious guilt concerning her early sexual experience—whatever it may have been—and her desire to flee her own sexuality which she fears. Certainly the unconscious seems to be trying to communicate that fleeing into celibacy is not the answer for Anna, for the boy bishop has a narrow cruel face and he bows from right—the "conscious"—to left—the unconscious side.

Rhys uses the bishop image at the mythic level also, since the hermaphrodite is a common archetype of *psychic wholeness*—the male-female, the conscious-unconscious merged in one complete SELF. Thus Anna, knowing that something is "overboard" tries to climb, to take flying strides, symbols representing both sexual activity and the attempt to reach higher levels of understanding. Anna's unconscious is obviously trying to convey that she must come to accept her sexual nature if she is to progress further in her psychic growth.

But the dream rises to a "climax of meaninglessness" as Anna wakes, everything still heaving up and down. After that, she keeps dreaming of the sea.

Part Four

One last revelation from the unconscious remains for Anna. Following her visit to the abortionist, Anna lies in bed hemorrhaging as her friend, Laurie, tries to decide what to do. A memory of an earlier sexual experience fuses with a memory of her childhood, evidently a time of carnival:

A pretty useful mask that white one watch it and the slobbering tongue of an idiot will stick out—a mask Father said with an idiot behind it I believe the whole damned business is like that—Hester said Gerald the child's listening—oh no she isn't Father said she's looking out of the window and quite right too—it ought to be stopped somebody said it's not a decent and respectable way to go on it ought to be stopped—Aunt Jane said I don't see why they should stop the Masquerade they've always had their three days Masquerade ever since I can remember why should they want to stop it some people want to stop everything.

I was watching them from between the slats of the jalousies—they passed under the window singing—it was all colours of the rainbow when you looked down at them and sky so blue—there were three musicians at the head a man with a concertina and another with a chak-chak playing There's a Brown Girl in a Ring and after the musicians a lot of little boys turning and twisting and dancing and others dragging kerosene-tins and beating them with sticks—the masks the men wore were a crude pink with eyes squinting near together squinting but the masks the women wore were made of close-meshed wire covering the whole face and tied at the back of the head—the handkerchief that went over the back of the head hid the strings and over the slits for the eyes mild blue eyes were painted then there was a small straight nose and a little red heart-shaped mouth and under the

mouth another slit so that they could put their tongues out at
you—I could hear them banging the kerosene-tins. . .

I was watching them from between the slats of the jalousies
dancing along dressed in red and blue and yellow the women
with their dark necks and arms covered with white powder—
dancing along to concertina-music dressed in all the colours
of the rainbow and the sky so blue—you can't expect niggers
to behave like white people all the time Uncle Bo said it's
asking too much of human nature—look at that fat old
woman Hester said just look at her—oh yes she's having a go
too Uncle Bo said they all have a go they don't mind—their
voices were going up and down—I was looking out of the
window and I knew why the masks were laughing and I heard
the concertina-music going (pp. 184-6)

Now all is revealed. In the festive mummery—rooted as are all
these celebrations in ancient fertility rites and the conflict between
good and evil, life and death—all that is brown or black is vital, earthy,
joyous. The white masks represent the outward appearance behind
which the reality mockingly hides. The masks the women wear are of
close-meshed wire, restricting, permitting only vacuous blue eyes and
painted heart-shaped mouths, the ideal of the white world, and by
extension, of the ego and superego.

But the masks of black sexuality grin out tauntingly from behind
the white masks of respectable hypocrisy. And Anna knows why the
masks are laughing!

Then in her delirium, Anna's mind seems to jump to another
carnival time and this episode merges all experience into the first
experience, the experience with Walter *or someone else,* and then
flows back to Carnival:

I'm awfully giddy—but we went on dancing forwards and
backwards backwards and forwards whirling round and
round

The concertina-man was very black—he sat sweating
and the concertina went forwards and backwards backwards
and forwards one two three one two three pourquoi ne pas
aimer bonheur suprême—the triangle-man kept time on his
triangle and with his foot tapping and the little man who

played the chak-chak smiled with his eyes fixed

Stop stop stop—I thought you'd say that he said

My darling mustn't worry my darling mustn't be sad—I thought say that again say that again but he said it's nearly four o'clock perhaps you ought to be going

You ought to be going he said—I tried to hang back but it was useless and the next moment my feet were groping for the stirrups—there weren't any stirrups—I balanced myself in the saddle trying to grip with my knees

The horse went forward with an exaggerated swaying lilting motion like a rocking-horse—I felt very sick—I heard the concertina-music playing behind me all the time and the noise of the people's feet dancing—the street was in a green-ish shadow—I saw the rows of small houses on each side in front of one of them there was a woman cooking fishcakes on an iron stove filled with charcoal—and then the bridge and the sound of the horse's hoofs on the wooden planks—and then the savannah—the road goes along by the sea—do you turn to the right or the left—the left of course—and then that turning where the shadow is always the same shape—shadows are ghosts you look at them and you don't see them —you look at everything and you don't see it only sometimes you see it like now I see—a cold moon looking down on a place where nobody is a place full of stones where nobody is

I thought I'm going to fall nothing can save me now but still I clung desperately with my knees feeling very sick (pp. 186-7)

Now we can surmise that at some carnival time before she was sixteen, Anna had somehow participated in the celebrations, caught up in the debauchery and excesses which left her feeling damned—"no-thing can save me now"—and "feeling very sick." We may further assume that whatever had happened had resulted in her being brought to England to "start all over again." We may also conclude that the memories of a funeral where "they said so young to die" (p. 97) con-cerned the death of someone she had loved and lost as punishment for her "sin," just as the loss of Walter has been punishment for later sin. We know that though she had attempted to control her sexual urgings (the rider in the saddle trying to balance herself), that she took, has taken, and will take again the "turn to the left." The "shadow", however, is always there (the other self) and the cold moon (the female principle) looks down on a "place where nobody is"—a "place full of stones" (the male archetype) "where nobody is" (the nothing-ness of woman).

This, then, for woman, is the undeniable despair, the ultimate death. Desirous, sexual by nature (the infection is in the blood, Rhys really says), needing man to complete her identity,[30] her SELF-ness, woman, in a world of crude pink-masked men with "eyes squinting near together near together squinting," has no real hope!

Then Anna's dream is suddenly over, the crisis past. The doctor and Laurie laugh and chat as Anna ". . .lay and watched it and thought about starting all over again. And about being new and fresh. And about mornings, and misty days, when anything might happen. *And about starting all over again, all over again.* . . (p. 188. Emphasis added.)

With this last paragraph, we have come full circle in the life and truth of Rhys's story of a tart. Anna Morgan, literally translated "grace or spirit from the sea," has told us, and hopefully herself, the truth in her voyage into the dark. In so doing she has forced us to face an honest and inescapable issue: if a woman's nature is such that, like Laurie and Anna herself, she really "likes it," " 'why shouldn't she [as Anna says] be a tart? It's just as good as anything else, as far as I can see.' " (p. 127).

Nevertheless, even as we admit the validity of both the question and the answer, Rhys leaves Anna's " 'Oh *God* . . .do leave me alone, do leave me alone,' " still haunting us. But, on the verge of helpless pity for Anna and all women like her, we are brought up short, remembering Maudie's comment early in the story concerning Zola's *Nana:* " ' . . .a man writing a book about a tart tells a lot of lies one way and another. *Besides, all books are like that—just somebody stuffing you up.*' " (p. 10. Emphasis added.) Then we remember Anna herself saying to Joe, the American, " ' . . .You didn't know my father. Because my real name isn't Morgan and I'll never tell you my real name and I was born in Manchester and I'll never tell you anything real about myself. *Everything that I tell you about myself is a lie . . .*' " (p. 125. Emphasis added.)

Thus Rhys permits us no false sentimentality. She forces us back to an ultimate theme, the unanswered question of her previous novels: "What, then, is truth?"

And suddenly, with a flash of insight, we realize the trick that Rhys has played—that all that has gone before in the discussion of this novel has been but half-truth. For hidden in "the story of a tart" is a subterranean myth already subterranean in its own right! Through her youthful protagonist, Anna Morgan, taking her personal voyage into the dark of her unconscious, Rhys has also taken her receptive reader on a journey far beyond the myths of Greece and Rome, a journey permitted by details already discussed. Rhys, the myth-maker, has penetrated the dark, unconscious racial memory of a long-forgotten time. A prehistoric time when the *Female Principle* dominated. A time when the Sun-Moon-Sea-Mother goddess in all her manifestations was worshipped. A time when the Judaic-Christian patriarchal myth (which permits no goddesses) had not yet subdued the Graeco-Olympian mythology, which itself had absorbed or destroyed the more ancient Celtic religions of goddess worship. The myths of these Celtic religions, almost lost in the mist of time, continue celebrated to this day in secret bardic Welsh tradition, the heritage of both Anna Morgan the heroine and Jean Rhys the author.

THE MYTHS OF "ANNA" OR
THE GODDESS LOST

It is the name of *Anna* which gives us insight to Rhys's bardic undercurrents and leads us to comprehension of a major theme she has been at pains to develop in almost overlooked detail. For *Anna* assumes overwhelming significance in ancient mythologies, metamorphosing as it does in various and complicated ways. For example, the *Anna* of Celtic myth, the Sea-Moon goddess, becomes the Irish *Ana,* the Great-Good Mother in beneficent mask or "Morrigan" the "Great Queen" in maleficent guise, a composite and fearful trinity-of-fate.[31] This is the same goddess also known as Danu or Danann or Buanann from whom the pantheon of Celtic gods derives its name—Tuatha De Danaan. In the Celtic (Gaelic) mythology, this Ana or Aine or Anann has been called the queen of Heaven, "mater deorum Hibernensium"—mother of the Irish gods.[32] Other derivations of Anna exist in the Sumerian *Ama* (mother) and in contracted form in Ma-ri (the fruitful mother), a goddess worshipped by Egyptians before 1000 B.C. Ma-ri-enna is the "fruitful mother of Heaven," which becomes Miriam, Mirianme. Ultimately, the ancient "fruitful mother of Heaven," mother of the gods, will become the Virgin Queen of Heaven, Mary the mother of

Christ. But before this, in Graeco-Roman myth, Anna emerges in complex synthesis as Minerva the Moon-goddess, as Athene, Ariadne, and even as the Great Mother, Urania.[33] The importance of the name Anna in pre-Judaic-Christian myth is summarized by Robert Graves: " . . .indeed if one needs a single, simple, inclusive name for the Great Goddess, Anna is the best choice. To Christian mystics she is 'God's Grandmother'." (*The White Goddess,* p. 372).

This process of transition from the ancient, female-centered myths into the conquering masculine theogonies is easily illustrated in Hebrew myth, as Anna (Earth-Sea-Moon-Mother-goddess) becomes Rahab, the priestess of primordial chaos. This priestess is subdued by God in the beginning of time and is gradually denigrated to become only the temptress, the mistress of fleshly corruption, a motif which will dominate Judeo-Christian attitudes concerning woman. Eventually, Anna-Rahab reincarnates as "Hannah," the mother of Biblical Samuel, her name now signifying "full of grace, mercy, prayer." (Graves, p. 480). Thus, mythically, the "Great Goddess" is progressively reduced from a virtual Earth-Mother, ruler of Sun, Moon, Sea, to a vitiated, non-threatening, male-engendered woman who waits upon her Lord with grace and prayer! This is the same process by which Ma-ri-enna, the ancient Mother of Heaven, becomes Mary, a vessel for God, and *through Him* is elevated to become a *virginal* Queen of Heaven, by virtue, ironically, of being the human mother of God Incarnate.

If more proof is needed to validate the significance of Anna's name, her surname Morgan—Celtic in origin, a contraction of the "Morrigan" mentioned above, in its own form meaning "from the sea"—should clinch the point.

In such manner, subliminally playing upon unconscious racial memories, Rhys evokes her myth, drawing her reader back into time when woman was not dominated by man but rather when man himself worshipped the life-giving and death-dealing female principle, paying homage, both spiritual and sexual. It is at this level of unconscious impact that *Voyage in the Dark* becomes art in the highest sense, its poetic power undeniable.

II

Now, aware of the underlying mythos, the reader synthesizes already suggested details of Anna's memories. Tall, thin, Maudie

Beardon—the "minstrel" who "rules"—suggests the Celtic bards who secretly and at risk of life preserved the myths of the great and terrible White Goddess, even as they accommodated them to the encroachments of the cold, sterile, masculine, Teutonic-Judeo-Christian world. Like the Goddess herself, who triumphed cruelly over men who denied her power or withheld due homage, Maudie also triumphs over the men who use her, knowing that "the thing with men is to get everything you can out of them and not care a damn." Similarly, the irony of Ethel Matthews, that unattractive, exploitive, stand-on-her-own-feet woman, whose name in its Teutonic-Hebraic form means "God's noble gift," emerges simultaneously as a sad comment on the debasement of the life-giving female force and as a caustic comment on the "creation" of a man-centered theogony, a neutered woman who makes her own way in a masculine world and is at once approved intellectually and scorned emotionally and sexually. Thus Maudie and Ethel become horribly mutated avatars of the Great Goddess.

More importantly, within the framework of this Anna myth, unexplained ambiguities concerning Anna Morgan become clear. For example, Anna's resentment over Walter's concern with her virginity (cf. p. 60) takes on added dimension. For the Anna of ancient myth was never a virgin in the current sense of sexual purity, only in the sense of not having been tainted by marriage.[34] All goddess worship was traditionally rooted in fertility rites honoring the sacred creative principle. Man copulated with priestesses—and woman in general—as a form of worship. But as Christianity triumphed, the physical worship of the fecund goddess was supplanted by the spiritual worship of the Virgin Mary. Thus Anna's: " 'Why did you start about that . . . What's it matter? Besides I'm not a virgin if that's what's worrying you,' " evokes memories of a time that "you've always known, always remembered, and then you forget so utterly, except that you've always known it. . . ." This memory was of a time when the dual sensual and creative nature of woman was not only recognized but honored, worshipped, fulfilled.

Likewise, Anna's remark to Joe—" 'You're a liar. . . . you didn't know my father. Because my real name isn't Morgan and I'll never tell you my real name and I was born in Manchester and I'll never tell you anything real about myself. Everything that I tell you about myself is a lie . . .' " (p. 125)—assumes significance beyond wounded pride. That is, her " 'You didn't know my father' " suggests that in a matrilinear society, fatherhood is unaccountable, unimportant. Further, one cannot know the father of the goddess who is herself "God's Grandmother" and the "universal mother."[35] Of course, Anna's "real name" can never be known since the female principle assumes such various forms as illustrated above. However, Anna was indeed "born in Manchester," as she declares. In her present avatar (the Anna who finds herself mocked by and at the mercy of the Walters and Joes of the world), she has been created "in the camp of man," that fortified citadel erected by the upstart patriarchal systems, epitomized by the masculine Victorian world.

III

The final detail tying this mythic interpretation irrefutably together, lies in our increased understanding of the dream sequence discussed above (cf. pp. 71-3). Within the framework of Celtic mythology, we can now understand the significance of the island and the trees of Anna's dream: "Somebody said in my ear, 'That's your island that you talk such a lot about.' And the ship was sailing very close to an island, which was home except that the trees were all wrong. These were English trees, their leaves trailing in the water." (p. 164). For in Celtic myth, as the Great Mother was systematically dethroned, becoming in man's evolving scheme the principle of darkness, cold, temptation, she was imprisoned below the sea ("Why didn't you bloody well make a hole in the water?" *Voyage*, p. 164), or banished to islands where she waited to lure men to destruction. Thus the myths of the Sirens, the Lorelei, thus Anna Morgan's, "And how do you know what it's like to try to speak from under water when you're drowned?" (*Voyage*, p. 98).[36]

But in earlier times, the goddess of the sea (as a sexual symbol) promised love, fulfillment, life. Thus the islands, Anna's original home[37] (symbolic of her ancient earthy, sexual reality) represent to her an Eden, decayed though it may now be. But in her dream, the trees are all wrong. They are *English* trees. Now as Graves (p. 38) points out, "in all Celtic languages *trees* means *letters*" and any amateur philologist knows the common derivation of the words "books" and "literature" from the word "beech." Graves emphasizes the significance of this relationship, asserting that the study of mythology is "based squarely on tree-lore . . ." (p. 11).[38] Thus symbolically, the "wrong trees" signify the wrong letters, books, literature, myths. These are

English (Teutonic-Judeo-Christian) myths and therefore the island can never be Anna's home, her paradise.

In similar manner we extend the significance of the concluding details of the dream. The "little dwarf" in "priest's robes" wearing the blue ring which signified the cold, intellectual life becomes the "boy bishop" of "narrow, cruel face" or the masculine priesthood.[39] And suddenly, infringing on that awareness, we remember Anna's memory of an earlier life: "...Here's the punch Uncle Bo said welcome Hebe—this child certainly can mix a good punch Father said something to warm the cockles of your heart." (p. 51). We think of Hèbe of Graeco-Roman myth, cup-bearer to the gods, supplanted by Ganymede, the Trojan "boy" whom Jupiter installed in heaven in her place (suggesting again the perversion of the natural female order by man and his consequent literature).

IV

Finally, then, we arrive at an understanding of Rhys's increasingly focused and controlled mythopoesis. Having more or less consciously freed herself from the "utter misery" of her life in the writing of *Quartet* and the subsequent *After Leaving Mr. Mackenzie*, Rhys has become emotionally and psychologically strong enough to turn again to those writings of an earlier day, writings which generated at least as early as 1914 and possibly as early as 1910. Turning from the restricted male-centered vision of the first two novels, Rhys reconstructs the dim outlines of a female-centered reality which she had stumbled upon some twenty years earlier and which she had hinted at in the person of Julia's mother (*ALMM*), that dying old woman struggling for life. She takes her reader on a voyage, not chronologically but psychically, through her own maturing vision. Thus the male-dominated reality of a Marya Zelli (*Quartet*) yields to that of a Julia[40] (*ALMM*), who survives in that same male structure almost on the verge of important self-discovery. Julia in turn apotheosizes into Anna, who having recognized herself (at least subconsciously)[41] as her own "center" lies in bed following the abortion, thinking of "starting all over again."

Appropriately, all three women bear children—as does Zola's Nana—symbolic of their ancient natural, life-giving powers. But in the hands of Zola, the male writer, Nana the Golden Venus, in effect a sexually distorted creation of man's own needs, must be destroyed by her son for being what she is,[42] just as the ancient goddess Anna—Grandmother of God—was destroyed by the engulfing patriarchal system. A Marya or a Julia, the product of that same male construct, must "lose" her child, a kind of symbolic sacrifice upon the altar of the male-universe which denigrates her life-giving powers and denies her economic and emotional survival. Anna, however, close to the reality of her own primal nature—a nature which is *not* a reflection of the masculine order—deliberately aborts her child; not for lack of money, not as a sacrifice to the conventions of the patriarchal, hypocritical white world. Anna aborts her child, without remorse, because, in the tradition of the Great Goddess, she is at once *creator* and *destroyer,* an independent force bearing the burden of no man! It is only when she has unconsciously but irrevocably acted in accordance with this duality of her own nature, aborting that which would destroy her, that the truth hidden in her unconscious can manifest itself and she can emerge whole.

Conclusion

And so we arrive at full awareness of Rhys's art and myth. Building on Zola's novel of a fallen woman, Nana, who was punished for her sins against man and his society, Rhys creates her own "story of a tart," Anna, a product of the sins committed against her nature by man and the society which he dominates. In moving from the perverted "Golden Venus" of Zola's male conception to the West-Indian-by-birth Anna Morgan, Rhys plucks—from the depths of her unconscious—sad melodies of mythic strain from the lyre of time, evoking memories of ancient sin against the life-giving female force. And in the siren song of different time and different way, she lulls us into hope that for the Annas of the world there might still be "mornings, and misty days, when anything might happen." But this hope, says Rhys, if it exists at all, lies in their awakening from the evil dream. Awakening from the illusory dream of safety which so long has held them captive, to take responsibility for their own lives, in whatever terms are right for them.

V

Clearly, in the light of all this complexity, *Voyage in the Dark* cannot be examined in any depth as a forerunner of *Quartet,* even though we have proof of its early genesis. The Marya of *Quartet* is an older Anna only in a chronological sense. In the psychological sense, she is a psychically younger and historically newer woman than the almost primal Anna Morgan. For Marya, bound by the unseen halters of her Zeitgeist, Rhys could offer no comfort. But for Anna Morgan there is hope — not illusory comfort in the dream of love, but only the glare of self-knowledge which, at the very least, precludes self-delusion.

It is not in Marya, then, but in Sasha, of *Good Morning, Midnight,* that we will find the avatar of Anna.

Chapter 4

GOOD MORNING, MIDNIGHT [43]

THE LABYRINTH OF TIME

In her fourth novel, *Good Morning, Midnight*—the last she was to write before the holocaust of World War II changed completely the structure of society—Rhys concludes her exploration of the feminine consciousness. This time there will be no journey into the darkness of myth and symbol as in *Voyage in the Dark;* Anna Morgan has made that journey, along with Rhys and her readers. Now there remains only the necessity for *conscious acceptance,* without hate or fear or recrimination, of the truths already conveyed. Then Rhys will have achieved her integration of the feminine psyche, leaving woman (Rhys, heroine, reader) freed to embrace life more maturely on her own individualized terms. This completion will be realized in the person of Sasha (Sophia) Jansen, protagonist and first-person narrator of *Good Morning, Midnight.*

As she has done in previous novels, Rhys, in *Good Morning, Midnight,* almost obscures the complexity of her theme in the economy of plot. Again, because of this, critics ignore or oversimplify important details, even as they almost unanimously praise Rhys's art. Overtly, this is the least complicated of the four novels. Plot seems simple, untortured, in its flashback technique. Characterization is limited to Sasha herself, other characters ostensibly serving only as bit players filling out the scenes of her life's routines. Narrative control is superb, revealing Sasha's first person awareness of herself and the world she inhabits. So technically proficient has Rhys become that she literally conceals the fact that she has reintroduced in compressed form every concern of her previous novels. This time, though, she chooses to reveal her "truths" wholly and clearly, not through distorting mirrors as she has done heretofore. For her narrator, Sasha Jansen, unlike Marya and Julia and Anna, harbors no illusion, clutches no hope, asks no quarter. Her life, "which seems so simple and monotonous," has been reduced to "a complicated affair of cafes where they like me and cafes where they don't, streets that are friendly, streets that aren't, rooms where I might be happy, rooms where I never shall be, looking-glasses I look nice in, looking-glasses I don't, dresses that will be lucky, dresses that won't and so on." (p. 46). Sasha has, she is able to admit to herself, "no pride, no name, no face, no country. I don't belong any-where. Too sad, too sad. . .It doesn't matter, there I am, like one of those straws which floats round the edge of a whirlpool and is gradually sucked into the centre, the dead centre, where everything is stagnant, everything is calm. . ." (p. 44).

But in the midst of Sasha's searing insight into her reality, Rhys, as she has done time and again, plays her trick of questioning the truth of "truth": ". . . You imagine the carefully-pruned, shaped thing that is presented to you is truth. That is just what it isn't. The truth is improbable, the truth is fantastic; it's in what you think is a distorting mirror that you see the truth." (p. 74). Thus the reader is warned to look beyond overt truth, to analyze seeming distortions in order to discover that unconscious level which is "true" and where all details will synthesize and Rhys's thematic truth be revealed.

II

The plot of *Good Morning, Midnight* is simple. The time is late October, 1937. Sasha—middle-aged, very "Anglaise," on the verge of illness—having been made "very cold and very sane" and "very passive"—revisits Paris, the scene of significant events in her younger years. Ensconced in a room in Montparnasse—money borrowed from a friend, Sidonie, permitting her some extravagance and freedom from worry—Sasha walks familiar streets, visits familiar restaurants, seek-ing familiar faces from the bittersweet past. Immersed in memories, haunted by fear of aging, desiring death, she strikes up an acquaint-ance with the Ukrainian, Nicholas Delmar, meets his artist friend, Serge, from whom she buys a painting, and is picked up by René, a young gigolo intent on seducing her.[44] These superficialities of plot culminate in a final scene in which René attempts seduction, Sasha rejects and humiliates him, and he subsequently departs, leaving her stunned and confused by his failure to forceably violate her and steal her money. Appreciating this "sweet gigolo, from the depths of her heart," desiring and expecting his imminent return, Sasha, lying naked on her bed, finds herself, instead, confronted by the old *commis*, [45] "thin as a skeleton . . . cringing, ingratiating," who lives in the room next door. The novel ends with Sasha seeing him standing there in his white dressing gown:

> He stands there, looking down at me. Not sure of himself, his mean eyes flickering.
> He doesn't say anything. Thank God, he doesn't say anything. I look straight into his eyes and despise another poor devil of a human being for the last time. For the last time. . . .
> Then I put my arms round him and pull him down on to the bed, saying 'Yes — yes — yes . . . .' (p. 89. Punctuation exact.)

In this ending, which Francis Wyndham, in his introduction to *Wide Sargasso Sea* calls "brilliantly written and indescribably unnerving to read,"[46] critics have seen the culmination of the "Jean Rhys heroine," a woman who evolves from a hate-fear-filled adolescent, concerned only with her own suffering, to a compassionate, feeling woman whose "pity extends beyond herself to embrace all other sufferers."[47] Curiously enough, even as they praise the art and explain the significance of this act of Sasha's, every critic avoids the questions which the ending raises, as well as many other details upon which the dénouement rests. To successfully resolve this final scene and do full justice to Rhys's art, we must carefully analyze the four sections into which Rhys divides her novel, interweave each of these sections, and finally, relate them to the nuances of the earlier novels. Then we will arrive at the "truth" that is "improbable," the "truth" that is "fantastic" and understand the ambivalence inherent in Rhys's title, *Good Morning, Midnight*.

Part One

Part One of *Good Morning, Midnight*, seemingly so simple, is a masterpiece of complexity. Ten lines provide a description of Sasha's room, the street outside, the information that within her five days in Paris she has carefully arranged her "little life" into "a place to eat at midday, a place to eat at night, a place to have [her] drink in after dinner." Suddenly Rhys shifts the focus from the present to Sasha's memory of a catastrophic experience the previous evening when, in a public cafe, she had succumbed to maudlin weeping. "Unable to stop crying," Sasha remembers having gone to the "lavabo" where, staring at herself in the mirror, memories of the past had overwhelmed her: "dark streets, dark rivers, the pain, the struggle and the drowning"— images reminding the reader of the psychological gropings of Julia (*ALMM*) and of Anna (*Voyage*). Then deftly, Rhys merges Sasha's memory of the lavabo of the present with memories of a lavabo in Florence in turn merging with a Parisian lavabo of another time where one could buy drugs to "heal a wounded heart."

Thus complexly, in less than three pages, Rhys forces her reader to the knowledge that she has trapped us in a sequence of time from which we can never extricate ourselves. Using the technique already employed in *Voyage in the Dark*, where the beginning was the end of the story and the end the beginning, Rhys will make one day of Sasha's present overlap with another, merging those days with overlapping days of the past into a sense of timelessness. Thus, reaching the end of the novel, the reader will know that this cannot be the ending. As Sasha embraces the old man from the room next door, we clearly understand that Sasha, our first-person narrator, is not revealing the experience as it happens, in *media res* as it were, but that this is the beginning of a new life which will, however, continue in other rooms just like the one described in the opening lines of her narrative.

Recognizing the aesthetic superiority of Rhys's structure and the impossibility of ever ordering it completely—as futile an effort as attempting to impose order upon life, Rhys seems to imply—we can, nevertheless, abstract from the events which are "all washing about, like the bilge in the hold of a ship," (p. 168), the facts of at least a portion of Sasha's past and present.

There is, we learn, a woman friend, Sidonie, ("the enticer") who has "swooped down" upon Sasha after months of absence. Because she "can't bear" to see the way Sasha looks (" 'She's getting to look old. She drinks.' ''), Sidonie lends her money for this trip, urging her to buy new clothes, which she "certainly" needs. In Paris, living in the dark room with "more red curtains"—the one which Sidonie has chosen for her because she "imagines that it's [Sasha's] atmosphere" —Sasha maintains her link with reality and sanity through routine, liquor, and sleeping drugs. Lying on her bed in the room which is like all the others she has known, walking the streets she has walked before, Sasha dredges up the past.

In 1923 or 24 she had lived with her husband, Enno, just around the corner and had changed her name from Sophia to Sasha, hoping it would bring her luck. (This is the archetypal theme of name as essence.) Sometime before or after that—we never know—there was a French dress-house where she worked as a receptionist. "It was dreary" and she was fired by the English manager, "the real English type" whom Sasha knows at once and against whose taunting disdain there is no defense. Through such details, Rhys recapitulates a major theme of *Quartet* and *After Leaving Mr. Mackenzie:* the cold, hypocritical capitalist, always English, who exploits without pity the poor working girl trapped in the misery of her barren life.

One memory of the past triggers another and Sasha remembers other abortive attempts to fit into the mould of the respectable working girl—another former Rhys theme—being a shop girl in London, an American Express tour guide in Paris. She had tried but: ". . .they always see through me. The passages never lead anywhere, the doors will always be shut. I know. . ." (p. 31). And always, she remembers, there was the conspiracy of the hard, sad, rich; and the "freemasonry among those who prey upon the rich." With this last detail, Rhys indicates to the reader some of the self-knowledge which Sasha (Sophia means wisdom) has acquired. In no other novel has the heroine been able to admit that exploitation is not the prerogative of the rich.

One morning in the present, lying in the bath on the first floor, watching the cockroaches "crawling from underneath the carpet and crawling back again," Sasha remembers the ups and downs of her life in terms of rooms:

> That's the way it is, that's the way it goes, that was the way
> it went. . . .A room. A nice room. A beautiful room with bath.
> A very beautiful room with bath. A bedroom and sitting-
> room with bath. Up to the dizzy heights of the suite. Two
> bedrooms, sitting-room, bath, and vestibule. . . .Swing high

> . . .Now slowly, down. A beautiful room with bath, A room
> with bath, A nice room. A room. . . . (pp. 33-4)

But ultimately, Sasha knows that: ". . .All rooms are the same. All rooms have four walls, a door, a window or two, a bed, a chair and perhaps a bidet. A room is a place where you hide from the wolves outside . . . ." (p. 38).

The wolves that Sasha hides from are like that "extremely respectable" "old devil" she remembers who, five years earlier in London, had asked her why she hadn't drowned herself in the Seine, why she hadn't "made a hole in the water" since they all had considered her as dead anyway. But, "jam after the medicine," she had learned from the old man that she has a legacy of two pounds ten shillings a week for life, left by someone Sasha hadn't thought liked her at all. But as she sees the resentment in the "old devil's" eyes, Sasha knows that her benefactress had done it "to annoy the rest of the family."

With these details, Rhys returns us to episodes of *After Leaving Mr. Mackenzie:* Julia's relationship with her Uncle Griffiths and her sister, Norah, who was to receive money from "Aunt Sophie's will, and the will her mother had made." (*ALMM*, p. 105). This inheritance, we remember, was to free Norah from her life of drudgery. Now here is Sasha—obviously a namesake of Aunt Sophie—receiving money which will provide the necessities of life and enable her, supposedly, to more fully control her life. Ironically, however, while money promised life to Norah, for Sophia it had meant

> . . .the end . . ., the real end. Two-pound-ten every Tuesday
> and a room off the Gray's Inn Road. Saved, rescued and with
> my place to hide in—what more did I want? I crept in and
> hid. The lid of the coffin shut down with a bang. Now I no
> longer wish to be loved, beautiful, happy or successful. I
> want one thing only—to be left alone. No more pawings, no
> more pryings—*leave me alone*. . . . (p. 43. Emphasis
> Rhys's.)

And with thirty-five pounds of accumulated legacy, Sasha had tried to drink herself to death—a process she intends to continue when she returns to London (p. 34).

But for now Sasha is in Paris and on the seventh day, walking the

Boulevard St. Michel, she is "not at all sad" but she is "tired." Even as she thinks this, two men come up from behind and

> . . .walk along on either side. . . .One of them says: 'Pour-
> quoi etes vous si triste?'
> Yes, I am sad, sad as a circus-lioness, sad as a violin
> with only one string and that one broken, sad as a woman
> who is growing old. Sad, sad sad . . . . Or perhaps if I just
> said 'merde' it would do as well. (p. 45)

Amazingly, in these four sentences Rhys not only introduces an important minor character but, through her imagery, again summarizes details of *every previous novel*. Thus, in the men who accost Sasha, we are reminded of the "boy" who had followed and then rejected Julia (*ALMM*) after seeing her in the light of the lamp-post. The image of the lioness—no longer free and threatening but caged in a circus—the violin with only one string and that one broken evoke the mythic de-throned and broken Great Goddess implicit in *Voyage in the Dark*. The sad, aging woman is like the dying mother of Julia, old, sad, an anachronism (*ALMM*). And finally, Sasha's desire to reduce everything to "merde"—roughly an equivalent of the English "shit"—reminds us of *Quartet* and Rhys's groping with the problem of woman's need for a language to communicate the "butt-ends" of her life, denied as she is the four letter scatology of the male. Rhys will further develop these almost subliminal implications as the novel progresses.

The men who accost her, the "Russians," are introduced and as the three stop under a lamp-post to "guess nationalities," Rhys turns us again to the theme of heritage so important in all her novels. As she does so, bits and pieces of Sasha's narrative fall into place. Now we understand the hotel-keeper's questioning of her passport: "What's wrong with the fiche? I've filled it up all right, haven't I? Name So-and-so, nationality So-and-so . . . . Nationality—that's what has puzzled him. I ought to have put nationality by marriage." (p. 14). We know, also, why the Russians "tactfully" refrain from guessing her nation-ality. There is something odd about Sasha; she does not look Anglo-Saxon in spite of her name, in spite of her hat which "shouts 'An-glaise.' " Similarly, Sasha's concern with dyeing her hair, with having "educated" hair becomes more than just a vain concern with age and the desire to look younger. Remembering Anna (*Voyage*) who was called "hottentot" because of her hair and who alternately fought and embraced her "black" heritage—the heritage of the body, of life—we penetrate the ambiguities of this so patently 'Anglaise' Sasha, whose clothes shout "mad old Englishwoman," but who speaks the slang of the Parisian demimonde. This woman who had "no name, no face, no country," who doesn't "belong anywhere," (p. 44) is WOMAN, displaced, dethroned, denied, and thus fearful of her sexual essence. In the world created by man, she is doomed to be "the stranger, the alien, the old one," who asks herself "all the time what the devil I am doing here." (p. 54).

That this association with myth is mandatory is indicated by Rhys as Sasha and the Russians philosophize over drinks following the pickup. As Sasha shrewdly assesses her companions, she thinks:

> Now, for goodness' sake, listen to this conversation, which, after the second drink, seems to be about *gods and goddesses*.
>
> 'Madame Vénus se fâchera,' the short one is saying, wagging his finger at me.
>
> 'Oh, her!' I say. 'I don't like her any more. She's played too many dirty tricks.'
>
> 'She does that to everyone. All the same, be careful . . . What god do they worship in England, what goddess?'
>
> 'I don't know, but it certainly isn't Venus. Somebody wrote once that they worship a *bitch-goddess*. It certainly isn't Venus.' (p. 47. Emphasis Added.)

Certainly at this point, no one can raise the issue of "critic imposition," for not only does Rhys deliberately raise the subject of gods and goddesses but, with the specific reference to Venus, and even further to a bitch-goddess, returns us again to the overtones of the myths of Anna (cf. p. 78), in all their permutations. For Venus, the Latin goddess of love, was Aphrodite (the foam-born) of the Greeks. Aphrodite, in turn, was the Greek version of a more ancient sea-goddess, Marian, the merry-maid or mermaid (Graves, p. 395). This Marian metamorphoses into the Virgin Mary who was equated by the early Christian Gnostics with the Holy Spirit—a concept originally female in the Hebrew—or with *Sophia*, Wisdom (Graves, p. 157), which was also female in concept. Thus, in this brief reference to Venus, Rhys merges, even apotheosizes, the protagonists of all four novels into a single symbol for archetypal woman in all her mutation. That is, Marya becomes Julia becomes Anna becomes Sophia—all deriving in some form from the old Great Goddess and all, incidentally, the names of saints in the Catholic pantheon!

Other small details accord with the sea-goddess image: Sasha's constant references to fish; her preoccupation with trees, "slender, straight trunks of trees" (p. 52), "thin, frail trunks of the trees" (p. 56), trees that resemble the slender palm-tree sacred to Aphrodite (Graves, p. 395), and the birch-like hazel, which is the tree of Wisdom (Sophia) (Graves, p. 182). The death-dealing aspect of the terrible triple-goddess is reflected in Sasha's hatred for the English girl who calls her "that old woman":

> Never mind. . . .[she thinks] One day, quite suddenly, when you're not expecting it, I'll take a hammer from the folds of my dark cloak and crack your little skull like an egg-shell; out they will stream, the blood, the brains. One day, one day. . . . One day the fierce wolf that walks by my side will spring on you and rip your abominable guts out. One day, one day. . . .Now, now, gently, quietly, quietly. . . . (p. 52. Punctuation exact.)

The knowledge that the wolf, along with the pig and the cat were sacred to the Moon-goddess (Graves, p. 222) will explain Sasha's "pig" references and her memory of the pitiful cat with the "terrible eyes, that knew her fate" and was killed by a "merciful taxi."

Rhys will use that harrowing memory of the cat to force Sasha's memories "back, back, back. . ." to the baby which she bore, only to see it die. On the surface, this episode seems rooted in a comment on the economics of life—the need for "money, money, money." But underlying that overt comment, Rhys suggests again the old Earth-Mother motif. For in the lying-in hospital for poor people, with "people having babies all over the place," Sasha learns the truth of woman's essence. For woman there is

> . . . No Jesus, no Mother, and no chloroform either. . . .
> What, then?
> This.
> Always?
> Yes, always.
> She comes and wipes my forehead. She speaks to me *in*

93

a language that is no language. But I understand it.

Back, back, back. . . . This has happened many times.

What are you? I am an instrument, something to be made use of . . . .

She darts from one room to another, encouraging, soothing, reproaching. 'Now you're not trying. Courage, courage.' Speaking her *old, old language of words that are not words.* (p. 58. Emphasis added.)

Thus Rhys recognizes WOMAN in her essence, giving life—*Anna, Arrian,* "High fruitful mother."

Only one major mythic detail of *Part One* remains to be discussed, a detail which in turn will introduce imagery central to our understanding of the conclusion of the novel and to the completion of the process of Sasha's individuation (cf. pp. 79-83). On the fifth night of her stay in Paris, Sasha has a nightmarish dream of being trapped in the passages of an underground tube station in London. All around are signs reading:

. . . This Way to the Exhibition, This Way to the Exhibition. But I don't want the way to the exhibition—I want the way out. There are passages to the right and passages to the left, but no exit sign. . . . I touch the shoulder of the man walking in front of me. I say: 'I want the way out.' But he points to the placards and his hand is made of steel. I walk along with my head bent, very ashamed, thinking: 'Just like me— always wanting to be different from other people.' The steel finger points along a long stone passage. This Way—This Way—This Way. . . .

Now a little man, bearded, with a snub nose, dressed in a long white night-shirt, is talking earnestly to me. 'I am your father,' he says. 'Remember that I am your father.' But blood is streaming from a wound in his forehead. 'Murder,' he shouts, 'murder, murder.' Helplessly I watch the blood streaming. At last my voice tears itself loose from my chest. I too shout: 'Murder, murder, help, help,' and the sound fills the room. I wake up and a man in the street outside is singing. . .'C'est L'amour qui flotte dans l'air à la ronde.' he sings. (p. 13)

This passage is consummate artistry, for here summarized is the whole conflict underlying the warring mythologies of time. Sasha, Woman, is trapped in the long stone passage (tomb) of time from which there is no escape, only the implacable steel finger of man pointing the way. (This tube image also suggests the labyrinth, an archetype of the unconscious.) The little man, bearded, in a long white night-shirt is the father-god image insisting he is Sasha-Anna's father—although the Great Goddess had no father, was pre-existent. But the god is wounded —as Uranus the supposed father of Aphrodite was grievously wounded by his son, Cronus—symbolically murdered in that a new mythology henceforth prevailed. From the blood of the mutilated Uranus sprang the Furies, the Giants, the Melic Nymphs, themselves the basis for subsequent Greek mythology. But even the most ancient Greek myths of Uranus and Gaea (at once his wife and mother) were themselves new-comers, foisted upon more ancient Bronze-Age, semi-matriarchal societies which worshipped the Great Goddess. Hence, in her dream, Sasha—avatar of Anna—shouts "murder, murder, help, help." And when she wakens, the little man outside her window is singing of "love," the only answer to the ancient conflict between the female-male principles.

Sasha, of course, is unaware of all these implications, but immediately after the dream she introduces the man in the next room, the man who so constantly intrudes upon her consciousness, "this damned man" whom she doesn't like, but whom she will welcome to her arms in the last startling scene of the novel. "He is as thin as a skeleton. He has a bird-like face and sunken, dark eyes with a peculiar expression, cringing, ingratiating, knowing. What's he want to look at me like that for? . . . He is always wearing a dressing-gown—a blue one with black spots or the famous white one." (p. 14. Punctuation exact.) Later she notices his shoes outside his room, ". . . long, pointed patent-leather shoes, very cracked. . . . I wonder about this man. Perhaps he is a commercial traveller . . . a commis voyageur. . . ." The next morning, after a brief encounter on the stair landing, there is a knock on the door:

> . . .It's the commis, in his beautiful dressing gown, immaculately white, with long, wide, hanging sleeves. . . . He looks like a priest, the priest of some *obscene, half-understood religion.*
>
> At last I manage: 'Well, what is it? What do you want?'
> 'Nothing,' he says, 'nothing.'

He doesn't answer or move. He stands in the doorway, smiling. (Now then, you and I understand each other, don't we? Let's stop pretending.)

I put my hand on his chest, push him backwards and bang the door. It's quite easy. It's like pushing a paper man, a ghost, something that doesn't exist.

And there I am in this dim room. . . thinking of that white dressing-gown, like a priest's robes. Frightened as hell. *A nightmare feeling . . . .* (p. 35. Emphasis added.)

Later, when she meets the "commis" on the landing, he will scowl as he reverses the action and shuts the door on her.

Certainly, in this old man who will appear in six brief passages, Rhys has introduced a character not to be taken only at face value. The skeleton image reminds us of the old thin man, "so thin that he was like a clothed skeleton" (*ALMM*, p. 188) that Julia saw immediately after her strange encounter with the "boy" who rejected her. His bird-like face and sunken eyes are curiously evocative. Obviously he is priest-like; the two robes—blue with black spots or the "famous white one" which frightens her like something from a nightmare—seem to have specific significance. (We remember the boy bishop of Anna's dream— *Voyage,* pp. 164-5—wearing the blue ring and the priest's robes.) His overtures, at first friendly, will eventually vary from dismissal to outright vilification just before the final scene.

Powerfully, in the figure of this old "commis," Rhys has managed to synthesize several images, so overlapping in their intent and application to Sasha as to be inseparable. Perhaps the foremost image arises from Sasha's description of him as a "commis voyageur" which, taken with his "bird-like face," suggests Hermes, herald of the gods and conductor of the souls of the dead, "past the gates of the sun and the land of dreams," to the dark realm of Hades. Sometimes seen as the swift wind, Hermes, with his winged hat and shoes, becomes a bird symbol, an archetype of transcendence. Thus Sasha's dream of the tube-labyrinth, explained above, together with the image of the old commis, indicates that she is ready for initiation into unknown worlds. By implication, this initiation will be only into that realm of shade reserved for the weary, outworn souls of men.

But beyond this image of Hermes with all his mythic overtones, the old commis may be a "shadow" image, a reflection of aspects of Sasha which she consciously rejects or of which she is unaware. Hence, his "peculiar" eyes—"sunken, dark eyes with a peculiar expression, cringing, ingratiating, knowing"—may reflect Sasha's eyes which are hollowed, dark as though she takes drugs, eyes "like that kitten's eyes," "terrible eyes" that know their fate. The shadow image, in psychoanalysis, often reveals itself as at once threat and friend, frightening or revealing. This explains the ambivalent behaviour of the old man toward Sasha. Ultimately, so psychoanalysts tell us, the mature individual must recognize the shadow or the alter-ego, accepting and controlling it. Hence the lines: "(Now then, you and I understand each other, don't we? Let's stop pretending.)"

Additionally, this multifaceted character of the old man may serve as a Satan-figure to Sasha, a concretization of the struggle between her libido and superego. Or perhaps he is a projection of Sasha's animus, at once conciliatory and threatening. Certainly, as any of these, he will serve a priestlike function when, in the final scene, he officiates at the altar of SELF-acceptance, acting as mediator between Sasha's ego and her SELF. Lest these interpretations seem specious, forced, remember that Sasha, herself, will say: ". . .Nevertheless, all the little birdies sing—Psychoanalysis might help. Adler is more wholesome than Freud, don't you think? . . ." (p. 168). Furthermore, in a 1974 interview with *Mademoiselle,* Rhys said that she wrote because "if you write out a thing, it goes. . . it doesn't trouble you so much. . . . I suppose it's like psychoanalysis."

At any rate, at their initial encounters, Sasha is not ready for liberation, not yet prepared to turn to the darkness, to make the sacrifice of submission, renunciation, atonement—the symbolic acceptance of death. Without this acceptance, so say all the myths of man, religious and psychoanalytic alike, there can be no compassion, no fulfillment, no birth into light. Thus, not yet submissive, receptive, Sasha rejects the old commis and seeks out life.

Stimulated by her encounter with the Russians, denying the threat of age which haunts her in the image of "the little old woman" with the knowing eyes on the street and the girls who mock her in the bistro, Sasha dyes her hair ash-blonde, caught up in the game—"(At it again, dearie, at it again!)"—which she has avoided during the five years of her weekly two-pound-ten. To set off her new blonde hair, Sasha decides she must have a new hat. And with this seemingly insignificant detail, Rhys introduces a new motif, a new awareness into her personal myth. For the hat, Jung says, denotes the taking on of a new identity. And since the hat which Sasha buys is "fashionable," a reflection of the current society, she indicates her unconscious desire to be a part of that society which she has been rejecting. Thus Rhys, through Sasha, works toward that more mature understanding which admits that all things change and that there is never any going back.

Rhys creates agony and tension during the hat-buying episode as Sasha watches a customer in a shop:

> Her hair, half-dyed, half-grey, is very disheveled. As I watch she puts on a hat, makes a face at herself in the glass, and takes it off very quickly. She tries another—then another. Her expression is terrible—hungry, despairing, hopeful, quite crazy. At any moment you expect her to start laughing the laugh of the mad. (p. 68)

This is the agony of woman in a world where youth and beauty are the essence.

Shortly after, looking at herself trying on hats, Sasha feels she wears the same demented expression. But the girl in the shop she has chosen is sympathetic: " 'The hats now are very difficult, very difficult. All my clients say that the hats now are very difficult to wear. . . . But I think—I am sure—I shall manage to suit you.' " (p. 69). And finally, aided by the clerk, Sasha chooses:

> When I put on the third one she says: 'I don't want to insist, but yes—that is your hat. . . . Walk up and down the room in it. See whether you feel happy in it. See whether you'll get accustomed to it.' . . . We are alone, celebrating this extraordinary ritual.
>
> She says 'I very seldom insist, but I am sure that when you have got accustomed to that hat you won't regret it. You will realize that it's your hat.'
>
> I have made up my mind to trust this girl, and I must trust her. (pp. 69-70)

In this curious little incident between Sasha and the smiling, friendly priestess of the hats, Rhys seems to say that even in this strange contorted world of 1937—where the hats are very difficult to wear—it is possible to find an identity that is bearable, even comfortable *if* one can surrender fear, antagonism and replace it with trust. Symbolically, the shop-girl becomes a positive anima projection.

"Feeling saner and happier after this," Sasha goes to a nearby restaurant where she has a good meal and is pleased by the fact that no one notices her new hat. Then, desiring music, dancing—but voicing the eternal litany of woman in the male-oriented society: "But where? By myself, where can I go?"—she goes to the plush-resplendent bar where she is picked up by René, the gigolo.

René, on the surface, seems to serve merely as a masculine reflection of the Marya-Julia-Anna-Sasha woman, a counterpart upon whom the aging, cynical Sasha can vent all the cruelty and bitterness she has been forced to repress for so long. Ostensibly mistaking Sasha for a wealthy English woman because of her new hairdo, her hat and her fur coat, René accosts Sasha as she leaves the Dome, accompanying her to a nearby cafe. Here, in an attempt to win her sympathy—a maneuver quite familiar to Sasha—René confides his deep need to communicate with someone, a woman "who would put her arms around" him and to whom he "could tell everything." French-Canadian, though Sasha insults him by insisting he is Spanish or Spanish-American, he recites a wild tale of escape from the Foreign Legion, of his arrival in Paris the night before without papers, of his thought that perhaps she might help him get a passport that would get him to London where he has friends.

Sasha finds this parody of her own wild tales and dependency "so funny" that she laughs aloud. René laughs too, binding them in a kind of cleansing comraderie. As they leave for another cafe, Sasha admits the truth to herself: "There we are, arm in arm. . . . and when I think of my life it seems to me so comical that I have to laugh. *It has taken me a long time to see how comical it has been, but I see it now, I do.*" (p. 76. Emphasis added.) For the first time, Sasha not only sees her life—sadly yet hilariously reflected in the potpourri of events René has just recited —but accepts it for what it is. Not the tragedy upon which a Marya or a Julia would have insisted, but a kind of mad comedy.

Suddenly we realize that this gigolo is far more than just an adjunct to Sasha, a caricature in masculine form. This "mauvais garçon," this open, honest, conniving, on-the-make young man, this man with whom for the first time in her life she is not self-conscious, this gigolo who "doesn't look like a gigolo," whose hair is "untidy" but "nice" is the projection of Sasha's animus, that masculine personification of the unconscious. Because the animus is potentially double-natured, René may be negative, *"a mauvais garçon,"* *"méchant"*. Or he may function as a positive force which enables Sasha to bridge the gap between the ego and the unconscious, thus finding her inner SELF—*if she can be reached*. This is why René "must talk" with Sasha. This is the significance of the name, "René," symbolic of the "rebirth" of the vitalizing psychic force within Sasha. This also explains the significance of René's "untidy" but "nice" hair—unruly hair has been a prime concern of all of Rhys's protagonists. Thus this detail indicates that for the first time Marya-Julia-Anna-Sasha is on the verge of accepting herself for what she is, without rancor, rejection. Furthermore, this animus interpretation will also explain René's feeling that he is walking "with a child." (p. 79). That is, Sasha for the first time is child-like—free, receptive without defensive cynicism, no longer playing a role.

This episode which concludes Part One is reminiscent of a similar scene in *After Leaving Mr. Mackenzie* (pp. 187-8). Here the "boy" who has been stalking beside Julia sees her under a lamp-post, his "little eyes" searching her with "deadly and impartial criticism." " '*Ah, non, alors,* ' " he says, turning and walking away. Julia had not been ready for revelation and initiation; Sasha is on the verge! However, for the moment, Sasha rejects René's further advances:

> 'Rien à faire?'
> 'Rien à faire.'

She returns to her room, her bed, to "pull the curtains and shut the damned world out."

Part Two

Part Two of *Good Morning, Midnight* is a short, curious, artistically disappointing section in which Rhys simultaneously reviews the political Zeitgeist of the early twentieth century and summarizes themes of her previous novels. Through the Russians, Nicholas Delmar and Serge, the painter—puppets more than characters—she seems to imply that the solution to the hard realities of life does not rest in political systems. Hence Nicholas, the Ukranian-now-naturalized-Frenchman, who is at heart a monarchist—an alien in this ugly world of 1937—who would prefer a "queen, a princess" (note the return of the mother-myth), is ineffectual, reducing his idea of non-essence to "they have bad manners" (p. 103). Although he offers irrefutable justification for those who believe themselves to be victims of life:

You didn't ask to be born, you didn't make the world as it is, you didn't make yourself as you are. Why torment yourself? Why not take life as it comes? You have the right to; you are not one of the guilty ones,'' (p. 64)

and although he seems to fully accept himself just as he is, nevertheless he affects Sasha ambivalently:

I don't know why I don't quite like him. This gentle, resigned melancholy—it seems unnatural in a man who can't be much over thirty. . . . Or perhaps it is because he seems more the echo of a thing than the thing itself. One moment I feel this, and another I like him very much, as if he were the brother I never had. (p. 66)

Nicholas (ironically meaning ''victory of the people,'' a cliché of the Red Revolution) is a kind of objectified psychic death wish, ultimately representing one philosophical possibility for life, appealing but passive and restrictive. Rooted in an older ethic, ''correct, gloves in his hands,'' he lives by a code which will not allow a woman to pay her own way but will permit her to do without. Sasha clearly rejects this ethic: ''I can't stand this business of not being able to have what I want to drink, because he won't allow me to pay and certainly doesn't want to pay himself. It's too wearing.'' (p. 103). Immediately after, however, Sasha sees, in the figure of the dishwasher in her ''coffin'' of a room behind the bar, the fate of woman who must pay her own way: ''Bare, sturdy legs, felt slippers, a black dress, a filthy apron, thick, curly, untidy hair. I know her. This is the girl who does all the dirty work and gets paid very little for it. Salut!'' Through this girl, Rhys makes further observation concerning the socialist-communist movements dedicated to the masses: ''. . . Why should I be sorry for her. . . . don't her strong hands sing the Marseillaise? And when the revolution comes, won't those be the hands to be kissed? Well, so Monsieur Rimbaud says, doesn't he? I hope he's right. I wonder, I wonder, I wonder. . . .'' (p. 105).

Echoing this doubt, Rhys uses the Jewish painter, Serge, to make much the same comment concerning the hopes of the ''revolution.'' ''Of the extreme left,'' able to understand and communicate with everybody—but basically ''not giving a rap for anything,'' so his friend Nicholas says—Serge represents the epitome of a type Rhys would have known well. Sensitive, artistic, seeing so clearly the ugliness and injustices of life, the Serges search for that which will alleviate the pain of the common people—primarily in some utopian system. Essentially, however, theirs is an intellectual allegiance. Hence Serge, having painted starkly the life he has lived and seen, finds that his paintings sell for unbelievable prices so that he is able to move from "la crasse" into "a beautiful, respectable" room. Less concerned with the economics of life than some, he is, nevertheless, "anxious and surly" when he thinks Sasha will be unable to pay for the painting she has chosen. Ultimately, he and Sasha part "amis," even though he absent-mindedly or arrogantly stands her up later in the evening, not to appear again in the novel. So much for the politics of life, Rhys seems to say.

Continuing to manipulate the plot and character to the end of message—making this the weakest section in any of her novels, I believe—Rhys uses Sasha's trip to meet Serge to evoke the memory of a man from Lille who had picked Sasha up during a bleak period after the first world war when she was, again, trying to drink herself to death. This episode permits Rhys to echo, without artistic conviction, observations from the earlier novels: (1) there is truth and exploitation on the part of both male and female; (2) man is capable of pity for woman's plight; (3) nevertheless, he resents and fears woman's economic hold on him.

From the episode of that man, faceless but with the ever-recurring blue-stoned ring on his finger, Rhys maneuvers us back to her mythic theme as Sasha, thinking of the masks that people wear, finds the walls of Serge's room lined with masks from the Congo:

> He takes [one] down and shows it to me. The close-set eye-holes stare into mine. I know that face very well; I've seen lots like it, complete with legs and body. . . . That's the way they look when they are saying: 'What's this story?' Peering at you. Who are you, anyway? Who's your father and have you got any money, and if not, why not? Are you one of us? Will you think what you're told to think and say what you ought to say? . . . (p. 92)

Here, encapsulated, is both the Victorian ethic and the myth of woman-dethroned. Clearly Rhys is stirring her *pot au feu.*

With the Congo masks, Rhys manages to merge Sasha with Anna (*Voyage*) and we are in the islands, listening to the gramaphone

> . . . grinding out 'Maladie d'amour, maladie de la
> jeunesse. . . .'
>
> I am lying in a hammock looking up into the branches of
> a tree. The sound of the sea advances and retreats as if a
> door were being opened and shut. All day there has been a
> fierce wind blowing, but at sunset it drops. The hills look like
> clouds and the clouds like fantastic hills. (p. 92)

This myth-motif, developed fully in the foregoing discussion of *Voyage
in the Dark,* is reinforced as Serge tells his story of the mulatto woman,
drunk, weeping, "like something that had been turned to stone." And,
Serge tells Sasha, though he had pitied the strange woman, tried to
reason with her, it was like "talking to something that was no longer
quite human, no longer quite alive." (p. 97). Thus, in reintroducing her
myth of ancient Woman, Rhys seems to imply, as Sasha is beginning to
realize, that the old way is fossilized, dead. And the "cruel child" who
had told the pathetic half-Negro woman that "she was a dirty woman,
that she smelt bad, that she hadn't any right in the house" (p. 97), had
spoken deadly truth—as the anima personification so often must.

Having somehow managed to restate every issue of her past
novels, however unconvincingly, Rhys resumes control of her material
and with a few deft strokes concludes Part Two. There are the paintings
of Serge in which "misshapen dwarfs"—modern, unnatural man—
juggle the "huge coloured balloons" in the circus of life; "the four-
breasted woman"—the double hate-love aspects of the Great Goddess
—is exhibited like a freak; the old prostitute, her kidneys now gone,
"waits hopelessly outside the urinoir," the "young one" stands under
the lamp-post as this charade called life continues.

There is the bar where Sasha has a "cringing desire" to justify her
existence to the waiter: "I am a respectable woman, une femme con-
venable, . . . Faites comme les autres—that's been my motto all my
life. Faites comme les autres, damn you." Suddenly she realizes the
truth:

> *And a lot he cares—I could have spared myself the trouble.*
> But this is my attitude to life. Please, please, monsieur et
> madame, mister, missis and miss, I am trying so hard to be
> like you. I know I don't succeed, but look how hard I try.
> . . . Every word I say has chains round its ankles; every
> thought I think is weighted with heavy weights. . . . Think

how hard I try and how seldom I dare. Think—and have a bit of pity. . . . (p. 106. Emphasis added.)

But, in the midst of her self-pity, Sasha also remembers that "sometimes it was sunny . . . Walking along in the sun in a gay dress, striped red and blue. . . I won't walk along that street again." (p. 108). Then the cinema, where Sasha laughs "till the tears come" at a mad, inane comedy, "exactly the sort of thing that happens to me." Then she is home, unrolling the painting she has bought for six hundred francs: " . . . the man standing in the gutter, playing his banjo, stares at me. He is gentle, humble, resigned, mocking, a little mad. He stares at me. He is double-headed, double-faced. He is singing 'It has been', singing 'It will be'. Double-headed with four arms." Rhys leaves us with this image of the double-headed, double-faced man, the anima-animus united, the realized SELF, singing "truth": " 'It has been', 'It will be'." He stares at Sasha; she stares back at him, thinking "about being hungry, being cold, being hurt, being ridiculed, *as if it were in another life than this.*" (p. 109. Emphasis added.)

Sasha is now ready to make the final journey down the streets and into the rooms of her life.

Part Three

Part Three of *Good Morning, Midnight* might well be titled "Rooms," for in this section, Sasha revisits the rooms of her life and in so doing reveals to the reader—as to Sasha herself—the truth of ambiguities raised in former novels. As Sasha's thoughts revert to rooms she has known in Holland, we learn that Sasha and Enno had married in the crazy aftermath of the Armistice, each believing the other to have money and Sasha burning to escape the drabness of her life in London. Enno had supposedly been a "Chansonnier," a journalist, a soldier, but he is now without a job or money. The money for which Sasha had written home has been denied, the family sending a note that she must be mad. Living from hand to mouth, caught up in the sentimentality of marriage—naively or perhaps determinedly believing in "love"—Sasha's life is at first "smooth, soft and tender," melancholy, revolving around "making love." Quickly, though, stranded without funds, wearing "shabby clothes, worn out shoes," circles under her eyes, Sasha discovers "what things are like underneath what people say they are,'' realizing that economics are the controlling factor and that woman's lot is not to talk, not to cry, not to go out, *only to wait!*

Finally established in Paris in a room crawling with bugs, surrounded by questionable friends—one of whom suggests not so subtly that Enno should pimp for his own wife—Enno walks out on Sasha, taunting her with " 'You don't know how to make love,' he said. That was about a month after we got to Paris. 'You're too passive, you're lazy, you bore me. I've had enough of this. Goodbye.' '' (p. 128). This is a theme which Rhys has introduced before in her novels, the masculine denigration of woman's sexual performance. Again we are struck by the fact that there is no antithetical equivalent of "emasculation," no masculine epithet similar to the feminine image of "castrating bitch" for man's sexual rejection of woman. Yet Rhys reveals a truth which most women know—women suffer sexual indignity as surely as do men.

Having left Sasha feeling physically rejected and concerned that she is pregnant and permanently abandoned, Enno nonchalantly returns three days later with money and a bottle of wine. Without explanation or apology, he casually takes her to bed. Sasha, nearly a quarter of a century later, remembers the hurt, also remembers that she had truly loved him:

> But it wasn't all that that mattered. It wasn't that he knew so exactly when to be cruel, so exactly how to be kind. The day I was sure I loved him was quite different.
>
> He had gone out to buy something to eat. I was behind the curtain and I saw him in the street below, standing by a lamp post, looking up at our window, looking for me. He seemed very thin and small and I saw the expression on his face quite plainly. Anxious, he was . . .
>
> . . .When I saw him looking up like that I knew that I loved him, and that it was for always. It was as if my heart turned over, and I knew that it was for always. It's a strange feeling —when you know quite certainly in yourself that something is for always. It's like what death must be. All the insouciance, all the gaiety is a bluff. Because I wanted to escape from London I fastened myself on him, and I am dragging him down. All the gaiety is going and now he is thin and anxious . . . (pp. 129-30)

Through Sasha's poignant memory, Rhys suggests that "love," for woman, is rooted in a maternal instinct of compassion which acknowledges the vulnerability of man, even in a world which he seems to dominate.

That maternal nature of woman is further emphasized in Sasha's pregnancy. Life has improved for the Jansens. Enno has work. Sasha gives English lessons, reads a lot, has many friends—prostitutes by implication—and revels in her approaching motherhood, refusing to think beyond that point or about money or about being alone when the baby comes. Ironically outside in the street the man sings, " 'J'ai perdu la lumiere . . . .' " And then, without explanation, the baby is dead.

Now Sasha knows that " 'God is very cruel . . . a devil, of course.' " God—not economics, not abortion—has become the agent of loss, and for Sasha, life will never be the same:

> Now the lights are red, dusky red, haggard red, cruel red. Strings plucked softly by a man with a long, thin nose and sharp, blue eyes.
> Our luck has changed and the lights are red. (p. 140)

> A room? A nice room? A beautiful room? A beautiful room with bath? Swing high, swing low, swing to and fro. . . . This happened and that happened. . , .
> *And then the days came when I was alone.* (p. 142. Emphasis added.)

> Did I love Enno at the end? Did he ever love me? I don't know. Only, it was after that that I began to go to pieces. Not all at once, of course. First this happened, and then that happened. . . . (p. 143)

Yet, those were the days when Sasha could still face life, drink coffee in a cafe, get drunk on half a bottle of wine:

> But they never last, the golden days. And it can be sad, the sun in the afternoon, can't it? Yes, it can be sad, the afternoon sun, sad and frightening.
> Now, money, for the night is coming. Money for my hair, money for my teeth, money for shoes that won't deform my feet (it's not so easy now to walk around in cheap shoes with

very high heels), money for good clothes, money, money. The night is coming. (p. 144)

And "always the same stairs, always the same room," until the inheritance, the hole to hide in. "And there is always tomorrow . . . . .And when I have had a couple of drinks I shan't know whether it's yesterday, today or tomorrow." (p. 154). Thus ends Part Three.

Part Four

Having finally, in Part Three, reduced the truth of her life to its bittersweet essence: love-desertion, laughter-tears, poverty-wealth, body-spirit, life-death, Sasha is ready in Part Four to make her complete psychic breakthrough, to welcome the midnight which must precede the dawn of her new day.

This process will be facilitated in the person of René, animus-shadow-alter-ego all wrapped in one, who comes to Sasha's room, unbidden and unwelcome. In the room, the contradictory nature of René (a reflection of Sasha's own unconscious) is revealed. He is openly sexual, reveling in this "nice, charming room" which contains nothing but beds. He is frank, seemingly guileless, talking of his rich American, even as he carefully eyes Sasha's ring (the "thin gold ring with a red stone in it" of Julia's mother, *ALMM*, p. 133). Sasha, excited and stimulated by his presence (the animus in its positive form is an activating psychic force), agrees to meet him later in the evening, cynically accepting the fact that he is after money—which she does not have. "Prancing and smirking" though she is, Sasha determines for the first time not to don her mask of make-up, her illusion of youth: " 'No, I won't do a thing, not a thing. A little pride, a little dignity at the end, in the name of God. I won't even put on the stockings I bought this afternoon. I won't do a thing—not a thing. I will not grimace and posture before these people any longer.' "

Meeting René and feeling "so natural, so gay . . . just as if I were young—but really young. I've never been young. When I was young I was strained-up, anxious. I've never been really young. . . ," Sasha goes with René to a former haunt, the "Pig and Lily"—a name which ironically evokes contradictory images of the pagan worship of the Sow-Pig (associated with Demeter-Aphrodite) and the Christian Resurrection. Here René, serving as a kind of mirror image of a youthful Sasha, chatters on about "chic" places, "chic" tailors, the "gold-mine" awaiting him just across the channel where "at least fifty percent of the men are homosexual and most of the others not liking it so much as all that. And the poor Englishwomen just gasping for it, oh, boy!" (p. 157).

René's conversation is pornographically sexual. He discusses with Sasha guiltlessly, enthusiastically, the "techniques of the métier," the tricks of the trade. Sasha is drawn to this "poor devil, so alive, gay, healthy, so as if he didn't drink too much," but she is, nevertheless, prepared for the proposition he finally makes:

'Listen. I've told you this from the start—nothing doing. Why do you go on about it? It's stupid.'

'A pity,' he says, indifferently, 'a pity. It would have been so nice. You wouldn't have been disappointed in me.'

(But supposing you were disappointed in me.) (p. 159)

In this last line Rhys takes us back to the maggot-fear of sexual rejection which man has buried in woman's brain. But René understands her fear of humiliation and inadequacy: " 'You know, you needn't be afraid of me. I'd never say cruel things to you, nor about you either. I'm not cruel to women—not in that way. You see, I like them. I don't like boys; I tried in Morocco, but it was no use. I like women.' " With this emphasis, Rhys tells the truth, not only of René but of the animus, which he represents. Psychically, so Jungian analysts say, the animus is not a threat to the anima. It does not desire to supersede. Rather its purpose is to merge, to complement, to become one with its other half, masculine and feminine uniting. It is only when woman permits her animus to dominate, refusing to listen and respond to the feminine part of herself, that it becomes literally a death force. This psychological truth is at the root of the subsequent discussion, wherein Sasha confesses to René that she is a "cérébrale," a mind, an intellect. René rejects this, asserting that Sasha "feels" better than she "thinks." He goes on to define a "cérébrale" as " . . . a woman who doesn't like men or need them. . . . a cérébrale doesn't like women either. . . . The true cérébrale is a woman who likes nothing and nobody except herself and her own damned brain or what she thinks is her brain. . . ." (p. 162).

Here, then, we have the animus—projected in the image of René— attempting to show Sasha that she may be "in fact, a monster."

Governed by her "inner man"—negative, cold, whispering to Sasha and Julia and Marya and even Anna, "you are hopeless; life is hell"— Sasha cannot hear the suggestions of her unconscious which will permit the two parts of the SELF to merge. Thus Sasha, not wishing to understand and annoyed by the turn the conversation has taken, abruptly decides to go to the Exhibition. She tells René:

> 'Well, I'm going. You needn't come if you don't want to. I'll go by *myself.*'
>
> I want to go by myself, to get into a taxi and drive along the streets, to stand by *myself* and look down at the fountains in the cold light.
>
> 'But of course,' he says. 'If you want to go to the Exhibition, *we'll* go. *Naturally.*' (p. 163. Emphasis added.)

So, though Sasha longs to escape the moment of truth, to be alone, René accompanies her, naturally—as the inner selves should merge, into One-ness not Alone-ness.

In the ensuing events of the evening, further details of René as projection of Sasha emerge. He, like Marya and Anna in England (Sasha's fur coat insulates her), does not belong in the cold of Paris; he is tropic born. René, like Sasha, is selfish, manipulative, and when he begins "to whistle, like a little boy . . . loud, clear and pure," the "trickster" image comes through strongly. He, too, has known Sasha's "very rich woman" who made up fairy stories—as he and Sasha make up their own fairy stories of life. But above all, René is physical, sexual, determined to seduce Sasha. Finally, drunk and pushed to the limit of her emotional resources, reassured by René's gentleness, Sasha admits that her refusal to take him to her room is the result of overwhelming fear:

> 'You want to know what I'm afraid of? All right, I'll tell you. . . . I'm afraid of men—yes, I'm very much afraid of men. And I'm even more afraid of women. And I'm very much afraid of the whole bloody human race. . . .
>
> And when I say afraid—that's just a word I use. What I really mean is that I hate them. . . . I hate the whole bloody business. It's cruel, it's idiotic, it's unspeakably horrible. *I never had the guts to kill myself or I'd have got out of it long ago. . . .*' (pp. 172-3. Emphasis added.)

In this last line, Sasha reveals a complex fact: that this hatred of the human race, this hatred of life which seems to consume her is only the coating which hides the poison. The horror with which Sasha's mind cannot cope, which must at all costs be kept at bay, is the *blackness of life,* "cruel . . . idiotic . . . horrible," which is really the *nothingness of* death. This is the existential theme with which Rhys struggled in such detail in *After Leaving Mr. Mackenzie.* So threatening is the recognition of this idea that Sasha cannot verbalize it, only admit it inwardly, as she does before the outburst quoted above. As René asks, " 'Then what are you afraid of? Tell me. I'm interested. *Of men, of love? . . . What, still? . . . Impossible,* ' " (p. 172. Punctuation exact and emphasis added), indicating that we are not to accept the almost platitudinous response which Sasha will *verbalize,* Sasha *inwardly* answers with truth. "You are walking along a road peacefully. You trip. You fall into blackness. That's the past—or perhaps the future. And you know that *there is no past, no future, there is only this blackness, changing faintly, slowly, but always the same.*" (p. 172. Emphasis added.)

This inward admission continues in an inner dialogue—presumably with an alter-ego-shadow self: "I know all about myself now, I know. You've told me so often. You haven't left me one rag of illusion to clothe myself in. But by God, I know what you are too, and I wouldn't change places. . . Everything spoiled, all spoiled. Well, don't cry about it. No, I won't cry about it. . . Let it be destroyed. Let it happen. Let it end, this cold insanity. Let it happen." (p. 173). And these last lines become double-edged. Let the bleakness called life end *or* let this cold insanity of the "cérébrale," the intellectual-dominated ego, be destroyed. For Sasha, dominated by the negative forces within her, knows that she is " . . . lying in a misery of utter darkness. Quite alone. No voice, no touch, no hand. . . . How long must I lie here? Forever? No, only for a couple of hundred years this time, miss. . . ." (p. 173).

But even as she wallows in the truth of her woman's pain, René breaks through with truth of his own. He, too, has suffered; he bears the scars of despair as absolute as hers from ear to ear:

There is a long scar, going across his throat. . . . A long, thick, white scar. It's strange that I haven't noticed it before.

He says: 'That is one. There are other ones. I have been wounded.'

It isn't boastful, the way he says this, nor complaining. It's puzzled, puzzled in an impersonal way, as if he is asking me—me, of all people—why, why, why?

Pity you? Why should I pity you? Nobody has ever pitied me. They are without mercy.

'I have too,' I say in a surly voice. 'Moi aussi.'

'I know. I can see that. I believe you.'

'Well,' I say, 'if we're going to start believing each other, it's getting serious, isn't it?'

Once more, in a few strokes, Rhys offers for our comprehension momentous truths far ahead of her time, even our time. For here she acknowledges from deep within herself that woman is not the only victim. Knowing this, woman must, she implies, evade the trap of egocentrism and achieve the maturity of understanding and compassion—not only for man but, by extension, for herself, inasmuch as René is her projection. But Rhys indicates that she has no illusions about the difficulties involved:

'What happened to you, what happened?' [René] says. 'Something bad must have happened to make you like this.'

'One thing? It wasn't one thing. It took years. It was a slow process.'

He says: 'It doesn't matter. What I know is that I could do this with you'—he makes a movement with his hands like a baker kneading a loaf of bread—'and afterwards you'd be different. I know. Believe me.' (p. 175)

The animosities between women and men, the disassociation of woman's psyche—again the double-edged knife—are not the product of a single careless act, a matter of days. They are the product of the slow, almost indiscernible process of many years. Thus, the healing of these life-threatening wounds will be neither easy nor quick. However, Rhys seems to suggest in her imagery that the real union of men and women, the integration of the female psyche, is possible and offers the bread of life.

Again, however, Sasha resists the inevitable, telling René, "Leave me alone. I'm tired . . . ." at which René starts to laugh.

The concluding scene with René in Sasha's hotel room summarizes the Jungian nuances of René as psychic projection of Sasha. Having said goodnight and mounted the stairs to her room, the landing light has suddenly clicked and Sasha is unable to get her key in the lock. Crossing the pitch-black landing to the head of the stairs, Sasha discovers that someone is there waiting and calls out, " 'Qui est là?' "

> But before he answers I know. I take a step forward and put my arms around him.
> I have my arms round him and I begin to laugh, because I am so happy. I stand there hugging him, so terribly happy. Now everything is in my arms on this dark landing—love, youth, spring, happiness, everything I thought I had lost. I was a fool, wasn't I? to think all that was finished for me. How could it be finished?
> I put up my hand and touch his hair. I've wanted to do that since I first saw him. (p. 177)

Aesthetically, Sasha's sudden, overwhelming passion lacks conviction, if the scene is accepted only on the literal level. For example, there has been no indication of mounting sexual frustration, no sign of repressed physical attraction on Sasha's part as the evening has progressed. Nor have we been prepared by a mounting anxiety concerning her age, her attractiveness, to accept her passion for René in terms of the sexual renewal he overtly promises—love, youth, spring, happiness. On the contrary, Sasha's progressive acceptance of age, of life, of death, makes this explanation an obvious over-simplification—*the fairy tale created by man that aging woman will give all for sexual fulfillment.*

Patently, then, in the light of René's symbolic significance already developed in detail, we must realize that Sasha's unexplained passion is an archetypal manifestation of her overwhelming urge toward self-knowledge, an urge that has been irresistibly stirring throughout the night. Thus Sasha welcomes René, who literally and symbolically opens the door to her room!

Once René has shut the door, however, Sasha's ego asserts itself, the "spotlight" goes on over the bidet, over the bed, the "damned room" grins at her, and Sasha again rejects René, asking him to leave. At this point, René becomes "méchant," revealing the negative, threatening side which can emerge in the animus-shadow when the ego misunderstands or ignores its message: " 'Well, I'm not going,' he says. 'I want to see this comedy. You'll have to call for someone to put me out. . . . Au secours, au secours,' he shouts in a high falsetto voice.

112

'Like that. . . .If you want to make yourself ridiculous.' '' As Sasha struggles, he continues: '' 'But what do you think I am—a little dog? You think you can first kiss me and then say to me ''Get out''? You haven't looked well at me. . . . I don't like it. . . that voice that gives orders.' '' And Sasha thinks, ''Well, I haven't always liked it either—the voice that gives orders.'' (p. 181). Patently ''the voice that gives orders'' is Sasha's ''inner man,'' the arrogant, cynical, death-dealing, negative animus of the ''cérébrale.''

The struggle between Sasha and René continues, and it is evident that René will triumph:

> 'You think you're very strong, don't you?' he says.
> 'Yes, I'm very strong.'
> I'm strong as the dead, my dear, and that's how strong I am.
> 'If you're so strong, why do you keep your eyes shut?'
> Because dead people must have their eyes shut.
> I lie very still, I don't move. Not open my eyes. . . .
> 'Je te ferai mal,' he says. 'It's your fault.'
> When I open my eyes I feel the tears trickling down from the outside corners. . . .
> I can't speak. . . .
> I feel his hard knee between my knees. My mouth hurts, my breasts hurt, because it hurts, when you have been dead, to come alive. (p. 182)

While overtly this is sexual surrender, the covert meaning lies in the fact that Sasha *opens her eyes*, refusing the image of death. In the surrender of her conscious will, and the cleansing tears which she now sheds, Sasha has ''come alive.'' But though Sasha has surrendered her will, though, as she tells René, she ''understands,'' the ''high, clear, cold'' voice she hears speaking is not the tender voice of her womanly self, but the inner voice of cynicism, experience, intellect which tells her that to humiliate is to control and to control is to triumph. She hears this voice speaking the cruel words:

> 'Of course I understand. Naturally I understand. I should be an awful fool if I didn't. If you look in the right-hand pocket. . .you'll find the money you want.'
> . . . 'You mustn't think,' I say, 'that I'm vexed about

anything, because I'm not. Everybody's got their living to earn, haven't they? I'm just trying to save you a lot of trouble.' (p. 183)

But another voice, the struggling ego, is crying out, "Don't listen, that's not me speaking. Don't listen. Nothing to do with me—I swear it. . . ." (p. 183). Still the words emerging from Sasha's mouth are deadly: " 'I loved all the various stories you told me about yourself. Especially that one about your wounds and your scars—that amused me very much.' " (p. 183). Suddenly René has gone "very still," his weight is no longer on her, he is standing up: " 'Yes, you're right,' he says. 'It would be a waste of time.' " (p. 184). And like the "boy" who rejected Julia, (*ALMM*) without word or look, René is gone.

With the shutting of the door, Sasha curls up like a child in the womb, seeing and accepting the truth of what she really is, not a "cérébrale" but a "child" hurt, crying, capable of laughter, joy—a force for the first time! Yet, despite this certain knowledge, the stronger self, which has ruled her ego for so long, taunts Sasha cynically:

> Her voice [the cérébrale] in my head: 'Well, well, well, just think of that now. What an amusing ten days! Positively packed with thrills. The last performance of What's-her-name And Her Boys or It Was All Due To An Old Fur Coat. . . . Go on, cry, allez-y. . . . Now, calm, calm, say it all out calmly. You've had dinner with a beautiful young man and he kissed you and you've paid a thousand francs for it. Dirt cheap at the price. . . . And you've picked up one or two people in the street and you've bought a picture. Don't forget the picture, to remind you of—what was it to remind you of? Oh, I know—of human misery. . . .' (p. 185)

Listening to the mocking voice, Sasha thinks of the painting she has bought and understands that it reflects much more than "human misery":

> He'll stare at me, gentle, humble, resigned mocking, a little mad. Standing in the gutter playing his banjo. And I'll look back at him because I shan't be able to help it, *remembering about being young, and about being made love to and making love, about pain and dancing and not being afraid of*

death, about all the music I've ever loved, and every time I've been happy. I'll look back at him and I'll say: 'I know the words to every tune you've ever played on your bloody banjo. Well, I musn't sing any more—there you are. Finie la chanson. The song is ended. Finished.' (p. 185. Emphasis added.)

In this passage, hidden in careful, evocative detail is the clue to life —and the answer to the terrible "blackness" that is life-death—which Sasha finally permits herself to accept: to truly live one must accept life in all its ramifications and *not be afraid of death,* that maggot in the brain of all human kind. This abjuration of fear, this willingness to face death, is the *sine qua non* of the rite of initiation, that archetypal rite of death and rebirth without which there is no psychic growth. That is, in the words of Dr. Joseph L. Henderson, a foremost American Jungian:

> . . . the novice for initiation is called upon to give up will-ful ambition and all desire and to submit to the ordeal. He must be willing to experience this trial without hope of success. In fact, *he must be prepared to die;* and though the token of his ordeal may be mild . . . or agonizing . . . the purpose remains always the same: *to create the symbolic mood of death from which may spring the symbolic mood of rebirth.*[48]

Once more, however, on the verge of initiation, the alter-ego, Sasha's negative animus, calls her back mockingly:

> She says: 'I hate to stop you crying. I know it's your favourite pastime, but I must remind you that the man next door has probably heard every damned thing . . . And another thing, . . . if he's taken all the money—which he almost certainly has—that'll be a lovely business, won't it? . . . Go on, look. You might as well know.' (p. 186)

Sasha blows her nose, goes over to the dressing-case, feels in the pocket:

> . . . Two hundred franc notes, a mille note.
> 'Well! *What* a compliment! Who'd have thought it?'

[says the alter-ego.]

'I knew,' I say, 'I knew. That's why I cried.'

I get the tooth-glass and half-fill it with whisky. Here's
to you, gigolo, chic gigolo. . . . I appreciate this, sweet
gigolo, from the depths of my heart. . . . So here's to you.
And here's to you. . . . (p. 186)

****

Sasha is very drunk—dream images surround her. The goddesses
and gods—Venus, Apollo, even Jesus—are dead in the machine-like
world of steel and lights and "eyelashes stiff with mascara." The music
is loud—"hotcha-hotcha-hotcha"—and Sasha knows the music and can
sing the song. She has another drink to stop "the damned voice" in her
head. Suddenly, "She has gone." [the damned cérébrale]. Now alone,
all intellectual resistance quelled, Sasha yearns for "the sweet gigolo"
to return:

'Come back, come back,' I say. Like that. Over and over
again. 'You must come back, you shall come back. I'll force
you to come back. No, that's wrong. . . . I mean, please come
back, I beg you to come back.'. . .

Come back, come back, come back. . . .

This is the effort, the enormous effort, under which the
human brain cracks. But not before the thing is done, not
before the mountain moves. (p. 188)

This last paragraph returns again—and finally—to the psychic struggle
which has raged within Sasha during the past ten days of her life. The
merging of the conscious with the unconscious—that massive upheaval
during which the intellect must finally release its controlling hold—is
the result of Sasha's enormous psychic effort and of her bitter experience. Now, "the thing done," Sasha echoes again and again: "Come
back, come back, come back. . . . He hesitates. He stops. I have him."

With all inhibition gone, all negation of her earthy, vital, even
ugly,woman-SELF relinquished, Sasha rushes to unlock the door—even
leaving it ajar—to undress, to compose herself on the bed:

. . . I lie there trembling. I am very tired.
Not me, no. Don't worry, it's my sale cerveau.

I think: 'How awful I must look! I must put the light out.'

But it doesn't matter. Now I am simple and not afraid; now I am myself. He can look at me if he wants to. I'll only say: 'You see, I cried like that because you went away.'

(Or did I cry like that because I'll never sing again, because the light in my *sale cerveau* has gone out?) (p. 189)

And then he is there, at the hotel, coming up the stairs; now the door is open; he comes in. *But it is the old "commis"!*

I lie very still, with my arm over my eyes. As still as if I were dead. . . .

I don't need to look. I know.

I think: 'Is it the blue dressing-gown or the white one? That's very important. I must find that out—it's very important.'

I take my arm away from my eyes. It is the white dressing-gown.

He stands there, looking down at me. Not sure of himself, his mean eyes flickering.

He doesn't say anything. Thank God, he doesn't say anything. I look straight into his eyes and despise another poor devil of a human being for the last time. For the last time. . . .

Then I put my arms round him and pull him down on to the bed, saying: 'Yes—yes—yes. . . .'

II

As these final words of Sasha ring in our ears, Rhys once more weaves her mythic magic, in much the same way as she had done with *Nana* in *Voyage in the Dark*. For Sasha's " 'yes—yes—yes. . . .' " echoes the beginning and ending words of Part Three of James Joyce's *Ulysses*, the words of Molly Bloom, half-British, half-Spanish, who affirms—in internal monologue and half-dreaming revery—a passionate acceptance of life, even as she yearns for the days now long past. Thus, through our knowledge of Molly, Rhys gains depth for

Sasha, merging time and place and people as she has done structurally throughout *Good Morning, Midnight.* Furthermore, in evoking Molly's words, thereby turning our attention to *Ulysses,* Rhys returns us finally to the mythic theme, using Joyce's[49] well-known concepts regarding the recurrence of myth in modern life to reinforce her own mythic emphasis. Additionally, with the implicit reference linking Ulysses' wanderings with Bloom's and Molly's, Rhys can further link *Voyage in the Dark,* wherein Anna searches for her spiritual center, with *Good Morning, Midnight,* wherein Sasha, a wanderer and an alien, finally returns to her own symbolic "faithful Penelope," the symbol for the synthesis of SELF. Thus Rhys emphasizes the eternal archetypal journey of discovery, the ultimate theme toward which the body of her work has pointed.

Previous critics of *Good Morning, Midnight* have been content to accept this final scene between Sasha and the old *commis* for its shock effect alone. In so doing, they have completely overlooked the significance of Rhys's careful detail, ignoring her supreme artistic control. Sensing the power of this dénouement, many critics have offered a kind of obtuse, if not enlightening praise. Francis Wyndham, for example, resolves the final scene in this way: "This involved episode is worked out with great subtlety; its climax, which brings the novel to an end, is brilliantly written and indescribably unnerving to read."[50] Mellown, summarizing others, sees Sasha's acceptance of the disgusting old man as Rhys's device for revealing Sasha's change from a "longing-for-death dipsomanic" to a mature woman who has developed "a compassionate understanding of the human situation." (Mellown, pp. 462 & 7). In presenting this theory of the maturing woman, he admits (obviously feeling uneasy about what Rhys has actually done) that the supposed change is more "suggested than defined" and "comes only on the last page of the novel," thus, it seems to me, imputing a lack of aesthetic control and an unconvincing character motivation. Gerald Kersh (*SR,* July 1, 1967) seems to interpret the ending as an objective correlative of Sasha's "spiritual disintegration." Only Paul Piazza, seemingly unaware of his perception, puts his critical finger squarely on the crux of the problem—of this particular ending and of the novels in general—when he writes: "A summary of Jean Rhys's plots is inadequate, even depressing; yet reading the stories proves a surprisingly exhilarating experience . . . *not a scene, not a word, is wasted.*"[51] Thus he raises the basic critical question concerning Rhys's works: how, if she writes so depressingly of human experience, can Rhys elicit such a sense of exhilaration in so many of her readers?

The answer, of course, lies in what we have uncovered in the course of this study: Rhys speaks to her readers, discerning or otherwise, at the level of the unconscious, at the level of myth. In so doing, she creates, not rhetoric, but poetry of the highest order. Thus, Sasha's final, almost horrifying act of surrender—which if taken at face value, offers only a kind of *deus ex machina* or rabbit-out-of-the-hat solution—becomes, in the light of Rhys's careful preparation, a masterpiece of double intention: *the culmination of Sasha's psychological confrontation and the end of Rhys's mythic quest.* Understanding Rhys's manipulation, we can interpret the ending simply but completely in this way:

Sasha, the "novice for initiation," stripped of all pride and reservation, lies on the symbolic altar of her bed, awaiting her symbolic death (sex is often referred to as the "little death") from which, hopefully, will spring a symbolic rebirth. Or, in other terms suggested within Rhys's careful development, Sasha's ego lies naked, receptive, prepared to embrace positively the SELF, so long imprisoned in the darkness of her unconscious.

However, instead of the young "boy" image she has been prepared to accept as the SELF of her youth, Sasha must endure the final humiliation of accepting the SELF that actually is the reflection of her aging, knowing psyche. So there he stands, the old *commis*, "like a priest, the priest of some obscene, half-understood religion" (p. 35), the trickster-initiator-shadow-animus-SELF. He does not wear—a detail which is of utmost importance to Sasha—the blue robe, the robe of sterile intellectuality with its "black spots" (p. 14), which would be the demons of her darker nature. He wears the white dressing gown, the priestly robe of white.

This priestly robe[52] which so frightened her previously has antithetical symbolic significance. Whiteness, archetypally associated with the sun, signifies not only purity but intuition, particularly the intuition connected with the after-life. Thus white in its most essential form connotes the spiritual center. But conversely, white in its negative quality of fire (the heat of the sun), symbolizes death and, curiously, eroticism. (This antithesis is more generally exemplified in the black/white image.) Hence Sasha welcomes, in the name of life *or* death (for the initiate upon the altar can only *hope* for a resurrection; and the confrontation with the SELF may be either life-healing or death-dealing), the priest, that *archetypal hermaphroditic image of the male-*

119

female force united. Brilliantly, Rhys does not let the projection of Sasha's SELF appear in the more typical Jungian female form; through the hermaphroditic image, Rhys can indicate at once the integrated female psyche and, more generally, man-woman synthesis.[53]

Thus, as the old priest stands there in his robes—like herself, unsure, unspeaking—Sasha gazes straight into the "mean," "flickering," eyes, a reflection of her own, and "despises for the last time," "another poor devil of a human being"—either mankind in general or her feminine essence in particular!

III

But we are left with final ambiguity. For if this initiation into SELF is positive, life-giving, then Sasha has come to terms with SELF and life; her agony of mind and spirit is stilled. She will live the rest of her days compassionately, with love for herself and others. If, on the other hand, this confrontation with SELF is—as it often is—death dealing, if the promise of resurrection is illusory and there is only further darkness, then Sasha faces a symbolic death and can never emerge whole. She will be trapped in the delusory fantasies of a fragmented SELF which can only lead her into further estrangement.

Which is it to be for Sasha? Rhys does not permit us, within the context of the novel itself, to know. Herein lies the ambiguity of narrative focus discussed earlier (cf. pp. 88-89). Is Sasha telling us, after the fact, the truth of events which have brought about her psychic rebirth? Or does she spin a megalomaniac tale (the result of a split psyche) in which she fantasizes that she has solved the riddle of life?

This ambiguity is summarized in the paradoxes inherent in the title of the novel, *Good Morning, Midnight* and in Emily Dickinson's brief poem which serves as epigram to the novel and from which the title was taken:

Good morning, Midnight!
I'm coming home,
Day got tired of me—
How could I of him?

Sunshine was a sweet place,
I liked to stay—

But Morn didn't want me—now—
So good night, Day!

The oxymoronic quality of "good morning, midnight" is obvious and points up implicit questions raised throughout the poem. Is this final act of Sasha's a welcome to the dawning of the final darkness of psychic and spiritual death? Or is it the welcoming of that nadir of night after which will come the day? WE SIMPLY CANNOT KNOW! [54]

And, ultimately, Rhys seems to say, it does not matter. For the inescapable truth of existence is this: The day will follow night. The night will follow day. "There is always tomorrow" where "all rooms are the same." Hopelessly, in the modern, mechanistic, spiritless world, the damned lost souls of mortals roam sunless corridors of hell. The ancient mother-goddess is dethroned. Those newer goddesses and gods that held men's minds—"Venus" and "Apollo" and "even Jesus"—are dead. Endlessly the cycle will repeat, leaving us all, like the Goddess herself, trapped in the eternal labyrinth of time!

Chapter 5

Wide Sargasso Sea[55]

THE MISTY ISLE

From the lone shieling of the misty island
Mountains divide us, and the waste of seas—

In her final novel, *Wide Sargasso Sea*, Rhys redefines for herself her myth of woman's reality and postulates the only viable solution to problems inherent in that reality. Using a minor character created by another woman novelist struggling with the problem of identity one hundred and twenty years earlier, Rhys creates a masterpiece within the framework of another masterpiece. In so doing, she substantiates her recurring theme of merging, overlapping time and also brings added insight to Charlotte Bronte's nineteenth-century novel, *Jane Eyre*, a work Rhys intuitively responded to in terms which contemporary readers are just beginning to understand.

Without reservation, critics have hailed *Wide Sargasso Sea* as a rare, if not classic, piece of literature—secure, perhaps, in the vindication of the Royal Society of Literature award which it received. Again, however, as in the case of *Good Morning, Midnight*, the praise is generally vague, at best specious, indicating that while the power of the novel is irrefutable, the critics themselves do not truly understand the intellectual basis and the emotional symbolism of Rhys's art. Their reviews leave too many aspects ambiguous, debatable, unresolved.

For example, to use some representative criticism as a case in point, Gerald Kersh comments on the nature of this novel:

I have seldom read a novel that was more of a piece than *Wide Sargasso Sea*. To quote from it would be like offering a snipping of a tapestry—it might convey something of the texture, but it wouldn't enlighten the reader as to the pattern. . . .

It is not an easy book to classify, but whatever you choose to call it—tour de force, psychological suspense story, period piece, study in disintegration—it remains a work of high art and profound perception. (*Saturday Review*, July 1, 1967, p. 5.)

Laudatory but hardly revelatory!

In much the same manner, Walter Allen, after damning Rhys's other novels with faint praise, calls "her new novel . . . a considerable tour de force by any standard," but concludes that this novel does not "exist in its own right" needing *Jane Eyre* to "complement it, to supply its full meaning." (*New York Times*, June 18 1967, p. 5.) In examining character, Allen sees Antoinette Cosway (Bertha Mason) epitomizing the "nature of the heroine who appears under various names throughout Jean Rhys's fiction." Mellown, however, in that curiously vague and contradictory paragraph already mentioned (cf. p. iii) interprets her as "a manifestation of the same archetypal figure" [Marya, Julia, Anna, Sacha (sic)] and yet as "a positive character who is not to be confused with anyone else. . . . not, like the other Rhys heroines, Woman with a capital W." Both critics question the function of Rochester, Allen seeing him "as shadowy a figure as Charlotte Bronte's Bertha Mason" and Mellown as a kind of puppet without "individuality," like all "Rhys's men. . . creatures with physical desires who have the power of simple, logical thinking." No critic really examines the functions of the minor characters; no one addresses the problem of title; only the most superficial attention is given Rhys's decision to use Charlotte Bronte's characters; and the implications of that decision for her ultimate theme have been completely ignored. And these are only a few of the complications demanding critical attention.

Certainly it would seem that if *Wide Sargasso Sea* is the example par excellence of Rhys's work and—in the opinion of many—the culmination of her previous work, we might well expect to find at least the complexity of the other novels! Therefore, once again a careful analysis of the parts seems essential in order to ascertain the impact of the whole.

The complexity of *Wide Sargasso Sea* is evident in Rhys's choice of heroine for the culmination of her *oeuvre,* the mad Bertha Mason Rochester of Charlotte Bronte's *Jane Eyre*. Bronte presents her as a shadowy creature, at once beast and human, whose existence as imprisoned wife is exposed only as Rochester and Jane are about to be married and whose function is ostensibly to fire Thornfield Hall, bringing about the blinding and subsequent maiming of Rochester. However, in Rhys's compassionate and myth-moulding hands, this indeterminate figure of doom becomes the compelling Antoinette Cosway, the young Jamaican Creole heiress who reveals in retrospect the debacle of her life. Through her memories—presumably during lucid periods in that room where Rochester has imprisoned her for many years—we learn that she is the daughter of Annette Mason, who was the beautiful and younger second wife of Alexander Cosway. He, implicitly, had died from debauchery about the time of the Emancipation (1834), when Antoinette was nine or ten. Subsequently, Antoinette, her still-young mother, Annette, and the young imbecile brother, Pierre, had lived a lonely and frightening five years at isolated Coulibri Estate with only the company of a few former slaves.

Poverty-stricken, almost hopeless in spite of her defiance, the young widow, Annette, had been inexplicably wooed and wed by wealthy Mr. Mason who had come to the West Indies to make a killing in the collapse of the West Indian economy. A genial and generous man, he permits Annette to refurbish the plantation, while he introduces new English customs and friends. Haunted by her fears of the blacks who, she tells Mason, ''can be dangerous and cruel for reasons you wouldn't understand,'' Annette sees her fears realized—her family driven out by sullen, rioting ex-slaves. In a horrifying night of fire and frenzy, Pierre is killed, Annette's parrot burned alive, and Antoinette wounded by a black friend and playmate, Tia.

Falling seriously ill and recovering six weeks later with her memory of the events impaired, Antoinette learns that her brother is dead and her mother mad, sexually at the mercy of blacks hired to care for her, she later discovers. Mr. Mason—her ''white pappy'' as she calls him—is evidently sincerely fond of Antoinette and assumes his moral obligations to her, sending her to convent school, making provisions that would make her ''happy. . . secure,'' and leaving her at his death an estate of thirty thousand pounds. After his father's death, her step-brother Richard Mason—perhaps as part of the arrangement intended by his father—connives a marriage of convenience for

Antoinette with Edward Rochester who, under English law, thus gains control of her estate.

Rochester, we learn subsequently through his own narration, is the younger son of an uncaring father who has, in essence, condemned him to marry an heiress or to endure penury. Having come to Jamaica to claim his bride, Rochester falls ill of a fever and within a week of recovery finds himself married to the seventeen or eighteen year old Antoinette and on his way to an alien but beautiful estate in the Windward Isles once owned by Antoinette's mother and now presided over by the former slave Christophine.

Inevitably succumbing to the lure of the island and his lovely though exotic bride, Rochester at first revels in the sexual experience of the honeymoon and its attendant lethargy of mind. Then, already satiated, wary of the sensual and sensuous abandon he associates with the island and with his wife, he receives a strange letter from a man calling himself Daniel Cosway. Daniel asserts that he is Antoinette's half-brother and that their father has been a licentious reprobate, spawning bastards throughout the islands. He further insinuates that Antoinette's mother is a mad nymphomaniac and that Antoinette herself has "coloured blood" and had been sexually promiscuous before Richard had literally sold her to the innocent Rochester. Maddened by anger, fear, self-revulsion (this is one of the most complex parts of the novel, belying the gross over-simplification of critics), Rochester determines to take Bertha—the name he prefers for Antoinette—to England where he will punish and imprison her.

After a brief passage narrated by Grace Poole—a passage undeniably linking Rhys's novel with Bronte's *Jane Eyre*—the novel ends with the last thoughts of the now demented Bertha. Lying in bed, she waits for sleep to overcome her keeper so that she may escape her room, light the fire which will consume Thornfield, and ultimately, destroy herself.

Here, in barest detail, is the plot of *Wide Sargasso Sea*. But in reality, the plot is so inextricably tied with characterization, in turn so tied with myth, that this overview, complicated as it is, cannot even suggest the complex scheme. Let us, then, attempt to unravel the multihued strands of Rhys's tapestry, revealing beyond argument or specious praise, the intricate and brilliant workmanship of this unique weaver of myth.

Part One

THE ISLAND EDEN

So complicated yet artistically controlled is the first section of *Wide Sargasso Sea* that to separate the strands weaving through the overt plot line seems an almost impossible task. Perhaps the simplest way is to begin with the facts of Rhys's choice of time and setting and their significance to the early themes developed, particularly in her first novel *Quartet*. These primarily concerned the fate of woman trapped in the male-oriented Victorian ethic (cf. previous discussion of *Quartet*). Therefore, in choosing the West Indian setting in the period following the freeing of the slaves (1834), Rhys can reveal, simultaneously, not only the breaking up of a long-established social order and the consequent changes and animosities such upheavals engender, but, since the time of that chaos is coincident with the beginning of Victoria's reign and the unparalleled rise of the British Empire, she can sketch by implication the genesis of "Victorianism" in all its resultant power.

Certainly, given this insight, we must see Rhys's choice of Bronte's *Jane Eyre* as substrata for her own work as more than fortuitous. Rhys indicates the validity of this assumption in an interview with Hannah Carter for the *Guardian*, (August 8, 1968):

> The mad wife in *Jane Eyre* always interested me. I was convinced that Charlotte Bronte must have had something against the West Indies, and I was angry about it. Otherwise, why did she take a West Indian for that horrible lunatic, for that really dreadful creature? I hadn't really formulated the idea of vindicating the mad woman in a novel but when I was rediscovered I was encouraged to do so. (p. 5)

That the book had lain at the level of Rhys's unconscious for some time is obvious, if the material in the October 1974 *Mademoiselle* interview is accurate:

> When her husband [her third, Max Hamer, a retired naval officer and a poet] got sick, someone gave them the cottage in Devon and there they lived until he died. After his death, she could not endure being there alone and went to London, had a heart attack and entered a convalescent home. She

came back to Devon where, she says, "no one ever wrote to me. I suppose they thought that after being sick, I'd never work again." She was obsessed, however, with Mrs. Rochester but every time she tried to put her on paper wrote the same words over and over again. "I'd go up and down the kitchen corridor," she said, pointing to a short hallway furnished by a bookcase choked with old Penguin paperbacks, "reading ancient books like *King Solomon's Mines.*" Then a man, the friend of a friend, heard about Jean Rhys and started to call. He encouraged her—"it was funny, he doesn't even like my books, says they're ephemeral"—and she finished *Wide Sargasso Sea.*

"I can't think it was altogether coincidence. I feel more and more as if we're fated. . . ." (p. 210)

In these last lines, Rhys suggests again the inevitable workings of the unconscious upon the artist's conscious.[56] Perhaps she never consciously understood what she would accomplish when she chose that "horrible lunatic" created by Charlotte Bronte as her final protagonist. But the fact remains that in using the Victorian masterpiece of *Jane Eyre*—the supposed autobiography of a proud, poor, virtuous young woman who survives in the ugly Victorian milieu—Rhys illustrates and deepens her previous themes, in the process achieving mythopoesis. Borrowing from Bronte (herself victimized by the sordid Victorian world which serves as the backdrop for *Jane Eyre*) the mad prisoner-wife, Bertha, Rhys creates from that shadowy horror her vivid original character of Antoinette, at once adding dimension to *Wide Sargasso Sea* and to the hundred year old *Jane Eyre*. For in the final analysis, Rhys's Antoinette will colour our understanding of Bronte's Rochester, while Bronte's Jane Eyre—never mentioned in Rhys's novel—will implicitly contribute to the final understanding of Rhys's Antoinette, of Rhys's Rochester, and ultimately, of Rhys's own mythic theme.

This process of reinforcement should not, of course, be unexpected. Rhys has employed it successfully in earlier novels. For example, we have seen how reference to Zola's *Nana* reinforced character and theme in *Voyage in the Dark;* Dickinson's poem, used as epigram and source of title in *Good Morning, Midnight,* reflected Rhys's philosophical complexity; the Joycean echoes of Molly Bloom in the same novel directed our understanding of Sasha's final surrender. And all these allusions worked together to point up Rhys's mythic progression. So, in the same manner, Rhys will permit Bronte's *Jane Eyre* to serve a similar purpose for *Wide Sargasso Sea.*

II

This process of allusion becomes immediately obvious in *Wide Sargasso Sea,* as we examine further ramifications of time and place revealed in Antoinette's memories of life at Coulibri both before and after the freeing of the slaves. For the young Antoinette, the world is one of sharp class distinction. The "white people"—obviously meaning the English West Indians—"close ranks" "when trouble comes." But Antoinette and her family are "not in their ranks," the English Jamaican ladies never approving of pretty, young Annette Cosway who had come from French Martinique.

Antoinette's world is also one in which worth is determined by money: the blacks, now freed from slavery if not from misery, stand around to jeer at her mother in her shabby riding clothes because "they notice clothes, they know about money." In this new economic world ostensibly occasioned by the emancipation, old orders have been swept away. The West Indian aristocracy founded on wealth derived from slavery is now bankrupt, despised and hated not only by pious English who have long sought the abolition of slavery but by the blacks who have suffered for so long. Black Tia, Antoinette's young friend, summarizes the value system of white and black alike: " . . . Real white people, they got gold money. . . . Old time white people nothing but white nigger now, and black nigger better than white nigger." (p. 25). The new aristocracy is "proper" English, with beautiful clothes, money, and, as Christophine says: " '. . . the Letter of the Law. Same thing as slavery. They got magistrate. They got fine. They got jail house and chain gang. They got tread machine to mash up people's feet. New ones worse than old ones—more cunning, that's all.' " (pp. 26-7). The social world of the West Indies is riven with hatred, malice, suspicion, poverty, and envy.

Mason

In the midst of this implicit madness, Mr. Mason looms as a rock of reason, generosity, moral superiority—the English virtues at their best. Although he has made money in the Indies, an "estate in Trinidad . . . the Antigua property," he patently has not come to exploit the natives or the land. After marrying the young widow, Annette, he improves and makes his home at Coulibri, having rescued the Cosways from "poverty and misery." He employs black servants, seeing them as "children" who "wouldn't hurt a fly." So sure of himself, so "without a doubt English," Mr. Mason (he is never given a first name) passionately loves his beautiful wife, "so without a doubt not English but no white nigger either." Nevertheless, liberal though he seems, he frowns when Antoinette indicates her knowledge of native promiscuity (p. 34); he "lectures" Antoinette about her "coloured" relatives, making her reticent and ashamed.

Secure in his English superiority and protected by his naiveté concerning the nature of the blacks, Mason is brave, protecting his family during the night of horror and facing down a machete-wielding black, "not frightened but too astounded to speak." Later, as the blacks close in with sticks and torches Antoinette remembers that ". . . Mr. Mason stopped swearing and began to pray in a loud pious voice. The prayer ended, 'May Almighty God defend us.' And God who is indeed mysterious, who had made no sign when they burned Pierre as he slept —not a clap of thunder, not a flash of lightning—mysterious God heard Mr. Mason at once and answered him. The yells stopped." (p. 43).

After the escape from Coulibri, Mason provides a "tidy pretty little house" for his now mad wife who has rejected her husband with all the fury of her soul. He visits Antoinette, bringing her gifts, kissing her, eyeing her "carefully and critically," as he has her educated by the nuns for the position in life he plans to provide for her—a life based upon marriage which in turn is based upon the money, half his fortune, which he provides for her before his death.

These details of character reflect the prototype of Julia's Uncle Griffiths (ALMM), who, like Mason, had married impulsively and never regretted it. Thus Mason, like Griffiths, represents that older, basically decent order from which will rise, with the ascendency of the British Empire, the new "Victorian."

Annette

Threaded within the straightforward character of Mason, Rhys weaves a counterthread in the complexity of his wife, Annette, whom

129

he has loved, indulged, and protected. Thinking of the marriage of her mother and Mason, Antoinette remembers: ''. . . Yes, she would have died I thought, if she had not met him. And for the first time I was grateful and liked him. There are more ways than one of being happy, better perhaps to be peaceful and contented and protected. . . .'' (pp. 36-7). Thus Antoinette implies that her mother has willingly accepted all that Mason offered, having gone so far as to sell her ''last ring'' to get money for the ''new white dress'' which would make her exciting and acceptable and thus assure the affluent life she desired. It is only when the blacks finally fire the house, burning her son, the helpless Pierre, that Annette turns on her husband as her wedding ring symbolically falls off. Then, in a frenzy, she screams at Mason, calling him a ''fool, a cruel stupid fool'': '' 'I told you what would happen again and again. . . . You would not listen, you sneered at me, you grinning hypocrite, you ought not to live either. . .' '' (p. 40). Later, as she recovers from her fever, Antoinette will remember her mother screaming: '' 'Don't touch me. I'll kill you if you touch me. Coward. Hypocrite. I'll kill you.' '' (p. 47).

Mason, then, as Rhys develops him, is not a wicked villain bringing deliberate misery to Annette. He is only trapped in the narrowness of his white male reason which cannot listen to the warnings of those more attuned to the nature of the primitive. Only in his logic and lack of imagination is he at fault. But perhaps, in the long run, this is the greatest sin. At any rate, in Annette's reaction to her husband, Rhys seems to summarize a view that she had played with in *Quartet* and *After Leaving Mr. Mackenzie:* woman's hatred of man, while understandable, is nevertheless rooted in an unreasoning insanity which cannot be appeased and only results in further madness.

Continuing with the complexity inherent in the character of Annette, the overtones of name—Antoinette's as well—cannot have escaped the notice of those who have read thus far in this work. Here, in Annette, we have again a variation of ''Anna'' with all the overtones suggested in the chapter, ''The Myths of Anna'' (cf. p. 78). More significantly, in this novel, unlike the others, Rhys sets the avatars of the Great Goddess within a ''garden gone to bush,'' a world out of kilter where the ''devil is prince.'' Once, however, as Antoinette remembers, the ''garden was large and beautiful as that garden in the Bible—*the tree of life grew there.* But it had gone wild. The paths were overgrown and a smell of dead flowers mixed with the fresh living smell. . . .All Coulibri Estate had gone wild like the garden, gone to bush. . . ." (p. 19. Emphasis added.)

Curiously, though the "emancipation troubles" are blamed for all the misfortunes at Coulibri, "the estate was going downhill for years before that" (p. 29), and Antoinette "did not remember the place when it was prosperous." (p. 19). On the night of the conflagration, Antoinette sees the house burning and knows that though the memory will always remain, she will never see Coulibri again: "The house was burning, the yellow-red sky was like sunset and I knew that I would never see Coulibri again. Nothing would be left. . . . When they had finished, there would be nothing left but blackened walls and *the mounting stone. That was left. That could not be stolen or burned.*" (pp. 45-6. Emphasis added.) With those last two lines, we are alerted to a sense of reenactment, a theme which underlies the whole of Rhys's writings. All of this has happened before. The gardens of Coulibri, innocence, freedom, Eden, have been destroyed before. But in the ashes, indestructible, still remains the *mounting stone,* the composite symbol of "stair" and "stone", the former suggesting evolutive and spiritual ascension and the latter the state of harmonious, cohesive "being."

With this image of the eternal "mounting stone"—the antithesis of man's natural, logical concepts of change, decay, death—Rhys accepts, for better or worse, the cyclical nature of life and supplies the foundation for understanding the significance of the remaining characters who round out Antoinette's world. Through them, we will come at last to understand the conflicts within Antoinette which she cannot control and which will eventually destroy her.

Returning to the complex significance of Annette, the implicit religious overtones of the garden imagery and the nuances of the name Annette are further extended in other religious-symbolic detail. While the religious background of Antoinette seems to be Catholic—implicit in her Creole background and convent education—Annette's religious background is not so clear. Born in the French island of Martinique with all its overtones of voodoo, witchcraft, obeah; served by Christophine, the black Martinique slave reported to be "obeah" herself; Annette has, according to gossip, encouraged her first husband in his sexual excesses, accepted with "presents and smiles" his bastards, and otherwise observed "old customs . . . better dead and buried." (p. 29). That Annette Cosway is to be associated with sexual license is further indicated symbolically: " '. . . Her new husband will have to spend a pretty penny before the house is fit to live in—leaks like a sieve. And what about the *stables and the coach house dark as pitch* and the servants' quarters and the *six foot snake*—saw with my own eyes *curled up on the privy seat . . .* ' " (p. 29. Emphasis added.) The stables, the darkness, the snake clearly suggest the sexual, the vital, the fecund—all aspects associated with the female-principle. At best, Annette's is not a Christian implication. She implicitly rejects the Christian in the form of her old slave, Godfrey (the "peace of God"), the black Christian who knows "the devil prince of this world." (p. 19). But, revealingly, Annette sees Godfrey as "the old hypocrite," "a devil!"

Thus, in the person of Annette, Rhys again revives the myth implicit in Julia's old, dying mother, the anachronistic female-principle struggling for life long after she has ceased to be the "sweet, warm center of the world." (*ALMM*). Antoinette, like Julia of the earlier novel, has loved her mother, has sought to be near her, to hide within the safety of her soft black cloak of hair, even to turn comforter as she feels her mother's distress. But as her mother has changed in the shifting pressures, as she has turned inward, cold, distant (the two-sided nature of the Great Goddess), as she has focused her maternal instincts upon the doomed, imbecilic son (in essence betrayed the matrilineal order) instead of her daughter, Antoinette has retreated, seeking refuge elsewhere. When Annette sells her "last ring," symbolic of her female-dominating life principle, to buy security in the male-structured English society—the final abrogation of female independence—Antoinette is literally left at the mercy of those forces from which there can be no escape. Her demented mother in the "tidy pretty little house," learning that Pierre the son is dead, irrevocably rejects her. But long before that final rejection, alienated and frightened by the mother she has loved, Antoinette has turned to a surrogate mother, Christophine.

Christophine

Christophine, although her function is barely implied in Part One, is no minor character, her essence permeating the entire novel. Like her mistress, Annette, Christophine is not Jamaican, she is Martinique. Ageless, blacker than the other slaves—"blue-black with a thin face and straight features"—she has "a quiet voice, a quiet laugh (when she did laugh)" and speaks English and French fluently as well as the patois of the natives, which she uses in their presence. These natives are terrified of her, working for her without pay and bringing her "presents of fruits and vegetables." Antoinette, after her mother's marriage, learns the significance of the terror and the gifts. Christophine is "obeah"! Despite the bright patchwork counterpane in Christophine's room and her "pictures of the Holy Family and the prayer for a happy death," Antoinette comes to imagine that ". . . hidden in the room (behind the old black press?) there was a dead man's dried hand, white chicken feathers, a cock with its throat cut, dying slowly, slowly. Drop by drop the blood was falling into a red basin . . ." (p. 31).

Rhys, by imposing Antoinette's fears of "obeah" upon the ageless, serene, black Christophine—the play upon Christ-Christian is obvious[57]—has again conjured images of innumerable ancient religions, absorbed, gone underground, accommodated to forces temporarily dominant but eventually to be themselves submerged in a never-ending process. Thus Rhys reinforces the eternal process of rebirth suggested in the Anna-Annette-Antoinette name symbolism. And, having added Christophine to the pantheon, she further extends her thesis in the name and characterization of Antoinette's Aunt Cora.

Aunt Cora

Antoinette's Aunt "Cora," a name meaning "maiden" but etymologically linked to Nora (Julia's sister in *ALMM*), in turn a variation eventually traceable to "Anna," is the one person of whom generally amiable Mr. Mason does not approve. Of West Indian birth, although her family relationship is never clearly established, Aunt Cora had been one of the lucky ones—a slave-owner who had "escaped misery, a flier in the face of Providence." Because her English husband hated the West Indies, resenting even her letters to the family, Aunt Cora had been unable to help during the bad years, but " '. . . when he died not long ago she came home, before that what could she do? *She* wasn't rich.' " (p. 31). Obviously, with the death of her husband, Cora is independently well-off and free of a man's control.

Furthermore, during the traumatic events at Coulibri, Aunt Cora reveals herself as a sensitive, intuitive, courageous woman. Responsive to Mason's desire for affectionate appreciation from Antoinette, Cora points out to her niece this need. In arguments between Mason and Annette, Cora refrains from interfering, except in the matter of leaving Coulibri. Then, because she is wise in her knowledge of native psychology, she supports Annette in her decision to take Pierre and leave. But the riot develops that very night and Cora, dressed almost ceremoniously in her "black silk dress, her ringlets carefully arranged," is calm, assuring, protective. Putting her arms around Antoinette, she says: " 'Don't be afraid, you are quite safe. We are all quite safe. . .' " (p. 40), and "just for a moment" Antoinette shuts her eyes and rests her head against her shoulder, smelling the good scent of vanilla.

When Pierre is brought from his room, burned, almost lifeless, it is Cora who, stepping out of her white petticoats and tearing them in strips, ministers to him. In the escape from the burning house and grounds, with flames roaring and shooting up all around them, it is Cora who instructs Christophine, leads Antoinette, strengthens Annette: " 'Annette, they are laughing at you, do not allow them to laugh at you.' " (p. 42). When the parrot falls, "all on fire" and Antoinette begins to cry, it is Cora who says: " 'Don't look, . . . Don't look.' She stooped and put her arms round me and I hid my face. . ." (p. 43). At the moment when death seems inevitable and Mr. Mason is too astounded to speak, it is Aunt Cora who faces the threatening black man down:

> . . .'The little boy is very badly hurt. He will die if we cannot get help for him.'
>
> The man said, 'So black and white, they burn the same, eh?'
>
> 'They do,' she said. 'Here and hereafter, as you will find out. Very shortly.'
>
> He let the bridle go and thrust his face close to hers. He'd throw her on the fire, he said, if she put bad luck on him. Old white jumby, he called her. But she did not move an inch, she looked straight into his eyes and threatened him with eternal fire in a calm voice. 'And never a drop of sangoree to cool your burning tongue,' . . . (p. 45)

When Antoinette emerges six weeks later from her illness, it is to find herself safe, in Aunt Cora's house, cared for by her comforting hands.

Clearly, Cora is a nourishing, sustaining avatar of the ancient life-giving goddess—a financially independent image of poor Norah

134

(*ALMM*), bound to servitude by choice but also by her economic dependence—and an Anglicized equivalent of Christophine. But after the harrowing events at Coulibri, Cora looks "thin and old and her hair wasn't arranged prettily," and the recovering Antoinette shuts her eyes "not wanting to see her." Cora, however, is emotionally wise and economically secure, so knowing that "her health was not good and she needed a change," she leaves Jamaica to spend a year in England, perhaps, by implication, that clear, cold land where the blood runs slower and the heat of passion lies cool. Thus, Cora gone, Antoinette must also leave the "dark, clean, friendly house," which has sheltered her and find refuge in the convent, "a place of sunshine and of death" where the nuns preside and where Mother Superior, Sister Marie Augustine, tells even the Bishop who interferes in her domain to "mind his own business."

Sister Marie Augustine

The characterization of Sister Marie Augustine is the final major figure against whose background Rhys will finally permit Antoinette to emerge. Her part is brief but not minor. It is her image with which Rhys concludes Part One, leaving her words burned in our brain. Swiftly Rhys sketches her, first as she comforts Antoinette in the convent following a frightening encounter with her two coloured Cosway cousins:

> . . . 'You have cried quite enough now, you must stop. Have you got a handkerchief? . . . Now look at me,' she said. 'You will not be frightened of me.'
> I looked at her. She had large brown eyes, very soft, and was dressed in white, not with a starched apron like the others had. The band around her face was of linen and above the white linen a black veil of some thin material, which fell in folds down her back. Her cheeks were red, she had a laughing face and two deep dimples. Her hands were small but they looked clumsy and swollen, not like the rest of her. It was only afterwards that I found out that they were crippled with rheumatism. (pp. 52-4)

Next she appears as Antoinette wakens to see "Sister Marie Augustine sitting serene and neat, bolt upright in a wooden chair. The long brown room was full of *gold sunlight and shadows of trees moving quietly.*" (p. 57. Emphasis added.)

In the convent presided over by Sister Marie Augustine, the sisters are not very strict and the " 'bishop who visits them every year says they are lax. Very lax. It's the climate, he says.' " The nuns seem happy, their faces are serene. But Antoinette resents their cheerful faces: "They are safe. How can they know what it can be like *outside?*" However, when after a terrifying dream she tells Sister Marie Augustine—who has brought her to her private room for a calming cup of chocolate—"I dreamed I was in hell," this cheerful, serene woman replies: " 'That dream is evil. Put it from your mind—never think of it again,' and she rubbed my cold hands to warm them." (p. 61). Sister Marie Augustine knows "that dream," and the fear and cold it engenders.

Then, as Antoinette drinks her chocolate, the memory of her mother's funeral the previous year when they had all come home to drink chocolate and eat cakes causes tears to come to her eyes and she says, " 'Such terrible things happen. . . . Why? Why?' " Part One concludes with this scene and with Sister Marie Augustine's words:

> 'You must not concern yourself with that mystery. . . . We do not know why the devil must have his little day. Not yet.'
>
> She never smiled as much as the others, now she was not smiling at all. She looked sad.
>
> She said, as if she was talking to herself, 'Now, go quietly back to bed. Think of calm, peaceful things and try to sleep. *Soon I will give the signal. Soon it will be tomorrow morning.*' (p. 62. Emphasis added.)

With these final lines of Part One, Rhys leaves us with a sense of brooding, waiting tension. And with a flash of recognition, recalling this nun in white sitting in the "gold sunlight with the shadows of the trees moving quietly," we remember a strange passage from *Good Morning, Midnight* where Sasha, in agonizing awareness, knows she is " . . . lying in a misery of utter darkness. Quite alone. No voice, no touch, no hand . . . . How long must I lie here? For ever? *No, only for a couple of hundred years this time, miss. . . .*" (*GMM*, p. 173. Punctuation exact. Emphasis added.)

Once more we realize the supreme artistry of Rhys and see clearly

136

what she has done. In this brief characterization of Marie Augustine, whose name means "bitter, exalted mind," Rhys reveals the essence of the new avatar of Anna. Here, in new form, is Rhys's theme of evolution, assimilation, religion gone under ground. For just as early Roman Christianity had absorbed the Greek and Roman goddesses and gods into the Christian pantheon—yielding St. Venere, St. Artemidos, etc.—so the terrible Anu became, in early British Christianity, a nun! Robert Graves, tracing that development, states that there is a picture of this goddess, wearing a nun's habit, in the vestry of the Swithland Church. (Graves, p. 370.) He further suggests that, in the assimilative process, it was an easy matter to so "Christianize" a death-goddess, because the nuns were already veiled.

Thus, Sister Marie Augustine, the intellectualized-through-bitter-experience avatar of the Great Triple Goddess, broods her time. In the midst of her sisters, within the safety of the convent walls, unthreatened by the outside world now gone mad, she waits to give the signal ushering in the morning.

Synthesis

Now we are ready to synthesize the significance of all the mother-characters which have dominated Part One. In these characters, so vital and yet seemingly so incidental, Rhys has achieved a kind of matri-archal pantheon. Thus Christophine in her blue-blackness represents the most primitive, ancient earth-mother image, older than even the earliest western mythologies encompass. Rooted in forces beyond the understanding of Indo-European cultures, accommodating herself of necessity to the white man's myths, she nevertheless triumphs in her SELF-ness, rooted in a wisdom which knows that the essence of life is sadness, that "the little ones grow old, the children leave us," that "the loving man was lonely, the girl was deserted, the children never came back. Adieu." (The fullness of Christophine's character emerges in Part Two.)

In Annette we find a less ancient, less primeval force, still instinc-tually attuned, however, to the darker ancient passions. She is beauti-ful, vital, sexual. But ultimately she is doomed to symbolic madness because she has betrayed the female-principle, sold her independence, lost control of her passions and is therefore unable to assimilate, to survive outside the garden now gone rank and virtually destroyed.

137

Cora survives. Anglicized, independent, Woman in her own right but in mutated form, she sustains and nourishes, though eventually, she will "turn her face to the wall," passing on her ring of life to Antoinette—as Julia's mother had left her the ring—the same symbolic ring which Sasha (*Good Morning, Midnight*) wears.

Sister Marie Augustine, who also wears the gold ring of the nun, now rules. Within the very framework of the patriarchal god-system which would destroy her if it knew, protected from man economically and physically, she bides her time, awaits the day, and worships the Holy Family—*MOTHER* and son!

Two minor characters remain to be discussed before the outline of Antoinette focuses into wholeness: Maillote ("link in a chain"?), Christophine's only friend, and Maillote's daughter, Tia, Antoinette's playmate, friend, and enemy. Maillotte remains nothing more than a name—but a name which evokes the memory of another Maillote whose name was seen by Anna Morgan (*Voyage*) on a slave list and who, by implication, might have been responsible for Anna's mixed blood. In the light of such inference, black Tia assumes an important literal significance and also, symbolically, opens up another of Rhys's motifs. That is, Tia may well be one of the "bastards" which Annette had welcomed and therefore she would be one of Antoinette's coloured cousins. This would account at a literal level for Tia's venomous digs, her less than covert hostility, her malicious running off with Antoinette's "starched, ironed, clean" dress—leaving Antoinette the dirty one which Tia had worn—and her final act of hatred, the throwing of the jagged stone which wounds Antoinette on the night of escape from Coulibri. The symbolic significance of Tia in her final appearance is clear:

> Then. . . I saw Tia and her mother and I ran to her for she was all that was left of my life as it had been. We had eaten the same food, slept side by side, bathed in the same river. As I ran, I thought I will live with Tia and will be like her. Not to leave Coulibri. Not to go. Not. When I was close I saw the jagged stone in her hand but I did not see her throw it. I did not feel it either, only something wet, running down my face. I looked at her and I saw her face crumple up as she began to cry. We stared at each other, blood on my face, tears on hers. *It was as if I saw myself. Like in a looking-glass.* (p. 46. Emphasis added.)

Here, then, we have objectified the psychological trauma that has consumed the protagonists of Rhys's novels: *the fractured personality which is a result of the circumstances of life.* That this fractured personality finds objective expression in the "black" image of Tia echoes Rhys's emphasis on the black heritage as the vital, earthy component. But, in the psychic splitting of the SELF, that sexual essence must be rejected. Hence Rhys's image of blackness—the mirror image of Antoinette—reflects not only Rhys's and Antoinette's particular West Indian experience but, in all probability, the *unconscious acceptance of feminine nature as the "black," "evil" force which man has for so long attributed to woman.* That this black image of SELF may perhaps be rooted in woman's racial or sexual unconscious must at least be considered.

At any rate, with Rhys's marvelously conceived objectification of the split SELF, it is relatively easy to analyze Antoinette as a synthesis of Rhys's protagonists. She is (her name translates into "of inestimable worth") a sensitive, intelligent personality caught in the emotional cross-fire of contrasting cultures, conflicting religions, warring psyche —all of which are, ultimately, one and the same. In this light, then, we may summarize rather quickly the episodes of Antoinette's memories which thread in and over the background design of images already discussed.

Antoinette

Born and raised during the terrible events associated with the tortuous emancipation of the slaves in the British West Indies, Antoinette lives in a predominantly black culture ruled by a fearful and often vengeful white minority. The decay of this culture has been gradual, insidious, but the final conflagrations culminating in victory have left the plantations seared, the economy ruined, and the new breed of wealthy, morally "righteous" Englishman in control. Antoinette, herself, is, by heritage, Creole, though by implication of mixed blood. Her nature draws her to this island "garden" where grows "the tree of life." However, taunted by the blacks as a "white nigger," despised by the aloof Jamaican-English as the child of a "Martinique," envied by the "coloureds" who invent stories about her and her family, it is little wonder that Antoinette isolates herself, taking strange paths away from the bathing pool where she has played in innocence with Tia:

139

> . . . I went to parts of Coulibri that I had not seen, where
> there was no road, no path, no track. And if the razor grass
> cut my legs and arms I would think 'It's better than people.'
> Black ants or red ones, tall nests swarming with white ants,
> rain that soaked me to the skin—once I saw a snake. All
> better than people.
>
> Better. Better, better than people.' (p. 28)

Then, in the midst of her loneliness, alienated from her mother,
puberty is upon her. One night she dreams a patently sexual dream: "I
dreamed that I was walking in the forest. Not alone. Someone who
hated me was with me, out of sight. I could hear heavy footsteps
coming closer and though I struggled and screamed I could not move. I
woke crying. The covering sheet was on the floor . . ." (p. 27). The next
morning she awoke, "knowing that nothing would be the same. It
would change and go on changing. . . . Watching the red and yellow
flowers in the sun thinking of nothing, it was as if a door opened and I
was somewhere else, something else. *Not myself any longer.*" (p. 28.
Emphasis added.) Without further detail, Rhys imposes upon
Antoinette the figure of Anna Morgan (*Voyage*), who remembered that
it was Francine, her black friend, who had made her feel when she
"was unwell for the first time" that it was natural and "quite all
right."

Now in the spring of Antoinette's womanhood, the fruit of life
grows on the tree in the "garden" and the fruit has been tasted by
Antoinette. She, like Anna Morgan trapped in her girlish guilt, knows
the time of day, "when though it is hot and blue and there are no
clouds, the sky can have a very black look." (p. 28). She watches,
knowingly, as her beautiful newly married mother dances with her
"white pappy": ". . .There was no need for music when she danced.
They stopped and she leaned backwards over his arm, down till her
black hair touched the flagstones—still down, down. . . . and he kissed
her—a long kiss. *I was there that time too but they had forgotten
me* . . ." (p. 30. Emphasis added.) She hears the drums calling the
natives to festival and knows that it is not for a wedding celebration:
" 'not a wedding. . .there is never a wedding.' "[58] (p. 34).

Always, underneath the music of the native drums and the "smell
of deadflowers mixed with the fresh living smell" and Godfrey's pious
grumblings and Christophine's "gay" music with the "sad" words and
Annette's stormy words about hypocrites and devils, runs the fear of

death and the threat of damnation: " . . . (Godfrey said that we were not righteous. One day when he was drunk he told me that we were all damned and no use praying.)" (p. 34). And another day, "Myra came in . . . looking mournful as she always did though she smiled when she talked about hell. Everyone went to hell, she told me, you had to belong to her sect to be saved and even then—just as well not be too sure." (p. 36).

Then English Mr. Mason comes to bring order to chaos, to save them from poverty and misery, to provide " . . . English food . . . beef and mutton, pies and puddings." (p. 35). And Antoinette is "glad to be like an English girl" and holds in her mind the vision of her favorite pictures: " . . . 'The Miller's Daughter', a lovely English girl with brown curls and blue eyes and a dress slipping off her shoulders. Then I looked across the white tablecloth and the vase of yellow roses at Mr. Mason, so sure of himself . . ." (p. 36).

Suddenly, however, in the midst of her new found security, her black-white, old-new world collapses. But in the terror of that night of fire, two male images survive in her memory. Mannie, the "black English-man," despised by his own people, and Mason, the "white pappy." Both emerge from the inferno as figures of strength and courage. Certainly the nuances of this memory should not be minimized, obscure though they seem.

In Spanish Town, after her recovery from the lengthy illness, three more symbolic figures manifest themselves as Antoinette goes for the first time to the safety of the convent. The first two

> . . . were waiting for me under the sandbox tree. There were two of them, a boy and a girl. The boy was about four-teen and tall and big for his age, he had a white skin, a dull ugly white covered with freckles, his mouth was a negro's mouth and he had small eyes, like bits of green glass. He had the eyes of a dead fish. Worst, most horrible of all, his hair was crinkled, negro's hair, but bright red, and his eyebrows and eyelashes were red. The girl was very black and wore no head handkerchief. Her hair had been plaited and I could smell the sickening oil she had daubed on it. . .
> (p. 49)

> The girl began to laugh, very quietly, and it was then that hate came to me . . . (p. 50)

As the girl laughs, the boy says, " 'One day I catch you alone, you wait, one day I catch you alone.' " (p. 50). And the girl, " 'You don't want to look at me, eh, I make you look at me, eh, I make you look at me.' She pushed me and the books I was carrying fell to the ground." (p. 51).

Clearly these two frightening adolescents are to be seen as a projection of Antoinette's unconscious—the boy her animus, ugly, white, with small green eyes, a negro's mouth and, worst of all, the bright red Negro hair which proclaims him her kin. The girl is an alter-ego, the shadow of that inner self against which every Rhys heroine has struggled.[59]

The third symbolic figure to appear is Sandi Cosway, Antoinette's coloured cousin whose arrival sends the menacing pair fleeing. Sandi is a projection of that unified SELF which similarly could send the shadows fleeing. It is Sandi whom Daniel Cosway will accuse of being Antoinette's lover; it is Sandi whom the mad Bertha Mason will remember in her last thoughts at Thornfield Hall; it is Sandi who is the shadowy, ambiguous first love of Anna Morgan—the heroine of *Voyage in the Dark* who is closest in spirit to Antoinette. Thus, as Rhys has progressively revealed in her preceding novels, *it is the longing for, the search for, the finding of the integrated SELF* which is the beginning and the end of "being," and *the whole purpose behind the act of love*.

Safe from the threat without, within the convent walls Antoinette finds friends and impeccable models to emulate: Helene with the beautifully coiffed hair, Germaine of "impeccable deportment" and Louise of the beautiful teeth:

> . . . Ah but Louise! Her small waist, her thin brown hands, her black curls which smelled of vetiver, her high sweet voice, singing carelessly in chapel about death. Like a bird would sing . . .
>
> France is a lady with black hair wearing a white dress because Louise was born in France fifteen years ago, and my mother, whom I forget. . . liked to dress in white. (p. 56)

Here, in embryo are the characters, the illusions, the conscious and unconscious inclinations revealed in such a variety of ways in Rhys's preceding novels. But in this image of Louise is also the Rhys heroine's vision of the Lady of Death—*herself* as she can never be. It is this vision which Sasha (*Good Morning, Midnight*) admits to having loved when

René asks if she has ever loved a woman, and it is this vision which keeps her from an acceptance of the self that really exists.

In Spanish Town in her place of refuge, the convent, which is at once a "place of sunshine and of death," of "sun or shadow," where everything is "brightness or dark," all the ambivalences, the contradictions of Antoinette's childhood days are deepened. Here the nuns who are "not strict at all," teach about Heaven and Hell and about the saints who "were all very beautiful and wealthy" and all were "loved by rich young men." They also teach about modesty—as Antoinette learns to "cautiously" soap herself in the big stone bath where the girls wore "long grey cotton chemises" which reached to their ankles—and about "pushing down the cuticles" and "cleanliness, good manners and kindness to God's poor," and about "order and chastity, that flawless crystal that, once broken, can never be mended." (p. 55). But sometime—during the days and nights of prayers, "after the meal . . . and at the hour of our death, and at midday and at six in the evening, now and at the hour our death," (p. 57)—*something happens*, something so dreadful that Antoinette prays "for a long time to be dead." Only that, *too,* was a sin so she

> . . . prayed for a long time about that *too,* but the thought came, so many things are sins, why? Another sin to think that. However, happily, Sister Marie Augustine says thoughts are not sins, if they are driven away at once. You say Lord save me, I perish. I find it very comforting to know exactly what must be done. All the same, *I did not pray so often after that and soon, hardly at all. I felt bolder, happier, more free.* But not so safe. (p. 58. Emphasis added.)

Then after many months in the convent, when she is past seventeen and Mr. Mason has visited to talk about his plans for her, Antoinette suddenly knows that life with the sisters will soon be over. She is gripped with a "feeling of dismay, sadness, loss" which almost chokes her. That night she dreams again her horrifying dream:

> Again I have left the house at Coulibri. It is night and I am walking towards the forest. I am wearing a long dress and thin slippers, so I walk with difficulty, following the man who is with me and holding up the skirt of my dress. It is white and beautiful and I don't wish to get it soiled. I follow

143

him, sick with fear but I make no effort to save myself; if anyone were to try to save me, I would refuse. *This must happen.* Now we have reached the forest. We are under the tall dark trees and there is no wind. 'Here?' He turns and looks at me, his face black with hatred, and when I see this I begin to cry. He smiles slyly. 'Not here, not yet,' he says, and I follow him, weeping. Now I do not try to hold up my dress, it trails in the dirt, my beautiful dress. We are no longer in the forest but in an enclosed garden surrounded by a stone wall and the trees are different trees. I do not know them. There are steps leading upwards. It is too dark to see the wall or the steps, but I know they are there and I think, 'It will be when I go up these steps.' At the top I stumble over my dress and cannot get up. I touch a tree and my arms hold on to it. 'Here, here.' But I think I will not go any further. The tree sways and jerks as if it is trying to throw me off. Still I cling and the seconds pass and *each one is a thousand years.* 'Here, in here,' a strange voice said, and the tree stopped swaying and jerking. (pp. 60-1. Emphasis added.)

With this dream of inevitable defilement by a man whose face is black with hatred, this dream of hell for which Sister Marie Augustine gives what comfort she can, Rhys ends Antoinette's childhood, a far-cry from the ''happy childhood in a tropical state of nature,'' which Mellown describes (p. 472). She also ends the matriarchal emphasis of *Part One* and predicts the days of humiliation and degradation ahead for Antoinette, when she is forced to leave her place of refuge and enter the pitiless world of man.

But beyond the implications for Antoinette herself, Rhys has symbolized masterfully in Antoinette's dream the inevitable dethronement and ultimate defilement, if not living sacrifice, of the feminine-principle that she has traced previously: *i.e.*, the process whereby the Great Mother Goddess becomes sister to the god, wife of the god, mother of the god; becomes Mary the Virgin Mother becomes lady to be worshipped becomes, finally, prostitute and temptress to be reviled with hatred, even as she represents man's own creation and his un-governable lust. Thus Rhys ends Part One by predicting—or explaining —the sequential misery of Antoinette, Marya, Julia, Anna, and finally Sasha, all of whom have been seeking the path to the lost garden.

Part Two

THE SNAKE IN THE GARDEN

Having left the reader at the end of Part One awaiting tensely Sister Marie Augustine's "signal" for "tomorrow morning," Rhys continues with the opening lines of Part Two her weaving of myth. Permeating the details of Rochester's marriage to Antoinette in Spanish Town, mythic overtones lift the reader out of the limits of fixed time and place, giving the first-person narrative of Edward Rochester an impact far beyond the cliché of the "gothic."

Overt facts of his marriage to Antoinette are few and clear. We learn that arriving in Jamaica, Rochester had been bedridden with fever for nearly three weeks. Not completely recovered, he had courted Antoinette for a week, playing the part he "was expected to play," bowing, smiling, kissing her hand, dancing, all of which "meant nothing" to him, anymore than did Antoinette herself. Finally the marriage is solemnized—though the morning before the wedding Antoinette had suddenly refused to marry him, "afraid of what [might] happen." But, playing his role, Rochester had "kissed her fervently, promising her peace, happiness, safety." Forthrightly, Rochester admits that his marriage to Antoinette has been an economic bargain. Her thirty thousand pound dowry has given him a "modest competence," freeing him from the necessity to grovel before his father and his elder brother. From Antoinette's inheritance he has, as yet, made no provision for her, though "that must be seen to." As he writes his father: "I have sold my soul or you have sold it and after all is it such a bad bargain? The girl is thought to be beautiful, she is beautiful. And yet . . ." (p. 70).

After the marriage in Spanish Town, among Antoinette's myriad female relatives—"Cousin Julia, Cousin Ada, Aunt Lina, thin or fat they all looked alike,"—the newlyweds immediately leave Jamaica for a small estate in the Windward Islands which had belonged to Antoinette's now dead mother. Part Two begins with their arrival in the small village called Massacre, the last stage of their "interminable journey." From here they will wend their way high above the blue-green sea through hills wild and green and menacing to Granbois (High Woods) where they will spend their "sweet honeymoon."

This abstraction of plot from the first fifteen pages of Part Two seems simple. It is not. For as she had done in the previous section,

Rhys has so skillfully interwoven fact and myth, present and past, character and symbol, that to strip them down to essence is next to impossible.

For example, the opening lines of Part Two seem a matter-of-fact summary of the events of the past few weeks of Rochester's life. At the same time, they immediately recall the "tomorrow morning" for which Part One had left us waiting. Further, as we read, "So it was all over, the advance and retreat, doubts and hesitations. Everything finished, for better or for worse" (p. 65), the nuances of ritual dance, the overtones of the mythic love chase tinge our consciousness. A few lines later, we are somehow attuned to the implicit significance of the honeymoon—symbolic death and hopefully, concomitant rebirth. This sense of ancient rite and timelessness is further reinforced as, with Rochester, we stand on the alien beach at Massacre where "something must have happened . . . a long time ago," though nobody remembers what or when. Impressions overwhelm us as the heavy rain beats down on the mango trees and the "sad leaning cocoanut palms," while the women sit outside their huts, watching, unsmiling, a "sombre people in a sombre place." Amélie, a little half-caste servant, disturbs us: "a lovely creature but sly, malignant perhaps, like much else in this place," watching Rochester with "delighted malice, intelligent . . . intimate." And Antoinette—her "too large" eyes disconcerting, long, sad, alien—seems as old as time itself. Young Bull, twenty-seven-years old with a "magnificent body and a foolish conceited face," somehow evokes memories of ancient sacrifice lost in the mists of time, where the "bull-man" or king in his various manifestations was sacrificed, to be resurrected in the form of his more youthful successor, thus assuring the continuity of life. Finally, as the sun blazes out, steaming the air, and the party prepares to depart for Granbois, a cock crows loudly—Rochester has listened to "cocks crowing all night"—and we comprehend the double-edged archetype: the cock with its Christian implication of betrayal and its more ancient implication as sun-symbol, the bird of dawn which heralds a new day.

Lest these interpretations seem specious, even themselves Gothic, Rhys carefully sustains her mythic nuances in the details of the journey to Granbois. As the road climbs upward, "on one side the wall of green, on the other a steep drop to the ravine below," Rochester feels menaced:

. . . the hills . . . those hills which would close in on you. . . .

146

> Everything is too much . . . too much blue, too much
> purple, too much green. The flowers too red, the mountains
> too high, the hills too near. And the woman is a stranger.
> Her pleading expression annoys me. I have not bought her,
> she has bought me, or so she thinks. I looked down at the
> coarse mane of the horse . . . *Dear Father*. The thirty thou-
> sand pounds have been paid . . . (p. 70. Emphasis added.)

In these lines the fear of the feminine (the hills, the fecundity,
Antoinette herself) is manifest, the threat of unconscious drives (the
horse) clear. Then, in the midst of the threat, seemingly as a heading to
the letter which Rochester is going to write his father, Rhys introduces
the image of "the Father"—man and god—as opposed to "the
Mother"—woman and goddess. From this point on, the emphasis of
the masculine—and the myths of the masculine—will become dominant, unfolding in an ultimate betrayal and sacrifice frightening in its
implications. This point will be fully developed at the conclusion of the
discussion of *Wide Sargasso Sea*.

For now, in the midst of threat, of his thoughts of "Dear Father,"
the air begins to cool and Rochester hears a bird whistle: " . . . a long
sad note. 'What bird is that?' She was too far ahead and did not hear
me. The bird whistled again. A mountain bird. Shrill and sweet. A very
lonely sound." Intruding into our consciousness come memories of
"the birds of Rhiannon!" Rhiannon, the Great Queen of Welsh mythology whose birds paradoxically awaken the dead and put the living to
sleep (we also remember that the Irish goddess Morrigane appeared in
the form of a bird).

Finally, at the little river which is the boundary to Granbois,
Antoinette comes into her own. For the first time Rochester sees her
smile "simply and naturally." For the first time he feels "simple and
natural" with her. Without hesitation, he drinks the "cold, pure and
sweet" water from the shamrock-shaped leaf from which Antoinette
has fashioned a cup. Significantly and symbolically, here at the river
signifying the flow of life, at the edge of the dark, mysterious forest (an
archetype of the feminine), Rochester drinks the clear cold water of life
(the unconscious) because, ironically, in the spell of the moment,
*Antoinette might have been "any pretty English girl and to please her I
drank.* " (p. 71. Emphasis added.) Clearly the birds of Rhiannon have
not sung to Rochester, either to awaken the dead to life or to lull the
living to sleep! When Antoinette says to him, "After this we go down

147

then up again. Then we are there," he cannot penetrate the truth which she would tell him, that one must die (go down) in order to be born into life. Instead he remembers her words as she rides ahead of him: " 'Oh England, England,' she called back mockingly and the sound went on and on like a warning I did not choose to hear." (p. 71).

Once at Granbois in the "shabby white house," among the shy and dignified but nevertheless savage servants, Rochester is insecure, out-of-place. In his room, carpeted, with a desk and paper and pens—"a refuge," he thinks—Rochester is reassured to find that "the door into her [Antoinette's] room could be bolted, a stout wooden bar pushed across the other."

In these details of the courtship, the trip, and the arrival, Rhys is covertly indicating that marriage for a man is a matter of economics, undertaken in a fit of fever, rooted in a charade of courtship, a charade which masks the lack of "love," concern, or any real sense of one-ness. *These things are the myths of women.* Furthermore, she implies through Rochester that the Victorian male is not at ease in the midst of the sensual, the sensuous, in spite of the myth he concocts to the contrary. Unlike a Mason of an earlier Zeitgeist—for whom there could be a union with Annette and all that she stood for, a union and commitment which would last even through the days of her madness—Rochester is tortured by his own inadequacies and his need to possess and to dominate, as well as by his Christian religion summarized in the words, "Dear Father".

Nevertheless, even the Rochesters succumb to the basic drives within them, and that night at Granbois, in the candlelight, with the fragrance of the flowers and the exhilaration of the champagne, Rochester sees how beautiful Antoinette is. They talk of England and the islands and of Antoinette's dreams of rats—which do not frighten her—and of how one night she had slept in the moonlight:

> 'There was full moon that night—and I watched it for a long time. There were no clouds chasing it, so it seemed to be standing still and it shone on me. Next morning Christophine was angry. She said that it was very bad to sleep in the moonlight when the moon is full.'
> . . . I wanted to say something reassuring but the scent of the river flowers was overpoweringly strong. I felt giddy.
> 'Do you think that too,' she said, 'that I have slept too long in the moonlight?'

Her mouth was set in a fixed smile but her eyes were so withdrawn and lonely that I put my arms around her, rocked her like a child and sang to her. An old song I thought I had forgotten:

> 'Hail to the queen of the silent
>   night,
> Shine bright, shine bright Robin
>   as you die.'

She listened, then sang with me:

> Shine bright, shine bright Robin
>   as you die.'

(pp. 83-4)

With the words of the song which Rochester and Antoinette sing, we return again to the theme of the Great Goddess Anna, "queen of the silent night"—as she was queen of the bright day before being banished into darkness by a usurping god. The last two lines rekindle Gaelic myths of Robin, Robin Hood, Robin-Good-Fellow, Merlin. Whatever the name, always there are the undertones of "devil," "ram," "phallus"—suggesting orgies of sex and sacrifice associated with ancient celebrations of the May Bride. (Graves, pp. 396-7).

Thus, almost at the moment of consummation, out of Rochester's unconscious, rises memory of a song bespeaking man's innate desire, yet dread, to serve the queen—to "die" in the sexual act, to find fulfillment outside the bonds and boundaries of self, even though this means a submersion, a symbolic death and emasculation. So there in Antoinette's dim-lit room, Rochester pours out two glasses of wine and tells her, "drink to our happiness, to our love and the day without end which would be tomorrow. I was young then. A short youth mine was." (p. 84).

The dawn of morning seems indeed to bring rebirth. The mood has changed; the air is fresh and cool. Christophine, imposing, regal in her rustling skirt, her yellow turban elaborately tied as though for a "feast day," brings coffee, urging Rochester:

> 'Taste my bull's blood, master.' The coffee she handed me was delicious and she had long-fingered hands, thin and beautiful I suppose.

149

'Not horse piss like the English madams drink,' she said. 'I know them. Drink drink their yellow horse piss, talk, talk their lying talk.' (p. 85)

And Rochester "drank another cup of bull's blood. (Bull's blood, I thought. The young Bull.)" (p. 86).

Then Rochester's surrender to the spell of Granbois seems complete. The weather is fine, the bathing pool enticing, the fever-weakness gone, the misgivings quieted: "It was a beautiful place—wild untouched, above all untouched, with an alien, disturbing, secret, loveliness. And it kept its secret. I'd find myself thinking, 'What I see is nothing—I want what it *hides*—that is not nothing.' " (p. 87). With these lines, in masculine context, Rhys returns to the theme of all her novels, the mythic quest, the attempt to return to the garden or in the more materialistic symbols of the male, to find the treasure. But Rochester, unknown to himself, has found the treasure, waking in the night to the sound of rain: ". . . a light capricious shower, dancing playful rain, or hushed, muted, growing louder, more persistent, more powerful, an inexorable sound. *But always music, a music I had never heard before.* " (p. 90. Emphasis added.)

This music is a music of night, words spoken in "whispers, in darkness, not by day." By day Antoinette is like "any other girl" smiling at herself in her looking-glass, but "at night how different, even her voice was changed. Always this talk of death. (Is she trying to tell me that is the secret of this place? That there is no other way? She knows. She knows.)" (p. 92). And Antoinette, understanding the secret, that death of "me" is necessary for life of "us," has "forgotten silence and coldness," has forgotten her convent training, has relinquished her innate fear and wariness and yields to the full passion of her now awakened senses:

'Why did you make me want to live: Why did you do that to me?'

'Because I wished it. Isn't that enough?'

'Yes, it is enough. But if one day you didn't wish it. What should I do then? Suppose you took this happiness away when I wasn't looking. . .'

'And lose my own? Who'd be so foolish?'

'I am not used to happiness. . . It makes me afraid.'

'Never be afraid. Or if you are tell no one.'

. . . 'If I could die. Now when I am happy. . . . Say die and I will die. You don't believe me. Then try, try, say die and watch me die.'

'Die then! Die!' I watched her die many times. In my way, not in hers. In sunlight, in shadow, by moon-light, by candlelight. . . . Very soon she was as eager for *what's called loving* as I was—more lost and drowned afterwards.

She said, 'Here I can do as I like', not I, and then I said it too. It seemed right in that lonely place. 'Here I can do as I like.' (pp. 92-3. Emphasis added.)

But in the midst of passion, that which passes for "loving" with man, Rochester reveals his fear, his resentment, his callousness toward the girl who has yielded herself to his lies:

'You are safe,' I'd say. She'd liked that—to be told 'you are safe.' Or I'd touch her face gently and touch tears. Tears—nothing! Words—less than nothing. As for the happiness I gave her, that was worse than nothing. I did not love her. I was thirsty for her, but that is not love. I felt very little tenderness for her, she was a stranger to me, a stranger who did not think or feel as I did. (p. 93)

Hauntingly Rhys summarizes here not only the unforgivable cynicism and disdain of Edward Rochester, but the unforgivable cynicism and disdain of men in general for their fellow female creatures. It is this seemingly innate cruelty which will make it so difficult for a Sasha (*GMM*), the only Rhys heroine to truly reach beyond herself, to make that leap into any kind of trust.

But Antoinette in her love is oblivious to cruelty, childlike, un-realistic in what she believes the world to be:

. . . she was not a stupid child but an obstinate one. She often questioned me about England and listened attentively to my answers, but I was certain that nothing I said made much difference. . . . Some romantic novel, a stray remark never forgotten, a sketch, a picture, a waltz, some note of music, and her ideas were fixed. . . . Reality might discon-cert her, bewilder her, hurt her, but it would not be reality. It would be only a mistake, a misfortune, a wrong path taken, her fixed ideas would never change. (p. 94)

And Rochester, unable to influence her at all, to in essence destroy the innocent child and the romantic framework upon which she and so many women build their dream castles, proves in Rhys's understanding hands what psychologists are now breathing as a new-found truth—that sexual excitement is generated by and rooted in hostility:

> Die then. Sleep. . . . I wonder if she ever guessed how near she came to dying. In her way, not in mine. It was not a safe game to play—in that place. Desire, Hatred, Life, Death came very close in the darkness. . . . (p. 94)

II

In the midst of the mounting passion-hostility which Antoinette and the alien ambiance have generated in him, Rochester receives the fateful letter from Daniel Cosway, the snake, as it were, in the garden. Impugning Antoinette's heritage, her mother, her father, Daniel ("God is Judge") Cosway takes upon himself the duty of "Christian" vengeance, with "God's help." In the brief letter, ostensibly the means whereby Rochester will be brought to mistrust Antoinette, Rhys continues the theme of the father-god, introduced earlier in Rochester's two simple words, "Dear Father." For in Daniel we see the prophet of patriarchal theology, who "honors his father" with vilification, who sees his Creator as a God of Vengeance, and who echoes the Judeo-Christian theme of woman as temptress, seducer, evil personified. However, even as he writes of his father, "the old devil," Daniel unwittingly emphasizes the matriarchal order in his "mother" now dead, and his "godmother" who has cared for him. Later, in a conversation with Rochester, he will say, curiously, "They call me Daniel, but my name is Esau" (p. 122), forcing the reader to remember Jacob's usurpation of rights belonging to the Edomites—supposedly worshippers of an older goddess cult. (Graves, p. 219).

In that same conversation with Rochester, Daniel's diatribe against old Cosway (the "cause" and the "way"!) reflects the myth of endless father-son hatred, hatred which may be rooted in the son's lust for his father's power *or* in his lust for his father's wife—which is, again, the longing for the treasure in the garden. But Daniel, himself, is free from woman, "demons incarnate" in his opinion, and vents his desire-hostility in fulminations against Antoinette.

Oddly enough, the letter he receives from Daniel does not "surprise" Rochester. He has, in fact, been expecting it. For having awakened in Antoinette all the passionate abandon of which she is capable—the consuming passion which is the essence of man's phantasies concerning woman—Rochester is caught in the dichotomy of that masculine myth which is epitomized in the Victorian morality. If woman is "pure," a "lady," she cannot know "evil" (sexual abandonment); if she is sexually abandoned, she must be "devilish" and a whore. Obviously this convenient categorization enables man to handle his ambivalence concerning the "worship" he feels proper for his mother and the "lust" he desires for his mistress. At any rate, it is easy to see that far from creating in Antoinette a heroine who is the victim of her "tropical hot blood reacting to the icy restraint of the North" (Mellown, p. 472), Rhys has, in fact, shown us a tragic fact of the man-woman relationship. That is, in Rochester she presents the tragedy of man who has within his grasp Woman, vital and whole, the essence of all his dreams if he can but recognize and accept it. And in Antoinette she suggests the sadness of woman who, despite her own fears and presentiments, ignoring the "inner voice," gives herself without reservation to the man who awakens her, only to be rejected and driven to madness by that awakener's sense of guilt and consequent hostilities.

Thus for woman, Rhys seems to say, there can be no "wholeness" within the male-construct. She must be saint or whore. And Rhys's heroines clearly choose the life of the body, though it brings pain, rejection, death. However, in her tacit evocation of myth, Rhys awakens in our mind the memory that in almost forgotten time, woman was goddess-holy-prostitute-woman all in one. Man reversed that natural order and the consequence has been, for woman—and himself —death.

Christophine, of course, that "free" woman rooted in an ageless wisdom, knows the inevitable outcome of Antoinette's self-abasement and her lack of emotional restraint. Preparing to leave this house—by implication antithetical if not destructive of all she stands for—Christophine cautions Antoinette: " 'Get up, girl, and dress yourself. Woman must have spunks to live in this wicked world.' " (p. 101). Dressed in a "drab cotton dress," having "taken off her heavy gold ear-rings," Christophine symbolically concedes that the old ways can be no more. She, herself, will retire to the house and garden bequeathed her by Antoinette's mother, where she will make her "lazy son" work for her, enjoying the rest which she has earned.

But before she leaves, Christophine ominously threatens Amélie, that "child" as Rochester calls her but who is, as Antoinette and Christophine know, "older than the devil himself and the devil is not more cruel." As Amélie, frightened at the thought of Christophine's "voodoo," creeps from the room, Christophine contemptuously dismisses her with : " 'She worthless and good for nothing. . . She creep and crawl like centipede.' " (p. 102). And with the creeping-crawling image, Rhys reveals the only true temptress, that woman who sells herself for evil and for gain—the taunting Lilith, alter-ego of Eve the Mother of Life!

III

The mythic significance of Christophine emerges most fully in the short section in Part Two in which the narrative focus shifts from Rochester to Antoinette. Some time must have elapsed—time is never clarified in Part Two—since the arrival of the letter and Christophine's departure from Granbois. Now in desperation over the scornful, silent rejection of her husband and the supposed mockery of the servants, Antoinette has gone into the mountains, past the rocks of "The Dead Ones," to seek aid from Christophine. "Warm and comforting," her clothes smelling of "clean cotton, starched and ironed," a far cry from the image of an obeah woman, Christophine offers the hard wisdom drawn from ancient memories of other times and places and the certain knowledge of men as they were and are:

'You ask me a hard thing, I tell you a hard thing, *pack up and go.* (p. 109).
. . . When man don't love you, more you try, more he hate you, man like that. If you love them, they treat you bad, if you don't love them they after you night and day bothering your soul case out. . . . *All women, all colours, nothing but fools. Three children* I have. One living in this world, each one a different father, but *no husband,* I thank *my God,* I keep *my money.* I don't give it to no worthless man. (p. 110. Emphasis added.)

Here, then, the female wisdom of the ages seems to say, is woman's only reality, her only hope: sharp, critical knowledge; emotional uninvolvement; sexual freedom and choice; her own gods; and above all, her economic independence!

But Antoinette is a romantic, has given herself passionately, is married in the church, does not recognize her own god and has had her economic independence destroyed or denied by English law. Thus Antoinette, a victim of illusions which Rochester has been unable to subvert, can only put her faith in such vagueness as a change of scenery —England where she "will be a different person" and where "different things" will happen to her—and a magic potion which will bring Rochester back to her. Despite all that Christophine can say—and disregarding her own dream-omens concerning the future—Antoinette begs Christophine for the magic necessary to return Rochester to her bed.

One final time Christophine offers the distillation of her accumulated wisdom:

> 'You talk foolishness. Even if I can make him come to your bed, I cannot make him love you. Afterward he hate you. . . . (p. 113)
>
> 'Listen *doudou che*. Plenty people fasten bad words on you and on your mother. I know it. I know who talking and what they say. *The man not a bad man* even if he love money, but he hear so many stories he don't know what to believe. That is why he keep away. . . . (p. 114. Emphasis added.)
>
> '*Have spunks and do battle for yourself*. Speak to your husband calm and cool, tell him about your mother. . .Don't bawl at the man and don't make crazy faces. Don't cry either. Crying no good with him. Speak nice and make him understand.' (p. 116. Emphasis added.)

But Antoinette, in the light of all sanity, succumbs to her unreasoning fear, her essential dependency, and pleads: " 'I will try again if you will do what I ask. Oh Christophine, I am so afraid. . . . I do not know why, but so afraid. All the time. Help me.' " (p. 116). Thus Rhys reveals, without hypocrisy or glossing, that woman is ultimately the victim, not of man but of herself.

And Christophine, betrayed by her own love for womankind, draws "lines and circles on the earth under the tree" and agrees to "do this foolishness," to tell Antoinette how to seduce Rochester.

155

IV

Meanwhile Rochester, caught up in his own disgust of Antoinette and all she stands for in himself, imagining the knowing scorn of his father and brother, remembering the tempting "blank smiling face" of the woman he supposes has tricked him, goes for a walk in the heat of the afternoon, deep into the forest:

> . . . you cannot mistake the forest. It is hostile. The path was overgrown but it was possible to follow it. I went on without looking at the tall trees on either side. Once I stepped over a fallen log swarming with white ants. *How can one discover truth I thought* and that *thought led me nowhere.* No one would tell me the truth. Not my father nor Richard Mason, certainly not the girl I had married. . . . I stubbed my foot on a stone and nearly fell. The stone I had tripped on was not a boulder but part of a paved road. There had been a paved road through this forest. . . . Here were the ruins of a stone house and round the ruins rose trees that had grown to an incredible height. At the back of the ruins a wild orange tree covered with fruit, the leaves a dark green. A beautiful place. And calm—. . . Under the orange tree I noticed little bunches of flowers tied with grass. . . Then I saw a little girl carrying a large basket on her head. I met her eyes and to my astonishment she screamed loudly, threw up her arms and ran. . . . I called after her, but she screamed again and ran faster. She sobbed as she ran, a small frightened sound. Then she disappeared. I must be within a few minutes of the path I thought, but after I had walked for what seemed a long time I found that the undergrowth and creepers caught at my legs and the trees closed over my head. . . .I was lost and afraid among these enemy trees. . . (pp. 104-5. Emphasis added.)

I have quoted this passage at length because it represents the pure poetry of which Rhys is capable, the essence of her mythic power. In a few lines Rhys not only synthesizes her multileveled myth but returns anew to themes of previous novels. That is, in one symbolic framework, Rhys can evoke the superstitions of the natives in their observance of "obeah," in turn conjure visions of ancient rites and culture in which Rochester intrudes like the snake who destroyed the "garden", and in the garden itself, in the ruined stone house surrounded by trees, suggest another level, the mythic quest. In turn, the child who flees from Rochester in terror becomes the "anima" or the guide who must finally lead Rochester to the treasure of himself.

And, compassionately, within this multileveled framework, Rhys explores the dilemma of man—a dilemma as searing as that which faces woman. In asking the supreme question, "How can *man* find truth?" she examines Rochester trapped in his culture and offers little hope. He will not learn truth from his "rational" masculine mentors—"not my father nor Richard Mason"—who teach small boys not to be vulnerable, to hide what they feel, to accept such teachings as "necessary" (p. 103) and, therefore, to be capable of betraying even their sisters. He will not learn it from "eternal" or even more human sources, for "if these mountains challenge [these views], or Baptiste's face, or Antoinette's eyes, they are mistaken, melodramatic, unreal." (p. 103). How, then, Rhys asks, in the midst of the alien forest where "enemy trees" (cf. The Myths of Anna, pp. 78-83) threaten and the undergrowth entraps, is a man to discover that the ruined stone house shadowed by the tree with beautiful fruit is perhaps the castle of the quest where the treasure may be found? For if one's little girl "anima" (the Jungian motif) is not yet mature or strong enough to confront the threatening "animus" but screams and runs away, then one can never find the way out of the forest and into the light—unless a guide appears to lead the way!

So Rhys sends Baptiste, a kind of Hermes-initiator image in his "blue cotton trousers pulled up above his knees and a broad ornamented belt round his slim waist," to conduct Rochester out of the forest and back to the light, back to Antoinette, his other half, the symbol of his sexual, feminine self—the "anima" which must be acknowledged and accepted before he can hope to understand deeper and more ancient mysteries.

But Rochester—like the heroines of the novels—must travel a long dark road of search and suffering and sacrifice before he finds his treasure, truth. For the time being, he can only read about "obeah", about zombies, about the Old Ones who "cry out in the wind that is their voice,. . . rage in the sea that is their anger." (p. 107). Thus Rhys prepares the stage for inevitable disaster.

Returning from a confrontation with Daniel Cosway, where all the disgust and loathing raging within him burns to a white-hot-coal at the mulatto's revelation concerning Antoinette and her coloured cousin,

Sandi, Rochester is coldly calm as Antoinette attempts the reasonable discussion and explanation which Christophine has advised:

> 'Will you listen to me for God's sake?' Antoinette said. She had said this before and I had not answered, now I told her, 'Of course. I'd be the brute you doubtless think me if I did not do that.'
> 'Why do you hate me?' she said.
> 'I do not hate you, I am most distressed about you, I am distraught,' I said. But this was untrue, I was not distraught, I was calm, it was the first time I had felt calm or self-possessed for many a long day.
> . . . 'Then why do you never come near me. . . . what reason have you for treating me like that? Have you any reason?'
> 'Yes,' I said, 'I have a reason,' and added very softly, *'My God.'* (p. 127. Emphasis added.)

God, then, says Rhys, is the real villain in the Garden—or rather God as man has created him. Man's God makes the sexual evil. But Antoinette, in her ancient femaleness, understands man's hypocrisy and the shallowness of his concept of God:

> 'You are always calling on God,' she said. 'Do you believe in God?'
> 'Of course, of course I believe in the power and wisdom of my creator.'
> She raised her eyebrows and the corners of her mouth turned down in a questioning mocking way. For a moment she looked very much like Amélie. Perhaps they are related, I thought. . . .
> 'And you,' I said. 'Do you believe in God?'
> 'It doesn't matter,' she answered calmly, 'what I believe or you believe, because we can do nothing about it, we are like these.' She flicked a dead moth off the table. (p. 128)

Then, in the "unknown and hostile" night, wearing her yellow silk shawl (yellow is the sacred color associated with the "sun"—a word which in Celtic and Germanic languages is *feminine* in gender, not masculine), Antoinette attempts her story of the long ago, in "the most beautiful place in the world" where "all the flowers in the world" were in her garden before "they" destroyed the "sacred place," the place "sacred to the sun!" (pp. 132-3). And in her story of Coulibri and the fearful night and the madness and her own consequent illness, Antoinette synthesizes for us once again the ancient memory of a time when the Sun-goddess reigned. A time destroyed, and lost forever, perverted even in the telling, but beautiful and haunting in the memory —until one remembers the poor mad goddess-woman, broken, sullied, taunted by those who do not love or understand!

Rochester, however, does not yet understand the holocaust which can end a world, and Antoinette realizes that her tragic story has left her husband unmoved:

> After a long time I heard her say as if she were talking to herself, 'I have said all I want to say. I have tried to make you understand. But nothing has changed.' She laughed.
> 'Don't laugh like that, Bertha.'
> 'My name is not Bertha; why do you call me Bertha?'
> 'Because it is a name I'm particularly fond of. I think of you as Bertha.' (p. 135)

With the reference to "Bertha," Rhys echoes again her myth motif concerning magic function of names. Symbolically Rochester, in re-naming Antoinette, strips her of her individual essence, domesticating and gaining control by denying her alien heritage. More importantly however, he unconsciously reveals his fear of all she represents to him. For as old as man's concept and awe of god-ness is his consequent belief that the real names of powerful and dangerous forces should never be uttered. Ironically, the name he chooses, solid, matronly "Bertha," derives from the Old German meaning "bright, shining one"—that is the Sun! As she has done repeatedly, Rhys suggests again the pre-eminence of the sun-goddess and the light-life-giving forces as feminine.

Unfortunately, as she herself has tried to tell Rochester, Antoinette had received a wound on that horrifying night at Coulibri, a wound which had spoiled her "for her wedding day and all the other days and nights." In other words, the goddess has suffered the mythic wound (usually associated in Western myth with the King or the Hero) which makes her unfit to rule. Hence she cannot be a life-force but is a harbinger of death. Thus the night of lust that follows—brought about, Rochester believes, by the presumably drugged wine Antoinette has given him—brings enveloping darkness for both Antoinette and Rochester.

<h1 style="text-align:center">V</h1>

Awaking in the dark from his dream of being "buried alive," of "suffocation"—Rhys suggests in this that copulation for the male means absorption, death—Rochester was

> . . . deathly cold and sick and in pain. I got out of bed without looking at her, staggered into my dressing-gown and saw myself in the glass. I turned away at once. I could not vomit. I only retched painfully. . . . After . . . some time I was able to go over to the window and vomit. It seemed like hours before this stopped. . . . (p. 138)

But in the cold light of day Antoinette is sleeping peacefully:

> . . . very beautiful, the thin wrist, the sweet smell of the fore-arm, the rounded elbow, the curve of her shoulder. . . As I watched, hating, her face grew smooth and very young again, she even seemed to smile. A trick of the light perhaps. (p. 139)

Loathing the image he has seen in the glass, repelled by the wife, Bertha, who has participated in the eroticism of the night, Rochester runs from the house, unable to remember where he ran or how he "fell or wept or lay exhausted." Returning home in the cool of the evening, he waits in his room, on his bed for Amélie who, he knows, will come:

> She came soundlessly on bare feet.
> . . . Her arm behind my head was warm but the outside when I touched it was cool, almost cold. I looked into her lovely meaningless face, . . . I pulled her down beside me and we were both laughing. That is what I remember most . . . She was so gay, so natural and something of this gaiety she must have given to me for I had not one moment of remorse. Nor was I anxious to know what was happening behind the thin partition which divided us from my wife's bedroom. (p. 140)

This, then, Rhys says, is Rochester's—and by extension the Victorian-hobbled man's—solution to the demons within his own bosom. Hating woman—his need for Antoinette and his loathing rejection of the forces she can arouse in him (i.e. the symbolic need to return to the womb)—he nevertheless seeks out woman. The woman he can sexually dominate without "remorse," without "complication"—the prostitute, the Lilith who will lie with him in laughter, take his "gift" of money, and depart as does Amélie. So Rhys has brought us full circle, having shown us the genesis of all the Heidlers (*Quartet*), the Mackenzies (*ALMM*), the Walter Jeffries (*Voyage*), who will embrace the myth of the "lady" and the "prostitute."

With this episode of Rochester and Amélie, Rhys also adds dimension to the little half-caste servant, making her at once the "true temptress" suggested previously and the "shadow self" of Rochester. Thus she becomes the evil, carnal nature (which to Rochester and men of his ilk is feminine, not masculine), representative of all those unmentionable forces that arise only in the black of night. By further extension, Amélie, whose resemblance to Antoinette Rochester has previously noted (p. 128), could become—were Rochester able to forget his fear and aversion of the sexual—a projection of the anima, the laughing, gay partner through whom he could become whole.

But not for Rochester this kind of consummation. Following his act of betrayal, the destruction of Granbois comes quickly. Antoinette, having listened on the other side of the wall, flees to Christophine in frenzy, although she tells Christophine nothing of what has happened. On the night of her return many days later, Antoinette seems a maddened demon—her eyes inflamed and staring, her face flushed, swollen, her feet bare. As Rochester attempts to restrain her from drinking, like some ancient savage goddess shrieking malediction, Antoinette

> . . . smashed another bottle against the wall and stood with the broken glass in her hand and murder in her eyes. . . .
>
> Then she cursed me comprehensively, my eyes, my mouth, every member of my body, and it was like a dream in the large unfurnished room with the candles flickering and this red-eyed wild-haired stranger who was my wife shouting obscenities at me. It was at this nightmare moment that I heard Christophine's calm voice. (p. 149)

With Christophine sanity prevails. Shortly, with Antoinette soothed and sleeping, she attempts to tell Rochester the events of the past days, how she has tried to heal the mental and emotional wounds of the poor wild creature she had found standing at her door. Wise in the ways of men and women caught in the spell of passion, remembering the ancient priestesses and priests who drugged and whipped themselves to ecstacies in the service of their goddesses, Christophine knows that the excesses of the night—those acts which loom so monstrous in Rochester's mind—are natural and to be expected. She laughs "a hearty merry laugh" as she tells this white man that "all that is a little thing—it's nothing." And then she tells her story of the husband who chopped off his wife's nose in the heat of passion:

> '. . . Rupert that man's name was. Plenty Ruperts here you notice? One is Prince Rupert, and one who makes songs is Rupert the Rine. . . . It's a pretty name eh—Rupert—but where they get it from? I think it's from old time they get it. . . .' (pp. 152-3)

And with the reference to Rupert-Robert-Robin, Rhys returns to the myths of the May Wedding when the male was sacrified, to be reborn, by implication, to love and song.

In the concluding dialogue between Christophine and Rochester, myth-reality, past-present, love-hate, truth-deception merge, coalesce, fade, as Christophine fights to save the girl she loves from her inevitable doom:

> '. . . Ah there is no God.'
> 'Only your spirits,' I reminded her.
> 'Only my spirits,' she said steadily. 'In your Bible it say God is a spirit—it don't say no other. Not at all. It grieve me to see what happen to her mother, and I can't see it happen again. You call her a doll? She don't satisfy you? Try her once more, I think she satisfy you now. If you forsake her they will tear her in pieces—like they did her mother.'
> 'I will not forsake her,' I said wearily. 'I will do all I can for her.'
> 'You will love her like you did before?'
> . . . I said nothing.
> *It's she won't be satisfy.* She is Creole girl, and *she have the sun in her.*' (pp. 158-9. Emphasis added.)

With these words, Rhys concludes her myth of the sun-goddess and attests a truth that man has twisted, perverted, rejected, but never escaped. It is *woman* whose sexuality "won't be satisfy!" It is *woman* who is regenerated by the act called love. It is man who is conquered, depleted, imprisoned. Hence in *Wide Sargasso Sea,* Rhys clarifies a theme only glimpsed in previous novels: that is, man's reversal of the facts of sexuality—and the ambivalencies it causes, in life and in myth. In this reversal, an Antoinette, by nature a creature of passion, must paradoxically be aroused by her husband before becoming a Circe who turns him into a beast! A youthful Marya must be "taught everything" by her husband, a man "natural as an animal" who makes her "come alive" (*Quartet,* p. 60). And, once "alive," then she is doomed by the masculine structure to become a "prostitute" who cannot resist a man. An Anna, a prostitute because she "likes it," will nevertheless have her sexual performance deprecated by the very man who uses and keeps her (*Voyage,* pp. 50-1). A Sasha must expect to lose her husband, though she is penniless and pregnant, because as he tells her, "you don't know how to make love," (*Good Morning, Midnight*); then she will prostitute herself for that same husband.

Thus man miraculously turns woman—to him the original temptress and tool of Satan and at the same time the Mother of All Life —into the frigid castrating bitch who can only be subdued when awakened by his sexual prowess. Similarly, man dethrones the powerful Mother-Goddess, once worshippped in sexual abandonment under the auspices of sacred prostitutes, and changes her into the Virgin Mary, wife without husband, worshipped by celibate hermaphrodites. The pursuer becomes the pursued becomes the pursuer in one unending circle. Truly, says Rhys, the world created by man boggles the mind! And Christophine, "a mask on her face and her eyes . . . undaunted," can only "walk away without looking back," leaving Antoinette to the fate foretold by her frightening dream.

VI

The fate decreed for Antoinette by Rochester, out of wounded pride, arrogance, and his love-hate ambivalencies, becomes, in fact, the reality created for Victorian woman in general. And nowhere is the callous, dehumanizing treatment more tersely described than by Rhys in the few lines in which Rochester sits drinking rum, thinking of the gossip which will follow wherever he goes, and plotting his revenge:

. . . I drank some more rum and drinking, I drew a house surrounded by trees. A large house. I divided the third floor into rooms and in one room I drew a standing woman—a child's scribble, a dot for a head, a larger one for the body, a triangle for a skirt, slanting lines for arms and feet. But it was an English house.

English trees. I wondered if I should ever see England again. (p. 164)

This is the house, the floor, the room in which poor "Marionette, Antoinette, Marionetta, Antoinetta" will lead her mindless existence, her body a match-stick puppet. And this is the world-apart-from-life which Victorian men will permit the women they cannot do without. A bed in a room in a house where their bodies may function, circumscribed and hobbled, but where their poor mad minds must not cry out and where they must listen to the sighing of the English trees, the truths permitted by that patriarchal society.

The last pages of Part Two are a crescendo of pain, an agony of remembrance as Rochester struggles with the "wild blast" of the gods of the universe and the devils of his own soul before he leaves Granbois. For the "wild blast" that passes "not caring for the abject trees," is not more pitiless than the vindictiveness of man as Rochester rages in chilling madness: " . . . I could not touch her. Excepting as the hurricane will touch that tree—and break it. . . . Vain, silly creature. Made for loving? Yes, but she'll have no lover, for I don't want her and she'll see no other." (p. 166). Yet clear beneath the tympanny of Rochester's hate run the sad flute notes of man's helplessness, of his longing for woman, the pure life-vessel which will assuage his grief:

. . . I'll watch for one tear, one human tear. . . . I'll listen. . . . If she . . . weeps, I'll take her in my arms, my lunatic. She's mad but *mine, mine*. What will I care for gods or devils or for Fate itself. If she smiles or weeps or both. *For me*.

Antoinette—I can be gentle too. Hide your face. Hide yourself but in my arms. You'll soon see how gentle. My lunatic. My mad girl. (pp. 166-7)

Rochester is given one irrevocable chance to understand and seize the secret that all the forces of nature and of his unconscious have sought to reveal. At the moment of departure from the "shabby white house" and the blackness of the "snake-like forest," Baptiste appears —as he had that day when Rochester had lost himself in the forest— and this time he is clearly a Hermes-initiator image:

> Baptiste looked very different. Not a trace of the polite domestic. He wore a very wide-brimmed straw hat, like the fisherman's hats, but the crown flat, not high and pointed. His wide leather belt was polished, so was the handle of his sheathed cutlass, and his blue cotton shirt and trousers were spotless. The hat, I knew, was waterproof. He was ready for the rain and it was certainly on its way. (p. 168)

Rochester senses Baptiste's dislike and contempt:

> . . . The same contempt as that devil's when she said, 'Taste my bull's blood.' Meaning that will make you a man. Perhaps. Much I cared for what they thought of me! As for her, I'd forgotten her for the moment. So I shall never understand why, suddenly, bewilderingly, I was certain that everything I had imagined to be truth was false. False. *Only that magic and the dream are true—all the rest's a lie. Let it go. Here is the secret. Here.* (p. 168. Emphasis added.)

Suddenly Rochester sees the truth and understands the secret for which man is always searching. Here is the treasure, the legendary golden treasure:

> *Blot out the moon,*
> *Pull down the stars.*
> *Love in the dark, for we're for the dark*
>   *So Soon, so soon.* (p. 170)

Like Sasha of *Good Morning, Midnight,* opening her arms to the dreadful, sad, pitiable *commis* who was her reality, Rochester knows what he must do: ". . . let's make the most and best and worst of what we have. Give not one-third but everything. All—all—all. Keep nothing back. . . ." (p. 170). This is the secret of love, the symbolic death of self through which the larger SELF emerges—male and female as one.

Understanding finally what he has almost lost, what Antoinette and all she stands for mean for him, Rochester cries out, " 'I have made a terrible mistake. Forgive me.' " But it is too late! The tragedy must be played out. Imploring her forgiveness, he sees the "hatred in her eyes" and his own hate springs up to meet it:

> . . . If I was bound for hell let it be hell. No more false heavens. No more damned magic. You hate me and I hate you. We'll see who hates best. But first, first I will destroy your hatred. Now. My hate is colder, stronger, and you'll have no hate to warm yourself. You will have nothing.
>
> I did it too. I saw the hate go out of her eyes. I forced it out. And with the hate her beauty. She was only a ghost. A ghost in the grey daylight. Nothing left but hopelessness. *Say die and I will die. Say die and watch me die.* (p. 171)

And at that moment of supreme hatred, the "nameless boy," the youthful image of the joyous SELF Rochester might have realized "leaned his head against the clove tree and sobbed. Loud heartbreaking sobs." (p. 171).

So Rochester leaves the place of mountains and of hills and of magic whose

> . . . secret I would never know. I hated its indifference and the cruelty which was part of its loveliness. And above all I hated her. For she belonged to the magic and the loveliness. She had left me thirsty and all my life would be thirst and longing for what I had lost before I found it. (p. 173)

But as he rides away:

> That stupid boy followed us, the basket balanced on his head. He used the back of his hand to wipe away his tears. Who would have thought that any boy would cry like that. For nothing. Nothing. . . . (p. 174)

Part Three

FAR FROM THE ISLAND HOME

After the intensity of Rochester's inner struggle and his brush with truth, Part Three seems anticlimactic, almost without purpose except to overtly link this novel with *Jane Eyre*. One's initial response is to wonder why Rhys felt it necessary to do this, since the details of her own plot and the complexity of her characterization make *Wide Sargasso Sea* a masterpiece in its own right. But as one finishes the brief, flat narration of Grace Poole which bridges the two works, it is clear that Grace functions as far more than a bridge[60]—that she, and the episode at Thornfield, are necessary to conclude the myth Rhys has been developing throughout her entire work.

For in the character of Grace Poole, brief as it is, Rhys shows us a representative victim and servant of that patriarchal world which now controls Antoinette's existence. Employed to care for the mad creature whom Rochester has brought home, Grace's services and silence have been purchased with money and threat—the tools of the Victorian ethic. As Mrs. Eff has told Grace:

> " . . . I am not prepared to treble your money, Grace, but I
> am prepared to double it. But there must be no more gossip.
> If there is I will dismiss you at once. I do not think it will be
> impossible to fill your place. I'm sure you understand." Yes,
> I understand, I said. (p. 178)

Here is the fear that Rhys has repeatedly shown haunts women who lack economic independence in a world of men: "Where do I go? What do I do?" Grace Poole has learned carefully her lessons of life in that man's world. As she tells Leah (the "weary"),

> ' . . . I don't contradict, I know better than to say a word.
> After all the house is big and safe, a shelter from the world
> outside which, say what you like, can be a black and cruel
> world to a woman. . . . The thick walls, keeping away all the
> things that you have fought till you can't fight no more. Yes,
> maybe that's why we all stay.' (p. 178)

Though she has given up the fight herself, Grace has pity and respect for the thin, shivering "girl who lives in her own darkness. I'll say one thing for her, she hasn't lost her spirit. She's still fierce. I don't turn my back on her when her eyes have that look. I know it." (p. 178).

As important to Rhys's myth as Grace Poole, is the physical setting of Thornfield, "this cardboard world where everything is coloured brown or dark red or yellow that has no light . . ." (p. 181), so unlike the world of "fire and sunset" and "flamboyant flowers" which Antoinette remembers. This "Thornfield" becomes an appropriate image for the archetype of the princess imprisoned within castle walls surrounded by impenetrable barriers. But for Antoinette there will be no Hero to return her to life, no rescue from the wicked lord of the castle. Alone, unmolested, she is to live out her days according to the will of Rochester, aided and abetted as he is by a law which does not permit even Antoinette's brother to "interfere legally" between a husband and his wife.

II

After Grace's brief introduction to Thornfield, the remainder of the novel is seen from the perspective of Antoinette—now Bertha—as her memories of past and present merge with the dreams which have haunted her through the years. Much of the time she is lucid. She watches Grace make the fires, count her money, drink her gin. She knows the details of her room with its high window through which she cannot see. One day in the tapestry on the wall she recognizes her mother, dressed in an evening gown but with bare feet. She knows that since "he" changed her name, "Antoinette" has drifted "out of the window with her scents, her pretty clothes and her looking-glass." (p. 180). She remembers the trip to England when "he" found her with the steward begging for help and then they gave her something to sleep and "we lost our way to England" because these passages in this cardboard house through which she roams when Grace is drunk and sleeping cannot be the England of her hope.

But Antoinette—as no one else can—knows how long she has been there:

Nights and days and days and nights, hundreds of them slipping through my fingers. But that does not matter. Time has no meaning. But something you can touch and hold like my red dress, that has a meaning.

> . . . I was wearing a dress of that colour when Sandi
> came to see me for the last time . . . . Sandi often came to see
> me when that man was away . . . Now there was no time left
> so we kissed each other in that stupid room . . . We had often
> kissed before but not like that. That was the life and death
> kiss and you only know a long time afterwards what it is, the
> life and death kiss. The white ship whistles three times, once
> gaily, once calling, once to say good-bye. (pp. 185-6)

Now in the memories of a poor mad woman—who sees so clearly—we
learn the truth of Antoinette—and of Anna of *Voyage in the Dark*. They
had both known love beyond restraint of moral codes—not as prostitutes for get or gain but as those who love without distinction of good or
evil. And that love, the giving of self, symbolizes their psychic wholeness. But circumstances tearing the lovers physically apart—or symbolically splitting the psyche—they must forever seek the mythic love, as
does Anna, or end in madness, as does Antoinette.

But Antoinette's madness is the madness of purpose. Lying in her
bed in the cold light of the English morning, she watches as the fire
crackles and spits, "the coal smoulders and glowers. In the end flames
shoot up and they are beautiful." (p. 179). All memories of past and
present coalesce in fire: her name written in "fire red" (p. 54) in the
convent in Spanish Town so many years before; the heat of the "hot
classroom, the pitchpine desks, the heat of the bench" (p. 53); the red
of her dress which spreads like fire across the floor. All tell her what
she must do. For she has known "that house where I will be cold and
not belonging, the bed I shall lie in has red curtains and I have slept
there many times before, long ago. How long ago? In that bed I will
dream the end of my dream." (p. 112).

And as time has merged and flowed throughout Antoinette's life—
and through all the novels Rhys has written—we know that the bed with
the red curtains in a cold alien house with a man whose "face [is] black
with hatred" as "he smiles slyly" (p. 60) is the fate reserved for all
those women trapped in a nightmare where "the seconds pass and each
one is a thousand years." That nightmare of coldness and hate can only
end in the conflagration of Antoinette's dream—a holocaust that will
ignite and destroy the cold world of Thornfield, as in another time,
another place, Coulibri was destroyed.

Inexorable as the hand of fate, calling on "Christophine," as the
only name for woman proffering hope, Antoinette will soon make her

way along the cold dark passages of night to light the fire which will usher in the light of a new day. Thus Antoinette will make her sacrifice to life and warmth and sun and SELF, leaping, in her phantasy, into the "pool at Coulibri" where Tia, her other half, still laughs and beckons.

Chapter 6

JANE EYRE [61]

One task remains in our discussion of *Wide Sargasso Sea:* to examine Rhys's accomplishment in superimposing her masterpiece upon that of *Jane Eyre.* But before proceeding to that end, let me acknowledge that I am aware that for some this analysis may be particularly troubling. Some will question the mythic emphasis, asking whether this can be valid *literary* criticism. Others will again evoke the ghost of authorial intent, suggesting that the interpretation advanced cannot be imputed to Rhys but is my personal critical imposition and, as such, cannot validly serve to illuminate either *Wide Sargasso Sea* or *Jane Eyre.* To this anticipated chorus, my only response *must* be that the analysis of *Wide Sargasso Sea* and *Jane Eyre* as an entity is for me inevitable — as Rhys implied that the writing of Antoinette's vindication was, for her, inevitable.

For whether Rhys was conscious of what she wrought through her use of the framework of *Jane Eyre* is not really, to me, of primary importance. The fact is, that in so clearly linking her novel with that of Bronte, she has turned our attention anew to a work gone stale, a work which has currently come to be dismissed by some as a kind of female tract on the rewards awaiting virtuous women. In the light of *Wide Sargasso Sea,* however, such reading is forever annulled and Bronte emerges clearly as a nineteenth-century predecessor of Jean Rhys, ordering and creating from the pressures of her unconscious an artistic world through which she could survive.

Thus it is, for me, that Rhys through her mythic progression has created not five but six novels — *Jane Eyre* emerging as the last — as well as the first. For me, *Jane Eyre* and *Wide Sargasso Sea* have become inextricable, as Jane Eyre, Antoinette Mason, Marya Zelli,

171

Julia Martin, Anna Morgan, Sasha Jensen, Charlotte Bronte, Jean Rhys and, in a sense, Helen Nebeker have become inextricable on the immutable sea of time. Rhys personally expressed this sense of the merging of time and person when she said of Mrs. Rochester (Antoinette-Bertha): ''. . . that woman is like me.''

So this section of *Woman in Passage* is written for those who have come thus far with Rhys and me to find that the experiences of life are at once unique and universalized, reflecting in various but always similar hues the mythology of the race. Others need not read!

II

Although a detailed exegesis of *Jane Eyre* is not the focus here, perhaps some overview of plot and character will aid those who have not recently read Bronte's novel to understand how Rhys, consciously or not, permitted that famous study to complete her personal myth.

Briefly, *Jane Eyre* purports to be the autobiography of a young woman of intelligence and passion, who despite her traumatic experiences as an unloved orphan overcomes adversity to become the happy, rewarded wife of the man she loves and whose child she bears. Told in retrospect from that standpoint of felicity, the cast of characters in Jane's involved plot includes Mrs. Reed, unloving aunt, who having tyrannized the child, Jane, for some ten years, sends her to Lowood School. Here, suffering humiliations and privations of every kind, Jane becomes an industrious student, blossoming under the benign care of Maria Temple, the head mistress, and befriending gentle, uncomplaining Helen Burns who dies of malnutrition and a lung condition.

Graduating at length from Lowood, Jane remains there as a teacher for a short time before leaving to take up a position as governess at Thornfield Hall. Here, in the forbidding setting, Jane ultimately falls in love with her employer, the forty-ish Edward Rochester, and finally, despite plaguing reservations, succumbs to his offer of marriage. Almost on the eve of her wedding, Jane awakens one night to discover a horrifying female apparition ripping to shreds the wedding veil, a gift to Jane from Rochester. Subsequently, Rochester attempts to convince Jane that she has had a nightmare, though the evidence of the veil is irrefutable.

Nevertheless, despite this and other warnings, Jane continues in her marriage plans. Then, at the church, in the presence of assembled guests, a stranger reveals the fact of Rochester's perfidy—his marriage fifteen years earlier to Bertha Mason, in Spanish Town, Jamaica. This woman, still living, is the demented figure of Jane's supposed nightmare, housed these many years in the guarded third story chambers at Thornfield.

Sanguine about his unforgivable deception, Rochester is determined to possess Jane in a mockery of wedlock or in open sin in the name of his overwhelming desire. Fearing her own nature, determined to be true to herself, Jane flees Thornfield and arrives, destitute and starving, at Moor House, the home of the Reverend St. John Rivers and his sisters, Mary and Diana. Assuming the name of Jane Elliott, Jane is taken in and nursed back to health by the gentle sisters and their old servant, Hannah. Eventually she becomes mistress in a small girls' school where she is happy until St. John, preparing to go to India as a missionary, proposes that she marry him, not out of love but as a companion and a servant to his God. On the verge of yielding to his importuning, Jane hears Rochester calling her name. Hastening back to Thornfield, she arrives to find the Hall a blackened ruin and Rochester, blind and maimed, living at Ferndean, a desolate farm. Content to love and serve him, mutilated though he is, Jane marries Rochester, becomes his eyes and his right hand and, two years later, is rewarded when Rochester's sight returns sufficiently for him to see his firstborn son laid in his arms.

Thus this "and they lived happily ever after" novel appears to be a sermon in how woman should live her live—antithesis, as some critics have pointed out, to the emotion-ridden lives of Rhys's prostitute protagonists, and particularly to the passion-possessed Antoinette of *Wide Sargasso Sea*. Such comparison is simplistic. For Rhys evokes the details of Jane's experience to illustrate ramifications of every theme which has been the focus of her own *oeuvre*. Let us, then, briefly (a full comparison demands another book!) see what Rhys has actually done.

Zeitgeist

The most obvious implication of *Jane Eyre* for Rhys's personal myth lies in the fact that the world presented by Charlotte Bronte is the image of the twentieth-century world Rhys has previously developed so carefully. Jane's nineteenth-century reality reflects, almost unchanged, the same social, moral and economic structure which not only

173

ultimately destroys Rhys's Antoinette, but which her Marya, Anna, and Julia will never escape. The world of Bronte's orphan Jane Eyre, of mistreated and nobly suffering Helen Burns, of Maria Temple that aloof and admired head mistress, of servant Grace Poole, is the same world which Rhys's Norah inherits and which her Marya and Julia and Sasha reject to their social and moral denigration. Bronte's sadistic young John Reed, who tortures and mocks his innocent cousin, Jane, evolves into Rhys's Heidler and Mackenzie; Rochester becomes the W. Neal James and the Walter Jeffries of a later generation.

Rochester

Just as the Zeitgeist of one novel reinforces that of another, so the characterization of a fifteen-year-younger Rochester caught in the "obeah" world of Granbois—where the fires of passion are subdued by the icy mind and vengeful god of the white man's world—adds dimension to Rochester of Thornfield. Thus the young, tormented lover of *Wide Sargasso Sea*, who almost grasps the secret of life is now Lord Edward Fairfax Rochester, old enough to be Jane's father, but still standing on the "crater crust" of his own inner fires. Because of Rhys's Rochester, we are able to understand the hypocrisy of Bronte's Rochester with a clarity probably denied Bronte herself, caught as she was in the pressures of her time and of her personal life. Thus, to us, Rochester stands revealed as a completely egocentric man who will go to any lengths to satisfy his own desires. We see him, having rejected and imprisoned the passionate Antoinette of Rhys's work, seeking assuagement of his lust with mistresses, although in self-pity he tells Jane that this was a "groveling fashion of existence." Despite his confession of debasement, Rochester will attempt to marry Jane illegally, making her in essence another of his mistresses. As certainly as he has sacrificed Antoinette to his personal vanity and sense of shame, we see that he will mercilessly sacrifice Jane in the name of love. He will do this oblivious to the shame that could result for Jane—her self-loathing, the contempt of his noble peers, and ultimately, given his reaction to the passion of Antoinette, his own rejection and disdain.

Obviously, because of Rhys's Rochester, we see a man who differs sharply from the one of whom Bronte's Jane had "made an idol," the man who had become for her the "whole world; and more than the world; almost her hope of heaven." (Chap. XXIV). We see Rochester as

174

a man who has learned no lessons from life, gained no understanding of himself or others. Narcissistically seeking his own image, he desires Jane because she is his "equal." He will hope to cleanse and rejuvenate himself in her virginity, making her his "angel and comforter." Nevertheless, forgetting his revulsion of the passion he had engendered in Antoinette, he will attempt to stir the flames of desire within Jane, seeking to render her "as madly in love" with him as he with her, knowing that "jealousy would be the best ally." (XXIV).

Jealous, possessive, dominated by his desire, Rochester means to claim Jane's "thoughts, conversation, and company— for life," making her another "marionetta," to dress, to transform into a creature whom he will "make the world acknowledge" as a beauty. Under the guise of love, he intends to imprison Jane as completely as he has the pitiable creature locked in his attic room. He tells her: " 'it is your time now, little tyrant, but it will be mine presently; and when once I have fairly seized you, to have and to hold, I'll just—figuratively speaking—attach you to a chain like this' (touching his watch-guard) . . ." (XXIV), an image as sinister in implication as the house and room Rhys's Rochester had drawn for Antoinette.

Yet in spite of all that he has done and still intends to do, Rochester feels that he is an innocent victim of fate: "I am not a villain . . . I am a trite commonplace sinner," he confesses to Jane. And feeling absolutely justified in his aims and motives—having passed a "law . . . that both are right," (XIV) he subverts his righteous, arrogant, masculine god to sanction his anticipated betrayal of Jane:

> '. . . It will atone—it will atone. Have I not found her friendless, and cold, and comfortless? Will I not guard, cherish, and solace her? Is there not love in my heart, and constancy in my resolves? It will expiate at God's tribunal. I know my Maker sanctions what I do. For the world's judgment—I wash my hands thereof. For man's opinion—I defy it.' (XXIII)

This, then, becomes not only Rochester's theme of justification, but the theme of the men of Rhys's novels. "Decent," god-fearing men, they salve their consciences by providing economically for the women they will use in the name of love.

In final condemnation of the composite Rhys-Bronte Rochester, even as he stands stripped as an intended bigamist and reveals to Jane the "facts" of his marriage to the woman who had "abused," "sullied," "outraged," "blighted" his life, he shows no sympathy nor compunction, only willful intent to accomplish his desires in the face of man and church:

> ' . . . you shall yet be my wife; I am not married. You shall be
> Mrs. Rochester—both virtually and nominally. . . . You shall
> go to a place I have in the south of France: a white-washed
> villa. . . . *There you shall live a happy, and guarded, and
> most innocent life.*' (XXVII. Emphasis added.)

Thus despite his own flight from a similar white house in another alien place, Rochester will take the woman he desires as paramour to an exotic place where he will literally create a prison—a happy, guarded, innocent existence—for the woman he betrays! In the light of this implicit villainy, the fall of Rochester's house, the loss of his vision, and the amputation of his hand seem tragic justice.

III

This triumph of justice—the punishment of Rochester—brought about by Bertha's burning of Thornfield underscores other aspects of Rhys's myth. We have already noted how the burning of Thornfield (cf. 168-9) was the inevitable consummation of Antoinette's life and love, the only possible resolution to her search for her alienated SELF. Additionally, Rhys allows the fire at Thornfield to evoke memory of the conflagration at Coulibri. In that fire Antoinette had seen her beautiful but decadent world destroyed. With the burning of his ancestral manor, Rochester, too, sees a world end—a world as steeped in decay as was the island home of Antoinette. Thus in *Jane Eyre*, the theme of Rhys concerning the cyclic nature of life, one order rising out of the ashes of another, is reaffirmed.

Simultaneously, in the blinding and mutilation which befall Rochester during the fire at Thornfield, Rhys's theme of the inevitability of Fate is reiterated and deepened. For in *Wide Sargasso Sea*, Rochester pronounces his own fate in that last confrontation with Christophine:

'And do you think that I wanted all this? I would give my

eyes never have to have seen this abominable place.'

She laughed. 'And that's the first damn word of truth you speak. You choose what you give, eh? Then you choose. You meddle in something and perhaps you don't know what it is.' She began to mutter to herself. Not in patois. I knew the sound of patois now. (*WSS*, pp. 161-2)

In this dialogue burned into the memory of Rochester, Rhys indicates, in the person and words of Christophine, a power beyond the comprehension of white man, uttered in a language older than man can remember. In the same way, in *Jane Eyre,* Jane's inner voice presages the penalty which must be paid for even the thought of adultery, spoken in what might well be called the language of man's genetic code: " '. . . you shall, yourself, pluck out your right eye! yourself cut off your right hand: your heart shall be the victim. . . .' " (*JE*, XXVII). Thus Rhys introduces an ancient theme of retribution, rooted in law beyond the making of man. Rochester, arrogant, compassionless in his youth, having failed to learn from experience in maturity, is fated to see in blindness—like Samson of old (XXXVII)—the ruins of his life, the result not of betrayal by woman (the perverted interpretation of the Samson-Delila myth in man's theology) but the punishment for his own "whoring" after false gods, for his hubris, for his ultimate betrayal of SELF.

Almost as an afterthought, Rhys seems to milk one final and intriguing implication from the punishment meted Rochester—the amputation of his left hand. In Part Two of *Wide Sargasso Sea,* in the scene between Rochester and Antoinette following her return from Christophine, Rochester, seeing Antoinette in the white dress he had admired but which, symbolically, has "slipped untidily over one shoulder" watches her "holding her *left wrist* with her *right hand,* an annoying habit." (p. 127). Since the left side always signifies the site of the feminine, unconscious drives, Rhys implies that Antoinette, in her attempt to please Rochester and "be reasonable," is trying desperately to hold her emotions in check. Subsequently, in Antoinette's dream sequence in Part Three just before she sets fire to the curtains, she becomes momentarily frightened and holds her *right wrist* with her *left hand* (p. 188), symbolizing her unconscious attempt not to let the emotions within her be stilled by the rational ego, the conscious intelligence which tells her she should flee the place. In a corresponding but ambivalent detail in Bronte's novel, Rochester not only is blinded but loses his *left hand* as well—symbolizing the maiming of his psyco-

177

sexual self [62] or of his feminine, intuitive powers. Because of that detail, we realize that Jane serves not only as Rochester's "eyes" in the literal sense but as his "eyes" or guide into those deeper things of the spirit generally associated with feminine perception: ". . . Literally, I was (what he often called me) the apple of his eye. He saw nature—He saw brooks through me; . . . field, tree, town, river, cloud, sunbeam . . . impressing by sound on his ear what light could no longer stamp on his eye." (XXXVIII).

Curiously, however, though it is the *left hand* which is gone, Jane makes clear that, as she had been Rochester's *eyes* for the first two years of their union, she is *"still his right hand."* Thus, what might have been glossed over as a defect of detail [63] or even a cliché on Bronte's part, becomes through the double emphasis of Rhys, an indication of awesome retribution. For if Jane controls both his unconscious female side (his eyes and the left hand symbols) *and* his conscious intellectual side (implicit in the right hand symbolism) then *Rochester truly has no psychic SELF*. Here at Ferndean (literally "the valley of the fern" and clearly feminine in imagery), he is as surely the prisoner of Jane's world as she would have been his in the "white-washed villa," in her "happy, guarded, and most innocent life."

Of course Rochester is not free to tell us the "truth" of his existence, a freedom Rhys permitted even the mad Antoinette. Jane tells his story, blithely and horribly emphasizing his dependent existence: " . . . He cannot now see very distinctly: He cannot read or write much: but he can find his way without being led by the hand: the sky is no longer a blank to him—the earth no longer a void." (XXXVIII). With these words of Jane's, so innocent in Bronte's hands, Christophine's final words to Rochester after he has pronounced his own curse seem to ring mockingly in our ears: " *'Read and write* I don't know. Other things I know.' She walked away without looking back." (*WSS*, p. 162). Truly the Goddess demands horrifying retribution from those who desert her worship!

IV

Jane

The most easily ignored and yet the most significant contribution of Bronte's *Jane Eyre* to Rhys's *Wide Sargasso Sea* lies in the character of Jane herself. For although Rhys can never introduce in her novel this young love of forty-ish Edward Rochester, it is in her that Rhys will culminate her theme—and ultimately, her myth of woman.

Ostensibly, the purpose of Jane would seem to be, if anything at all, simply an implied contrast of types: Antoinette, a hot-blooded young woman of tropical background who succumbs to her heritage and passion, thus reaping the whirlwind of madness; Jane, a "quaint, quiet, grave, and simple" governess whose life has taught her the lessons of "quiet discipline" and whose ultimate happy fate will be to "live entirely for and with what I love best on earth. . . . I am my husband's life as fully as he is mine." (XXXVIII).

Closer scrutiny, however, will deny this antithesis; the similarities will become striking. Both girls, for example, are essentially alone. Jane is an orphan; Antoinette's father is dead and her mother, having rejected Antoinette for the imbecilic son, first goes insane and then dies. Likewise, both Jane and Antoinette know well the meaning of humiliation in a world respecting beauty, wealth, and position. Jane is a "little toad," a "dependent" who "ought to beg"; Antoinette is a "white nigger," a "white cockroach." Antoinette withdraws into nature, knowing that it's "better than people"; Jane finds escape, is "happy at least in my way" reading Bewick's *History of British Birds* with its gothic images of "naked, melancholy isles." Jane, like the hot-blooded Creole Antoinette, is a child of passion, flying into "a picture of passion" at the menacing John Reed and receiving a wound in the head during the episode, just as Antoinette was wounded when the stone thrown by Tia struck her head.

Other similarities emerge. Both girls live in a world where God threatens. "God will punish you," Miss Abbot warns Jane, while Godfrey tells Antoinette that they are "all damned and no use praying." In girlhood, despite the hardships at Lowood, Jane finds love and encouragement in the essentially female environment under Miss Temple's supervision, just as does Antoinette in the convent at Spanish Town. An interesting parallel in the details of this school experience is that Maria Temple, that nourishing maternal figure who becomes Jane's "mother, governess and . . . companion," might well be an incarnation of Antoinette's Sister Marie Augustine who offers what solace and comfort she can in a world in which "the devil must have his day." Of course Maria Temple marries, but a "clergyman" of a distant county—not unlike Sister Marie Augustine who is married to a Christ of a distant heaven.

Perhaps the most important characteristic which Jane and Antoinette share is their need to love and be loved. Antoinette longs to reach out to her mother, values her friendship with Tia, remembers even in her madness her friends at the convent, and needs the love of Rochester so desperately that she longs to die rather than lose his love. Jane, too, knows that death is preferable to loneliness: "If others don't love me, I would rather die than live—I cannot bear to be solitary and hated."

Unfortunately, Antoinette's story essentially ends in the convent. After that, most of the details of her stormy marriage will be unfolded by Rochester—both in Rhys's work and in Bronte's—and hence the truth must always be suspect. Ironically, because fate has provided her with a fortune which makes her an economic asset in the world of the Rochesters and Masons, Antoinette has lost forever any hope of independence, autonomy. She will be sold, literally, into a bondage from which there will be no escape. Having achieved the *sine qua non* of the Victorian woman—money and husband—Antoinette's life is ended. Rhys simply could not make this point about Antoinette's fate with artistic integrity *except* through the similarities of Jane's early circumstances and the *contrast* of her ultimate victory.

For it is in the very fact that Jane is not a marketable commodity that she will be able to triumph. Because she has no money, no family position, her every effort must be expended in survival. Hence, alone and defenseless, she will learn as a child the penalty of undisciplined passion in her horrifying "red room" with its curtains of "deep red damask." At Lowood amidst the privations and hardships, she will learn to mask her feelings, to *appear* a disciplined and subdued character. Here she has placed within her reach "the means of an excellent education" which will give her another tool for survival. Conversely, Antoinette and the girls within the convent—because they are marketable commodities—will be taught to be "ladies," to do needlepoint (*WSS*, p. 54), to be modest, charitable, to have good manners and beautiful nails, since ultimately they will all be courted and "loved by rich and handsome young men."

Thus Rhys shows that, ironically, the *sine qua non* of the Victorian male—money and position—can bring, for women, only slavery. Freedom, then, for woman, is not to be found in beauty, wealth, position or marriage. Only a disciplined, educated, rational, opportunistic woman —who takes advantage of all that fate offers within the scope of her personal integrity and is faithful always to that inner voice which is her gift—can hope to prevail. And prevail Jane does! And it is in that prevailing, that triumph, that Rhys returns us once again, and finally, to the myth that has permeated not only *Wide Sargasso Sea* but is the searching of all her novels.

For in Jane Eyre Rochester, we have emerging the final avatar of the Great Goddess Anna, since "Jane," while translating in the Hebrew as "God's noble gift," in its more ancient form derives from Latin myths associated with "Jana" (Diana), the goddess of the woods and of the moon, who before she became the *wife* of the god, Janus, was the White Goddess, the *mother* of Janue (or Dianus or Jupiter). While the simple fact of Jane's name alone suggests Rhys's theme of the ancient mother goddess demoted from supremacy to, at best a kind of co-existence, we are not left with a mere single allusion to this theme. In fact, the avatars of Anna are numerous in *Jane Eyre*. Helen Burns, for example, translates into "the light" which "burns" and in derivation reminds us of Norah (*ALMM*), Julia's sister who, in the name of duty, cares for the ancient, dying mother. Maria (remember the complicated derivation of "Mary," cf. pp. 78-9) Temple's significance has already been pointed out. Additionally, at Marsh End, Jane will find the old servant Hannah, and the two young, graceful women, Diana and Mary, all variations of the name "Anna". Again, if the name symbology seems specious symbol hunting, remember the archetypal significance of names and Rhys's continuing emphasis of the motif.

Furthermore, there are other details which will strengthen the interpretation of *Jane Eyre* in Rhys's mythic terms. For example, in the episode which occurs the night before her wedding, having presentiments about the "Mrs. Rochester" who would be "born" the following day, Jane seeks the orchard where the old chestnut tree has been cloven by the storm. Lamenting its death and romanticizing its implications, Jane sees the tree, black and riven:

> . . . The cloven halves were not broken from each other, for the firm base and strong roots kept them unsundered below; though community of vitality was destroyed—the sap could flow no more: their great boughs on each side were dead, and the next winter's tempests would be sure to fell one or both to earth: as yet, however, they might be said to form one tree—a ruin, but an entire ruin.
>
> 'You did right to hold fast to each other, ... I think scathed as you look, and charred and scorched, there must be a little sense of life in you yet; rising out of that adhesion

at the faithful, honest roots: you will never have green leaves more . . . the time of pleasure and love is over with you; but you are not desolate: each of you has a comrade to sympathise with him in his decay.' (Chap. XXV)

Thus Bronte, through Jane, seems to indicate that the tree (symbol of life with the male and female principle harmonized, united) sundered as it is, will never again unfold green leaves or provide nesting places for birds who will sing "idyls" in her boughs. Nevertheless it *can* *endure*. Furthermore, the "cloven" halves of the blackened trunk may somehow offer sympathy and consolation to each other in the ruin which now has no center. But in the midst of Jane's sanguine, innocent romanticism,

> . . . the moon appeared momentarily. . . her disk was blood-red and half overcast; she seemed to throw on me one bewildered, dreary glance, and buried herself again instantly in the deep drift of cloud. The wind fell, for a second, round Thornfield; but far away over wood and water, poured a wild, melancholy wail: it was sad to listen to, and I ran off again. (Chap. XXV).

While Bronte's passage may be dismissed as merely gothic, the juxtaposition lends greater significance in the light of Rhys's overall myth of women. The images suggest that the ancient female principle, in the guise of the moon-goddess, knows the barrenness, the grief, if not the impossibility of such fragmented existence. But Jane, rejecting the "wild, melancholy wail" of truth because it is "sad" to listen to, runs off—as Rhys's heroines have consistently fled from "truth" attempting to reveal itself.

But just as truth cannot be denied, so the presentiment of the scene just described is fulfilled in Jane's discovery of Rochester's marriage. Jane, who had been an "ardent, expectant woman—almost a bride" became "a cold, solitary girl," her summer of life blighted by the winter of betrayal. Her faith "blighted," her "confidence destroyed," Jane tries to pray to God "words . . . that should be whispered; but no energy was found to express them: . . . 'there is none to help.' " So in Bronte once more a Rhys theme is repeated: *for Woman there can be no help from the god created by man*. This theme is reinforced subsequently, when rejecting Rochester's passionate and, to her, heart-rending appeal, Jane decides to leave forever the man she loves:

> That night I never thought to sleep; but a slumber fell on me as soon as I lay down in bed. I was transported in thought to the scenes of childhood; I dreamt I lay in the red-room at Gateshead; that the night was dark, and my mind impressed with strange fears. The light that long ago had struck me into syncope, recalled in this vision, seemed glidingly to mount the wall, and tremblingly to look: the roof resolved to clouds, high and dim; the gleam was such as the moon imparts to vapours she is about to sever. I watched her come—watched with the strangest anticipation; as though some word of doom were to be written on her disk. She broke forth as never moon yet burst from cloud; a hand first penetrated the sable folds and waved them away; then, not a moon, but a white human form shone in the azure, inclining a glorious brow earthward. It gazed and gazed and gazed on me. It spoke to my spirit: immeasurably distant was the tone, yet so near, it whispered in my heart—'My daughter, flee temptation!'
>
> 'Mother, I will.' (XXVII)

Like Antoinette, who in her moments of final agony had called for and received help from her ancient of days, Christophine, Jane too, is sustained by a feminine force. In her dream, which releases the unconscious depths, Jane sees and hears the voice of the goddess—a psychological or universal manifestation—and answers: "*Mother*, I will."

Similarly, at Marsh End, on the point of surrendering to the importuning St. John, Jane breathes out:

> 'Show me, show me the path!' I entreated of Heaven. I was excited more than I had ever been. . . .
>
> All the house was still. . . . the room was full of moonlight. My heart beat fast and thick: I heard it throb. . . .
>
> . . . I heard a voice somewhere cry—'Jane! Jane!Jane!' nothing more . . .
>
> 'Oh God! what is it?' I gasped.
>
> I might have said, 'Where is it?' for it did not seem in the room—nor in the house—nor in the garden: it did not

come out of the air—nor from under the earth—nor from overhead. I had heard it—where, or whence, for ever impossible to know! And it was the voice of a human being—a known, loved, well-remembered voice—that of Edward Fairfax Rochester; and it spoke in pain and woe wildly, eerily, urgently.

'I am coming!' I cried. 'Wait for me! Oh, I will come!' I flew to the door, and looked into the passage: it was dark. I ran out into the garden: it was void.

'Where are you?' I exclaimed.

The hills beyond Marsh Glen sent the answer faintly back—'Where are you?' I listened. The wind sighed low in the firs: all was moorland loneliness and midnight hush.

'Down superstition!' I commented, as that spectre rose up black by the black yew at the gate. 'This is not thy deception, nor thy witchcraft: it is the work of nature. She was roused, and did—no miracle—but her best.'

I broke from St. John, who had followed, and would have detained me. It was my time to assume ascendancy. My powers were in play, and in force. I told him to forbear question or remark; I desired him to leave me: I must, and would be alone. He obeyed at once. Where there is energy to command well enough, obedience never fails. I mounted to my chamber; locked myself in; fell on my knees; and prayed in my way—a different way to St. John's, but effective in its own fashion. I seemed to penetrate very near a Mighty Spirit; and my soul rushed out in gratitude at His feet. I rose from the thanksgiving—took a resolve—and lay down, unscared, enlightened—eager but for the daylight.

In this passage, Jane, hearing the voice of her beloved (the underlying "animus" implications of Rochester seem obvious but are incidental to this discussion) responds to her inner urgings—recognizing them as the work of nature which is *feminine* in essence and the source of Jane's new found force—breaks from St. John and, in her own words, *assumes her ascendancy*. This, then, is the day which Sister Marie Augustine foretold when, comforting Antoinette, she said: " 'Soon I will give the signal. Soon will be tomorrow morning.' " (*WSS*, p. 62). Despite her unconscious acceptance of truth, Jane still consciously accepts the masculine deity: "my soul rushed out in gratitude at His feet." Nevertheless, she is aware that she prays in a way different from St. John's and she penetrates near a "Mighty Spirit," which is not necessarily masculine.

This emphasis on the feminine principle as the source of strength and comfort is emphasized repeatedly after Jane departs from Thornfield. For example, set down and alone at Whitcross, Jane recognizes her dependency on the "universal mother":

> Not a tie holds me to human society at this moment—not a charm or hope calls me where my fellow-creatures are—none that saw me would have a kind thought or a good wish for me. I have no relative but the universal mother, Nature: I will seek her breast and ask repose.
> . . . Nature seemed to me benign and good; I thought she loved me, outcast as I was . . . I . . . clung to her with filial fondness. . . . I was her child: my mother would lodge me without money and without price. (XXVIII)

Of course Jane is unaware of the truth she has touched upon. Echoing her religious training and the myths of her Zeitgeist—as Rhys's heroines have echoed theirs—Jane returns verbally to the concept of God the Father, ironically and impossibly the "Source of Life."

In succeeding events, Bronte's details flesh out Rhys's myth. Jane, having faced—as have all the Rhys heroines—the spectre of actual starvation, arrives at Marsh End. Here, "worn to nothing," "thin," "bloodless," "a mere spectre," Jane is succored by Diana of "remarkable countenance. . . . instinct both with power and goodness;" by Mary, "more reserved. . .more distant;" and by Hannah, the reluctant and mistrusting servant. At Moor House, under the auspice of St. John, at once the brother and the master, these avatars of "Anna" harbor for a short time before taking up their roles as governesses and servants in the cruel world of economic survival. Thus, in the three women, harbored and safe though temporarily, Bronte resurrects Rhys's recurring motif of the goddess-gone-underground, in hiding, accommodating herself to the exigencies of time and circumstance. Just as Christophine retires from Granbois to her own little house, just as Sister Marie Augustine bides her time in the convent waiting for the new day to dawn, so Diana, Mary and the aged Hannah (the three faces of the triple-goddess) enjoy the safety at Moor House as temporary respite from the hardships which face them outside their little world.

St. John

It is in the brother, St. John, however, that occurs the greatest reinforcement for Rhys's theme of the goddess dethroned, subordinated, absorbed. The fact that "John" is a masculine variation of "Jane" evokes memory of the mythical process by which the ancient sun-moon-sea-mother goddess, becoming first an adjunct to a god-equal, was finally subjugated as wife and eventually absorbed in masculine essence. This process of progressive absorption is exemplified in various well-known myths such as that of Artemis (Diana) and her twin brother, Apollo, who usurps the role of ruler of the sun, banishing Diana to the darkness of the night in her role as moon-goddess; Hera (Juno) first sister and then wife of Zeus (Jupiter); and most relevant to the Jane-John symbology, the oak-god Janus (John), whose wife Jana (Jane) was originally his mother before he put her under subjection by marrying her.

With these nuances in mind, the significance of St. John to Rhys's myth is unavoidable. *St. John* not only symbolizes the Judeo-Christian triumph over the ancient goddess-worshipping cultures in the most general cultural sense, but in a more specific application, shows how the process was accomplished. For St. John, with his "Greek face," his "straight, classic nose," his reserved, "abstracted," "brooding nature," represents the triumph of asceticism and rationality over the instinctual and excessive which is traditionally associated with goddess worship.[64] As St. John cautions Jane about "yielding to the craving of . . . appetite" in a literal sense, she is aware of an alien quality in this man whose eyes are "difficult to fathom" because he uses them "as instruments to search other people's thoughts" rather than "as agents to reveal his own." (XXIX).

Unconsciously and symbolically acknowledging St. John's power, Jane instinctively chooses as an alias for Eyre (in derivation signifying appropriately either "to journey" or in an older etymology "nature" or "origin") the surname Elliott, meaning "the Lord is God." Nevertheless, hearing herself called Miss Elliott for the first time, Jane will give "an involuntary half-start at the alias," having "forgotten" her "new name," and she will emphasize to St. John: " '. . . it is the name by which I think it expedient to be called at present: but it is not my real name, and when I hear it, it sounds strange to me.' " And when he says: " 'Your real name you will not give?' " she replies, " 'No: I fear discovery above all things; and whatever disclosure would lead to it, I avoid.' " (XXIX). The similarity of this conversation to that of Anna and Joe (*Voyage*, p. 125), with the implication of both conversations for Rhys's theme, attests to the strong link between the two novels and suggests the unprobed depths of *Jane Eyre*.

This linking is further emphasized when we understand how Rhys's theme of the process of goddess absorption is deepened in the subsequent revelation of Jane's legacy and the consequent discovery of a blood relationship between John and Jane. Realizing that they are cousins, that "half our blood on each side flows from the same source," Jane in genuine joy feels that she has "found a brother . . . and two sisters," and determines to share her wealth with her new found family. But John protests that he will be her brother without such sacrifice and suggests that since she now has a dowry, she may want to marry. To which Jane vehemently replies " 'Nonsense again! Marry! I don't want to marry and never shall marry. . . . I know what I feel and how averse are my inclinations to the bare thought of marriage.' " (XXXIII). Upon her insistence that she desires only a brother, John agrees to accept her as his sister.

Later, having set in motion the division of her legacy, Jane sets about the renovation of Moor House, "happy," "jovial . . . amidst the bustle of a house turned topsy-turvy." It is obvious that Jane delights in her domestic skills, her creative restoration of the family home. In other words, Jane accepts her "femininity" as she has accepted her intelligence and her independent nature previously; thus she indicates her integrated female SELF-ness. St. John, however, takes only cursory interest in her accomplishments and denigrates her efforts by asking Jane if she were "at last satisfied with housemaid's work." St. John, like the Victorian men of Rhys's novels, believes that Jane should have "purpose," "ambition in life," beyond "domestic endearments and household joys," even as Jane insists that they are "the best things the world has!"

Curiously, both Bronte and Rhys seem to have realized a truth which, in the light of today's woman's liberation movements, is almost traitorous to breathe. That is that there is great satisfaction, creativity, joy in the nurturing process and that woman has been sold a bill of goods by men—and women—who demand that she find her meaning in life in his terms of competition and strife. Jane herself voices this idea in response to St. John's urgings that she turn "to profit the talents

God has committed to her safe-keeping:'' '' 'St. John,' I said, 'I think you are almost wicked to talk so. I am disposed to be as content as a queen, and you try to stir me up to restlessness! To what end?' '' (XXXIV). To the end, of course, that women abrogate their queenship and absorb themselves in the aspirations conceived by and insisted upon in a masculine world under the aegis of a masculine God. Jane sees this clearly and tells us:

> Now, I did not like this, reader. St. John was a good man; but I began to feel he had spoken truth of himself when he said he was hard and cold. The humanities and amenities of life had no attraction for him—its peaceful enjoyments no charm. Literally, he lived only to aspire—after what was good and great, certainly; but still he would never rest; nor approve of others resting round him. As I looked at his lofty forehead, still as pale as a white stone—at his fine linea- ments fixed in study—I comprehended all at once that he would hardly make a good husband: that it would be a trying thing to be his wife. (XXXIV)

Despite her insight, however, St. John's dominance increases daily over Jane. He takes over her schooling, "a very patient, very for- bearing, and yet an exacting master. . ." Soon he acquires "a certain influence" over her that takes away her "liberty of mind," and she finds that

> his praise and notice were more restraining than his indiffer- ence. I could no longer talk or laugh freely when he was by, because a tiresomely importunate instinct reminded me that vivacity (at least in me) was distasteful to him. I was so fully aware that only serious moods and occupations were accept- able, that in his presence every effort to sustain or follow any other became vain: I fell under a freezing spell. When he said 'go,' I went; 'come,' I came; 'do this,' I did it. But I did not love my servitude. (XXXIV)

And then one evening, at the playful insistence of his sisters, St. John kisses Jane. Remembering that experience ten years after the fact, Jane tells us:

> . . . St. John bent his head; his Greek face was brought to a level with mine, his eyes questioned my eyes piercingly—he kissed me. There are no such things as marble kisses, or ice kisses, or I should say my ecclesiastical cousin's salute belonged to one of these classes; but there may be experiment kisses, and his was an experiment kiss. When given, he viewed me to learn the result; . . . (XXXIV)

How clearly Bronte reveals what many women instinctively sense and what Rhys and at least her character, Anna (cf. pp. 57-8), knew: that man, in what passes with him as love-making, is cold, testing, essentially egocentric and without passion. This is Rhys's theme of the myth-distortion of man who, transferring his own "hard and cold" nature to the warm, passionate woman he fears, creates, in his own image, the "frigid woman" already discussed in terms of Rhys's protagonists. But Jane, as woman has done throughout the ages:

> . . . daily wished more to please him: but to do so, I felt daily more and more that I must disown half my nature, stifle half my faculties, wrest my tastes from their original bent, force myself to the adoption of pursuits for which I had no natural vocation. He wanted to train me to an elevation I could never reach; it racked me hourly to aspire to the standard he up-lifted. The thing was as impossible as to mould my irregular features to his correct and classic pattern, to give to my changeable green eyes the sea-blue tint and solemn lustre of his own. (XXXIV)

Increasingly despondent over her futile attempts to discover news of Rochester, Jane feels St. John's "ascendancy" over her increase and tells us, "I, like a fool, never thought of resisting him—I could not resist him." And it is then, when Jane is in her weakest, most vulnerable state, that St. John attempts the transition from *brother* to *husband*—the process by which Jane will be absorbed and stripped of her feminine essence and identity. As callously and selfishly as Rochester had sought to dominate and absorb Jane in the name of love, so St. John will subdue and absorb her in the name of duty to God:

> '. . . you are formed for labour, not for love. A missionary's wife you must—shall be. You shall be mine: I claim you—not

for my pleasure, but for my Sovereign's service. . . . Think like me, Jane—trust like me. . . . I can set you your task from hour to hour. . . .' (XXXIV)

But Jane resists St. John's powerful persuasion, knowing that if she succumbs to his arguments and marries him, she must "abandon half" herself, that he "has no more of a husband's heart" than does a rock, that in "all the forms of love" his "spirit" would be "quite absent" from her. She does, however, offer to remain his sister. St. John is adamant in the face of her resistance; the absorption in the name of man and his God must be complete, as his urgings to Jane reveal:

'. . . Simplify your complicated interests, feelings, thoughts, wishes, aims; merge all considerations in one purpose: that of fulfilling with effect—with power—the mission of your great Master. To do so, you must have a coadjutor—*not a brother;* that is a loose tie: *but a husband.* I do not want a sister; . . . *I want a wife:* the sole help meet I can influence efficiently in life and *retain absolutely* till death.' (XXXIV. Emphasis added.)

Fortunately Jane is wise enough to understand the portent of these words, to realize that as the wife of this formidable, severe, consuming man she would be

. . . at his side always, and always restrained, and always checked—forced to keep the fire of my nature continually low, to compel it to burn inwardly and never utter a cry, though the imprisoned flame consumed vital after vital—*this* would be unendurable. (XXXIV)

These words of Jane, of course, reflect exactly the penalty that Rhys's Rochester had inflicted upon the young bride whose passionate fire he was driven to extinguish but which, only banked and hidden inwardly, has already—though unknown to Jane—broken forth to consume his very world. Jane, sensing what Antoinette could not, takes "courage," realizes she is "an equal" and maintains her willingness to go with St. John as a fellow-missionary, as an equal, but not as his wife, not as part of him. St. John remains unmoved, insistent upon his own designs:

'It is what I want,' he said, speaking to himself; 'it is just what I want. And there are obstacles in the way: they must be hewn down. . . .

  . . . *it is a long-cherished scheme,* and *the only one which can secure my end.* . . . Refuse to be my wife, and you limit yourself forever to a track of selfish ease and barren obscurity.' (Emphasis added.)

With these ominous words, uttered by a man of "an austere and despotic nature" which had "met resistance where it expected submission," Bronte brings us in full circle to Rhys's theme of mythic dethronement. Woman, the "queen," must be subjugated and, if possible, completely absorbed. If this process is thwarted, if, like Jane, woman scorns this "counterfeit sentiment" of love, then, again like Jane, she must expect neither warmth, nor pity, nor friendship.

Jane, having openly expressed her "scorn" for John and his offer, understands that he will never forget the words she has uttered, that they will always be written "on the air between" them, and "their echo toned" in every word he speaks to her. In Jane's words concerning the subsequent relationship between herself and St. John, Bronte summarizes all the agony that will torture each Rhys heroine in her attempt to accommodate herself to the men who dominate her existence:

  . . . To me, he was in reality become no longer flesh, but marble; his eye was a cold, bright, blue gem; his tongue a speaking instrument—nothing more.

  All this was torture to me—refined, lingering torture. It kept up a slow fire of indignation, and a trembling trouble of grief, which harassed and crushed me altogether. I felt how, if I were his wife, this good man, pure as the deep sunless source, could soon kill me: without drawing from my veins a single drop of blood, or receiving on his own crystal conscience the faintest stain of crime. Especially I felt this when I made any attempt to propitiate him. No ruth met my ruth. *He* experienced no suffering from estrangement—no yearning after reconciliation; and though, more than once, my fast falling tears blistered the page over which we both bent, they produced no more effect on him than if his heart had been really of stone or metal. (XXXV)

How reminiscent is this of Rochester's treatment of Antoinette before he takes her from her island home to imprison her in the cold, dark rooms he has destined for her.

Furthermore, through these words which Bronte has allotted Jane, we are able to recall not only the pain of Rhys's Antoinette and Marya and Anna and Julia and Sasha, but we see the genesis of that masculine hatred which will oppress those sad, tortured, weak, gallant heroines and, by extension, woman in general. Masked as love at best, as indifference or disdain at worst, man's cold hatred of woman derives from his failure to subjugate and destroy. Jane, herself, voices her recognition of this hatred in her final refusal to submit to marriage:

' . . . If I were to marry you, you would kill me. You are killing me now. . . . Now, you will indeed hate me, . . . It is useless to attempt to conciliate you: I see *I have made an eternal enemy of you.*' (XXXV. Emphasis added.)

Understanding all this, the episode in Chapter XXV, wherein the fearful apparition of Bertha rends and tramples the expensive wedding veil Rochester has purchased for Jane, gains added significance. This becomes not the act of poor, mad Bertha symbolically destroying the marriage of her husband to another woman. Rather, this "woman, tall and large, with thick and dark hair hanging down her back," dressed in "gown, sheet, or shroud," whose "savage" face with its "red eyes" and "fearful blackened . . . lineaments" so frightens Jane, is the Great Goddess in her destructive aspect.[65] This is Rhys's goddess who, in the avatar of mad Bertha-Antoinette, has been first submerged and then destroyed in the symbolic act of marriage. Hence the frightful hag rips and tramples the *veil* which symbolizes the subordination and violation of the female-principle. She does not, however, threaten Jane. Thus, once more a seemingly minor detail of Bronte reinforces Rhys's fully developed myth—that of the goddess first subjugated then absorbed by the patriarchal order.

VI

There is one final nuance in connection with St. John and Jane's refusal to marry him that parallels another continuing Rhys theme. That is the emphasis on climate. Jane, in her conviction that she "should not live long in that climate" of India, suggests, in reverse, Antoinette and the other Rhys heroines who shiver and sicken in the alien cold associated with England. In terms of this double emphasis, the seeming trivia synthesizes a truth. For we realize that just as Rhys's emotionally undisciplined and essentially cold heroines could not bear the grey chill of the Anglo-Saxon world, so Jane, disciplined, educated, capable of fiery passion as well as deep, abiding love, knows that she could not long withstand the rigors of a place so alien in climate and morès, even without the unremitting pressures of a St. John. So again we find summarized in Bronte's characters a truth whch Rhys has arrived at in her own passage to maturity: one must, she says, in the final analysis, be true to one's essence. St. John, "cold," without "fervour," "Christian," "patient and placid," without "cheering smile or generous word," may with impunity seek out strange climes. But Jane, aware of the "fire" of her nature, the "imprisoned flame" which could consume her "vital after vital," knows that to go to India, with or without St. John, would be "almost equivalent to committing suicide." Jane, then, will escape the fate of an Antoinette, driven mad by emotional fire unleashed in the heat and fecundity of the tropics. And St. John, unlike the older Rochester who, to his misfortune, had gone whoring after the alien goddess of love in alien places, will never succumb to the fires of passion. As Jane clearly recognizes and forthrightly tells St. John—"the very name of love is an apple of discord" in the Christian's male-centered Eden.

So St. John will remain true to his nature and his God and our last image in *Jane Eyre* will be of this "firm, faithful," "devoted," "stern," "exacting," "warrior" of Christ, whose "glorious sun hastens to its setting." And with this foreboding image of a setting sun, the reader of Rhys's *Wide Sargasso Sea* will recall—almost with a shiver—the quiet, brooding, Sister Marie Augustine abiding the devil's "little day," as she waits for "tomorrow morning." (*WSS*, p. 62).

But before he leaves, alone, for India and this final resolution of his life, St. John will make one last effort to win Jane to his purpose, "all his energy gathered—all his stern zeal woke . . . resolved on conquest." And such is his power that Jane, despite her psychic wholeness, almost succumbs to his appeal to her spiritual nature as she had wavered in the face of Rochester's appeal to the physical:

> I stood motionless under my hierophant's touch. My refusals
> were forgotten—my fears overcome—my wrestlings para-

lysed. The impossible — *i.e.* my marriage with St. John — was fast becoming the Possible. All was changing utterly, with a sudden sweep. Religion called . . . (XXXV)

Then, at the point of surrender, with John's hand upon her head as in an act of consecration, Jane breathes out to "Heaven," " 'Show me, show me the path!' " Jane is saved. "Nature . . . roused . . . did . . . *her* best." (Emphasis added). Jane "assume[s] ascendancy," her "powers . . . in play." Mounting to her chamber "unscared, enlightened — eager but for the daylight (the "tomorrow morning" promised Antoinette by Sister Marie Augustine), Jane waits the dawn when she will find her way to life!

Chapter 7

THE MYTH OF RHYS

It is in this triumph of Jane that Rhys's Myth of Woman is concluded—as it could not fully be in terms of her own doomed characters. Ostensibly Jane's day has dawned! Not, however, before Thornfield— that mythic castle which has always imprisoned the sleeping beauty behind its thorny hedges—has been offered as a burnt sacrifice at the autumnal equinox and its former giant-master, blinded and mutilated, "deep buried in a wood," (XXXVII). There at Ferndean, in a "quite . . . desolate spot"—a setting reminiscent in detail of Antoinette's destroyed Coulibri and of the woods in which the young Rochester (*WSS*, p. 105) found himself lost and afraid before he was rescued by the unsmiling Baptiste—Jane finds her former master, her intended husband, her would-be lover, "desperate and brooding" like some "wronged and fettered wild beast or bird, dangerous to approach in his sullen woe." (How this recalls the strange imagery of Julia's wallpaper in the opening lines of *After Leaving Mr. Mackenzie,* cf. pp. 15-6). In this decaying and forbidding setting, "rich," her "own mistress," Jane can at last offer to the "desolate and abandoned" man—his life, "dark, lonely, hopeless," his "soul athirst and forbidden to drink"— companionship, the "sweetness of . . . consolation." With Rochester now: "there was no harassing restraint, no repressing of glee and vivacity . . . with him I was at perfect ease . . . Delightful consciousness!" (XXXVII).

Thus Bronte seems to arrive at the view Rhys had almost embraced with Sasha in *Good Morning, Midnight.* That is, through the ultimate union of Jane and Rochester, we find suggested the theme that when woman has achieved true SELF-hood, accompanied by financial independence, and when man has been humbled, permitted to see in

195

the midnight of his blindness what he has lost, then each may yield to the other that which will feed the famished spirit and light the bitter dark. In other words—to use the underlying patterns which Rhys has been at pains to develop in such varying ways—when the spirit and the body, the anima and the animus, the unconscious and the conscious, unite within each individual woman and man, balanced, harmonized, then the eternal seekers will find their lost Eden. Or, as Jane says of herself and Rochester, "We entered the wood, and wended homeward."

II

If Bronte's novel had concluded with these final words of Chapter XXXVII, Rhys's myth could have ended, as should all good fairy tales, with "and they lived happily ever after." But consistent with her refusal to yield to the obvious, the timeworn, in her own novels, Rhys forces us to realize, through the fusion of her myth with the details of Bronte's novel, that all is not what it seems at Ferndean. For the final chapter of *Jane Eyre*, pointedly labeled "Conclusion" by Bronte, suggests ambiguities and dilemmas of resolution which we have recognized throughout Rhys's novels. Though Jane has married Rochester and acknowledges herself—ten years after the wedding— "supremely blest," because "no woman was ever nearer to her mate . . . absolutely bone of his bone and flesh of his flesh," there are, nevertheless, ominous undertones to this overt state of felicity, some of which I have touched upon previously.

First of all, there is the unavoidable nuance of narrative focus, so important in each of Rhys's own novels. Everything concerning the details of married life derives from Jane's vision of that reality. Unlike Rhys's Rochester, Bronte does not permit her Rochester direct thought or speech. Blinded, mutilated, completely dependent (cf. pp. 177-8), Rochester's consciousness is never penetrated; he is denied the freedom of revelation permitted even the captive Bertha-Antoinette. We see him with Jane, "ever together," and ever the recipient of her "maternal" care:

> . . . blind the first two years . . . perhaps it was that circum-
> stance that drew us so very near—that knit us so very close!
> . . . Never did I weary of reading to him . . . of conducting

him . . . he claimed these services without painful shame or damping humiliation . . . He loved me so truly that he knew no reluctance in profiting by my attendance . . . .

Anyone aware of the corroding oppression of complete dependency must feel oppressed by Jane's blithe sanguinity. Furthermore, as Jane herself unwittingly—or chillingly—reveals that he often called her "the apple of his eye," we remember that it was the apple in the Garden of Eden which brought about man's death. Add to this Rochester's words—again reported to us by Jane—when she has given him her promise to marry him, crippled and old though he is. Jane says, "To be your wife is, for me, to be as happy as I can be on earth." To which he replies, *"Because you delight in sacrifice."* (Emphasis added). Thus Bronte suggests for us Rhys's goddess, dethroned, who has come into her own as much as is possible; she retains, as it were, the bleeding, living sacrifice of Rochester, which permits her constant maternal care.

In that living sacrifice, that captive recipient of Jane's oppressive care, we are returned to a theme progressively developed in Rhys's novels—the nature of woman as primarily maternal. This maternal nature is reinforced in our last image of Rochester who, recovering a minimum of sight, "can find his way without being led by the hand," and is able to see "when his first-born was put into his arms" that "the boy had inherited his own eyes, *as they once were—large, brilliant,* and *black.*" (Emphasis added).

In the midst of this ambiguity of horror and hope, realizing the triumph of the female-maternal spirit implicit in the birth of Jane's son, we are shocked into recognition of a further ambiguity, seeing clearly that Fate—another recurring emphasis of Rhys—rules Jane as implacably as it has Rochester. For the eternal cycle has begun again. Jane, triumphant, has borne the instrument of her own disaster. She has, mirroring the most ancient myths associated with the Great Goddess, given birth to the new king who must eventually be sacrified or himself become triumphant over his mother. The cycle cannot be stopped; woman and man carry within them the seeds of their own destruction. Each must subject the other or be sacrificed to the needs of the other, literally doomed to a living death as in the case of Rochester or to the death-in-life existence of every Rhys heroine.

And so we are forced to feel for Jane, as we have already done for Rochester, pity and horror in its classic tragic sense. For as surely as

Rochester, this "rock" of man's "fortress" is doomed to his fate, so Jane, that avatar of Anna the Great Goddess, is doomed to hers, finding fulfillment only within the desolation of a Ferndean—with its implicit female connotations—and only with a fettered, crippled mate. Thus there is no triumph, no ultimate hope for man or woman. The cycle continues endlessly. For the heir of Lord Rochester, born with his father's large, brilliant eyes, will not be mutilated, blind, dependent. He will eventually supplant his father, subject his mother, reach out for his own place in the world, a world which will be masculine in its focus.

This new Lord Rochester will become, ironically, the mid-Victorian aristocratic prototype from which Rhys will derive her masculine antagonists for her victimized protagonists. Young Rochester's generation will be that of a W. Neal James, the aristocratic seducer of the young Julia of *After Leaving Mr. Mackenzie.* And as we make the circle from Rochester to W. Neal James, we understand the significance of the latter name in its Teutonic, Celtic, Hebraic derivations (cf. p. 27): Walter the Teutonic "mighty warrior" who overcomes the Celtic "champion" Neal, to be in turn absorbed by the "powerful supplanter" James. Thus Rhys suggests the very process by which the ancient goddess had been dethroned and absorbed in evolving myths, leaving finally the supplanting Hebraic-Christian patriarchal myth triumphant. This triumph is objectified in the final image in *Jane Eyre:* St. John triumphant in his missionary efforts. But paradoxically, and again chillingly, Jane tells us that St. John's "glorious sun hastens to its setting"; his "toil draws near its close!"

With this image of decline in *Jane Eyre* we understand beyond equivocation Rhys's thematic genius. The myth is completed; that passage into maturity which she had begun so painfully in her first novel, *Quartet,* has been accomplished. For as she has done in each of her own novels, Rhys has brought us, in our increased understanding of *Jane Eyre,* once again full circle. We end where we begin and we begin where we should end! Jane's story, the ending of a cycle in which Jane has triumphed, is actually the beginning of another cycle in which man will gain ascendancy. From the ashes of Rochester's world will eventually rise that world now summarized in the term "Victorian"—the lingering hold of which will ensnare the heroines whose stories Rhys will weave. From Jane's happiness will derive the misery of the Maryas and Julias and Annas and Sashas, those later avatars of the ancient mother goddess.

Thus finally, in another ambiguity of beginning and end, Bronte's

Jane Eyre, which preceded Rhys's *Wide Sargasso Sea* by a hundred years, becomes not only the genesis of Rhys's magnificent twentieth-century novel, but is, by virtue of the fresh life and added depth given it by Rhys, actually the latest novel in her own sequential myth. In this curious reversal of beginnings and ends, Rhys's truths—arrived at so painfully during her journey into awareness and her resulting acceptance of SELF—find resolution in the person of Bronte's Jane. In Bronte's Jane is Rhys's almost archetypal woman—woman indepen-dent, freed from internal, cultural, economic pressures so that she stands complete, psychically whole, absolutely in control of that feminine reality which is hers uniquely (symbolically, all that is ascribed to the realm of the unconscious). Yet, ironically, Ferndean is desolate; Jane's husband is recovering his sight, hence moving toward independence; the birth of her son presages the cyclic disaster already detailed.

Chapter 8

CONCLUSION

So, once more, Rhys has ended just where she began. For in *Quartet,* Marya had lain in her room, deserted, defeated, the goddess with a wound in her head, while Zelli, dazed but "extraordinarily relieved," had moved out into the street triumphant, only to be picked up by *"encore une grue"* who will start again the never-ending cycle. In much the same way, Julia, in *After Leaving Mr. Mackenzie,* having taken Mackenzie for a hundred francs, walks out into the night to recommence the ugly cycle, with herself at once the victim and en-snarer. So, too, Anna, in *Voyage in the Dark,* more aware than the previous protagonists of what life is all about, cannot avoid her fate; she lies in bed recovering from her abortion and her brush with death, ready to start "all over again, all over again" the same old cycle of exploiter, exploited, exploiter. Even Sasha (*Good Morning, Midnight*), having found her way out of the dark tunnel of the night, welcomes to her arms the old *commis,* enacting again the everlasting drama of other rooms, in other places, in other times.

This, then, is the entangling seaweed in which Rhys leaves us floating, bound as inextricably as the eternal plankton holds the help-less sailors in currentless tropical seas. There is, we realize, no tri-umph, no ultimate hope. There is no way back to the island home, which may have existed only in dreams. All the gropings after truth and understanding are, in the long run, vain. The psychic journey from west to east, from death to life, from ignorance to understanding, cannot be completed. Those who make that journey must end in madness and death like the unfortunate, innocent Antoinette. The rest of us, sane and alive in the endless cycle, must remain adrift, becalmed. We are engulfed in waters unexpectedly chill in the heat of the day. Male and female, we are ensnared, alien and afraid, in the slimy weeds of the Wide Sargasso Sea!

FOOTNOTES

[1] *The Left Bank* (London: Jonathan Cape, 1927)—a collection of stories; *Postures* (London: Chatto and Windus, 1928); American title *Quartet* (New York: Simon and Schuster, 1929); *After Leaving Mr. Mackenzie* (London: Jonathan Cape; New York: Knopf, 1931); *Voyage in the Dark* (London: Constable, 1934; New York: William Morrow, 1935).

[2] Elgin W. Mellown, "Character and Themes in the Novels of Jean Rhys," *Contemporary Literature* xiii, 4(1972), pp. 458-74.

[3] 1972 *MLA Abstracts,* I, English, Rhys, 7448, p. 127.

[4] (New York: Vintage Books, 1974). All paginations in *Quartet* will be to this paper-back edition, as the one most generally available to the contemporary reader.

[5] For a careful discussion on style, see Thomas F. Staley, "The Emergence of a Form: Style and Consciousness in Jean Rhys's *Quartet,*" *Twentieth Century Literature,* 24(Summer, 1978), pp. 203-24.

[6] It is not my purpose here to undertake an extensive study of the Victorian Zeitgeist. A growing wealth of information is easily available, but for a generalized overview and extensive bibliography concerning aspects of the Victorian reality see *Suffer and Be Still,* ed. Martha Vicinus, (Indiana University Press: Bloomington and London, 1972). See also Selected Bibliography.

[7] In a letter to me dated September 20, 1978, Diana Athill writes: "she told me . . . she [Rhys] started *Quartet* because she was very angry with Ford and wanted to pay him back—though once it got going it took shape, and ended up not quite as she had expected. Obviously on that occasion the conscious mind was the boss, to start with, anyway."

[8] The near-intimacy of Lois and Marya, Marya's fascination with the "gay" life of Paris, and her awareness of "masculine" women have interesting implications.

[9] Rhys's onomastic approach, in essence the magic of naming, is evident in every novel, becoming ultimately fundamental to the focus of her personal myth. This will be discussed later, in detail.

[10] (New York: Vintage Books, 1974). All references will be to this edition as the one most generally available at this time.

[11] See *Bibliography* for selected background readings in Freudian and Jungian concepts. My discussion here is generalized from my own extensive readings in these areas and the literature relevant to such interpretations.

[12] A minor character says in *Quartet:* " 'Le mélange des races est à la base de l'évolution humaine vers le type parfait.' " (p. 33). Rhys's urge to throw off the Anglo-Saxon fairness of skin becomes increasingly obvious in subsequent novels.

[13] Rhys states in an interview with Mary Cantwell, *Mademoiselle,* 79(October, 1974), p. 208, "My son did die. It made a terrible impression on me and I had to bring it in. I think it was Somerset Maugham who said that if you write out a thing, it goes . . . it doesn't trouble you so much. You're left with a vague melancholy, but not utter misery. I suppose it's like psychoanalysis or a Catholic confession."

[14] In the same interview, Rhys acknowledged that Norah was based on her sister who cared for their sick mother and "didn't like her [Rhys]." (pp. 171 & 206).

[15] In an article for *The Times,* 17 May 1975, p. 16, Rhys wrote: "If you've often tried in the past to put yourself to sleep by repeating 'nothing matters, nothing matters at all', it's a relief when few things really do matter any longer. This indifference or calm, whatever you like to call it, is like a cave at the back of the mind where you can retire and be alone and safe. The outside world is very far away."

[16] That Julia remains surrogate for Rhys, reflecting Rhys's unconscious recognition of her own inability to effect change is suggested in a letter to me dated September 1, 1978, in which Diana Athill quotes Rhys's letter to her regarding my interpretation of *Quartet:* " 'But I would like to know what she [Nebeker] makes of the other books. I have often hated Mackenzie and wished I'd never written it. But so it goes.' "

[17] (New York: W.W. Norton, 1968). All references will be to this edition, although a Popular Library paperback edition is now available.

[18] Mary Cantwell, *Mademoiselle,* pp. 208 & 210.

[19] Rhys, Jean (rēs) *Current Biography Yearbook,* 1972, ed. Charles Moritz (New York: H.W. Wilson, 1972-3) pp. 364-5.

[20] Staley, *Jean Rhys: A Critical Study,* p. 8.

[21] The inability of Rhys to understand or to accept the truths she unravels for herself accounts, of course, for the twenty-some years delay in finishing and publishing this work (cf. pp. 43-7).

[22] Louis James, *Jean Rhys: Critical Studies of Caribbean Writers* (London: Longman Group Limited, 1978), pp. 40-1, concludes that Anna actually gives birth to a still-born child, attended by a midwife. I can see no evidence for this. More reasonably, this seems a post-abortion hemorrhage. The doctor is called after the fetus has been expelled, while Anna is unattended.

[23] This plot structure is, of course, implicit in Rhys's writing of the "Diary", a recounting of her experience *after the fact,* following the abortion itself. See my discussion, pages 47-8 and Rhys's chapter, "World's End and a Beginning," (*Smile Please,* 1979). See also Staley, *Jean Rhys. . . .* pp. 58-9 and Louis James, pp. 38-41 for a differing interpretation.

[24] Staley, *Jean Rhys . . .,* p. 4, writes: "One day in Paris in the 1920s she went into Sylvia Beach's Shakespeare and Co and found a book on psychoanalysis, but to her the man who wrote it was surely wrong. She hoped then that someday a man would write about women fairly—an unfulfilled hope which provided her with another impulse to write."

[25] In the *Mademoiselle* article, Rhys, when asked what she read, answered, " 'Contemporary French novels—I've forgotten their names. And I loved Maupassant, Anatole France, Flaubert. . . . I think French books helped me an awful lot [with form and precision]. They had clarity. Ford insisted—if you weren't sure of a paragraph or statement, translate it into another language. And if it looks utterly silly, get rid of it.' "

[26] Curiously, while female sexual rejection of man is referred to as "symbolic castration," there is no equivalent term of any nature for the male's rejection of a woman's sexuality.

[27] Rhys attests to her basic sexual inhibitions, inhibitions existing even in old age, when in her autobiography (*Smile Please,* 1979) in a chapter entitled, "Facts of Life," she writes of going into her doctor-father's consulting room and happening upon "several diagrams of a woman having a baby. I was so horrified that I shut the book, put it back and avoided going into his consulting-room again. As to the diagrams, I didn't believe them. Impossible." In the next paragraph, she writes of her dog Rex, having a "love affair while. . . taking him for a walk. . . . I watched, horrified, and must have shown my horror because several passers-by laughed at me. I managed not to cry in the street but as soon

as I got home I burst into tears.'' Her mother, she tells us, comforted her but did not enlighten her. Then, Rhys writes, ''After this I shut away at the back of my mind any sexual experiences, *for of course some occurred,* [italics added], not knowing that this would cause me to remember them in detail all the rest of my life. I became very good at blotting things out, refusing to think about them.''

[28] Psychoanalysts verify that many uninstructed young women believe the onset of menstruation to be punishment for sexual activity.

[29] See Staley, *Jean Rhys . . .,* p. 65, and James, p. 39, for differing but congruent interpretations of this episode.

[30] In the *Mademoiselle* interview, Cantwell says, '' '. . . You must have equated happiness with men,' '' and Rhys replies, '' 'Oh, no, no. But . . .I'm not sure whether men need women, but I'm perfectly sure women need men.' ''

[31] Robert Graves, *The White Goddess* (New York: Farrar, Strauss and Giroux, 1972), pp. 370-71; Alexander Macbain, *Celtic Mythology and Religion* (Edinburgh: Eneas Mackay, 1917), p.128; Charles Squire, *Celtic Myth and Legend, Poetry and Romance* (London: Gresham Publishing Co., Ltd., 1910) pp. 50-7.

[32] Squire, *Celtic Myth . . . .* p. 50.

[33] See Will Durant, *The Story of Civilization: Our Oriental Heritage,* Chapters VI - XII, for other myths of the Great Mother, i.e., Isis, Kali, Demeter, Ceres, Ma, Cybel and of goddess worship in general. Also see his *The Life of Greece.*

[34] Durant, *Our Oriental Heritage,* p. 235.

[35] Squire, *Celtic Myth . . . .* p. 51.

[36] There are many legends which suggest this banishing of the evil woman-goddess to the bottom of the sea. Interestingly, Charles Guyot published in 1926 in Paris his *La légende de la ville d'Ys,* a work based upon such a body of Gaelic legend. It is possible that Rhys, in Paris and reading extensively in the French literature of the day, might have been familiar with this story deriving from ancient texts of Dahut who, flouting Christian morality, indulging in pagan ritual and revelry, is sunk with her city, Ys, to the bottom of the ocean. Dahut embodies the many manifestations of the evil siren who gives herself to the devil and becomes the seducer, temptress, betrayer, doom of man.

[37] The Celtic-Gaelic myths of an afterlife in some paradisiacal isle in the West, the ''Happy Isles'' in the country of the setting sun (or possibly a land under Western waves) are numerous. See Macbain, Rhys, Squire, *Mabinogion,* etc.

[38] I cite Graves as an easily available source although other references are found in Macbain, Squire, Durant, Frazer, and numerous mythology references. Tree lore is a complex study and is, indeed, central in Gaelic bardic tradition, as for example, the ancient Welsh myth of *Câd Goddeu, The Battle of the Trees,* wherein the forces of Amaethon and Arawn clash over a white roebuck and a whelp stolen by Arawn, supposedly king of Hell. Interestingly, the battle is won when Gywdion is able to guess a *hidden name* of an opponent, thus subduing and controlling the forces of Arawn.

Groves were, of course, ancient seats of worship with special trees being of particular significance to various goddesses and gods. Note also how, from earliest time, as cities were conquered by invaders, the local god-images and temples, *along with the temple groves,* were irrevocably destroyed.

[39] Macbain, Squire. For a readable synthesization of the process of religious encroachment upon the Celtic theogonies, see Deirdre Cavanagh's translation of Charles Guyot's *The Legend of the City of Ys,* (Amherst: University of Massachusetts Press, 1979). The Notes to Maria Tmyoczko's "Introduction" contain excellent reference material for those seriously interested in the religious evolution of this legend. This work has become available only as I complete the final annotations.

[40] Both Marya (Hebrew for "bitter") and Julia (Juliana) derive from mutations associated with the Celtic "Ana".

[41] Rhys attests to her own lack of guilt over an abortion in *Smile Please,* p. 118: "After what was then called an illegal operation, . . . I didn't suffer from remorse or guilt. I didn't think at all like women are supposed to think, my predominant feeling was one of intense relief, but I was very tired. I was not at all unhappy. It was like a pause in my life, a peaceful time. . ."

[42] Ironically, Frazer (Sir J.G., *Adonis, Attis, Osiris.* London, 1907) notes that the virgin-goddess Nana conceived a son, Atys, by placing a pomegranate between her breasts. This son, beloved by Cybele (the mother-goddess and another form of Nana-Ana) was forced to emasculate himself in her honor.

[43] (New York: Vintage Books, 1974). All references will be to this edition as generally available.

[44] Mellow (p. 467) obviously confuses the Russian, Nicholas Delmar, with René, who says he is a French-Canadian, although Sasha insults him by saying he is Spanish or Spanish-American.

[45] Louis James, p. 29, it seems to me, completely misinterprets this episode. There is no indication that the rape is concluded, that René leaves Sasha "bleeding and hurt." The fact is that she stops him in the very act—and he leaves in disdain. Furthermore, although she wills him to come back, it is not René she sees standing over her bed as James says, but the old *commis*, in the white dressing gown, and it is he whom she pulls to her bed.

[46] Jean Rhys, *Wide Sargasso Sea* (New York: Popular Library, 1966). Introduction by Francis Wyndham, p. 9. This reference cited as presently most generally available.

[47] *Ibid.*, p. 10.

[48] Joseph L. Henderson, "Ancient Myths and Modern Man," *Man and His Symbols* (New York: Dell Publishing Co., 1972), p. 124, emphasis added.

[49] *Ulysses* was published in 1922 and there is no reason to believe that Rhys, knowing as she did the world of Montparnasse and Bloomsbury and participating in its artistic life, would not have been familiar with this literary milestone.

[50] *Wide Sargasso Sea,* "Introduction," p. 9.

[51] Paul Piazza, "The World of Jean Rhys," *The Chronicle of Higher Education,* March 7, 1977, p. 19.

[52] Interestingly enough, the ancient dress of the Druidic bard was pure white, "the proud white garment which separated the elders from the youth." Sir John Daniel, *The Philosophy of Ancient Britain* (London: William and Norgate, Ltd., 1927), p. 84.

[53] She can also re-evoke the mythic theme since Aphrodite, originally a mother goddess, and Hermes, at once messenger or herald of the gods and a Jungian symbol of Transcendence, conceived as offspring a delicate hermaphrodite, hence the name. Paradoxically, however, they also conceived, according to some ancient accounts, Priapus, God of Fertility. Aphrodite and her grotesque son, Priapus, were also the protectors of seafarers, goddess and god of the sea and the wind. This offers interesting implications for Anna's (*Voyage*) dream concerning this misshapen child carried in the coffin (cf. 71-73).

[54] The ambiguity cannot be reconciled even in terms of Rhys's life. For although she seems to have found some peace and contentment, particularly after her third marriage, leading her quiet life in Devonshire, her final days were unhappy. Diana Athill wrote me in a letter dated June 8, 1979, following Jean's death in May: "As often happens with very old people, it was not the actual death that was

distressing, but the crushing that life gave her in the last year, before the end. She was very miserable, totally unreconciled to old age, quite rapidly being reduced to nothing but fretfulness and distrust—that was terribly sad. After the fall which finally led to her death it actually became a little better, for the last three weeks—in that she had a series of small strokes so that her awareness became greatly diminished. Her actual death was very quiet—she just stopped breathing."

[55] (New York: Popular Library, 1966). Edition most generally available.

[56] See Rhys, *Smile Please*, pp. 19-94; James, pp. 45-62; Staley, pp. 100-20 for the explicit influence of Rhys's family history and childhood experiences upon the art of *Wide Sargasso Sea*.

[57] James notes that " 'Christophine' is the name of a vegetable in the Antilles; it would appear to be unusual as a girl's name. Like Antoinette and Tia, she comes to Jamaica as a stranger." (p. 63, #18).

[58] Rhys (*Smile Please*, p. 51), writing of her envy of the blacks, says: "Also there wasn't for them, as there was for us, what I thought of as the worry of getting married. . . . Black girls . . . seemed to be perfectly free. Children swarmed but negro marriages that I knew of were comparatively rare. Marriage didn't seem a duty with them as it was with us."

[59] James, writing from the framework of the West Indian culture with its complex racial conflicts, sees these images as "expressing all the terror of an unnatural union of black and white." (p. 55). His thesis that the conflicts of *Wide Sargasso Sea* emerge from the "trauma of history," rooted in generations of "accumulated hatred" between the races is perfectly justifiable. Rhys's use of this historical racial tension for her own purpose, the further piling of level of meaning upon level of meaning, is further evidence of her intuitive if not conscious genius. This is, after all, the essence of mythmaking.

[60] Rhys indicates the validity of this interpretation in her comment that ". . . Grace Poole, the nurse in *Wide Sargasso Sea*, . . . [got] more important than I intended. It happened beyond my will. . . ." (*Mademoiselle*, October, 1974), p. 208.

[61] Charlotte Bronte, *Jane Eyre*, ed. Richard J. Dunn, (New York: W.W. Norton & Co., Inc., 1971). This edition is based upon the third edition published in 1848—the last edition personally corrected by Charlotte Bronte. Chapters are cited for the convenience of readers using other editions.

[62] For an overview of this concept, see Helene Moglen, *Charlotte Bronte: The Self Conceived* (New York: W.W. Norton & Company, Inc., 1976), pp. 141-45.

[63] *Ibid.*, p. 141, footnote 25.

[64] Interestingly, the Midsummer Festival celebrating the summer solstice—a major Celtic and Teutonic time of worship—was Christianized into St. John's Eve and Day. (Macbain, p. 167).

[65] A 4th century A.D. mosaic, discovered in the Yorkshire Cotswolds and now housed in the Yorkshire Kingston-upon-Hull Museum, depicts a big-bellied, wild-haired, eye-reddened, naked Venus. Called the "Rudston Venus," this figure might well have served as the prototype of Bronte's description of the vengeful madwoman, had it not been discovered as late as 1933.

SELECTED BIBLIOGRAPHY

Primary Texts

Bronte, Charlotte. *Jane Eyre*. Ed. Richard J. Dunn. W.W. Norton Critical Edition, 1971.

Rhys, Jean. *After Leaving Mr. Mackenzie*. New York: Vintage Books, 1974.

_____. *Good Morning, Midnight*. New York: Random House, Vintage Books, 1974.

_____. *Quartet*. New York: Vintage Books, 1974.

_____. *Smile Please: an unfinished autobiography*. London: Andre Deutsch, 1979.

_____. *Voyage in the Dark*. New York: W.W. Norton, 1968.

_____. *Wide Sargasso Sea*. New York: Popular Library, 1966.

Secondary Sources

Allen, Walter. "Bertha the Doomed." *New York Times Book Review*, June 18, 1967, p. 5.

Cantwell, Mary. "A Conversation with Jean Rhys." *Mademoiselle*, 79(October, 1974) pp. 170-71 + 206, 208, 210, 213.

Cavanagh, Deirdre. *The Legend of the City of Ys:* a translation of Charles Guyot's version. Amherst: University of Massachusetts Press, 1979.

Daniel, Sir John. *The Philosophy of Ancient Britain*. London: William and Norgate, Ltd., 1927.

Durant, Will. *The Story of Civilization: Our Oriental Heritage*. New York: Simon and Schuster, 1954.

_____. _____: *The Life of Greece*. New York: Simon and Schuster, 1939.

Graves, Robert. *The White Goddess*. New York: Farrar, Straus and Giroux, 1972.

Henderson, Joseph L. "Ancient Myths and Modern Man." *Man and His Symbols*. New York: Dell Publishing Co., 1972.

James, Louis. *Jean Rhys: Critical Studies of Caribbean Writers*. London: Longman Group Limited, 1979. (Contains Selected Bibliography.)

Kersh, Gerald. "The Second Time Around." *Saturday Review*, July 1, 1967, p. 23.

Macbain, Alexander. *Celtic Mythology and Religion*. Edinburgh: Eneas Mackay, 1917.

Mellown, Elgin W. "Character and Themes in the Novels of Jean Rhys." *Contemporary Literature*, xiii, 4(1972), pp. 458-74.

Moglen, Helene C. *Charlotte Bronte: The Self Conceived*. New York: W.W. Norton and Co., Inc., 1976.

Piazza, Paul. "The World of Jean Rhys." *The Chronicle of Higher Education*, March 7, 1977, p. 19.

Squire, Charles. *Celtic Myth and Legend, Poetry and Romance*. London: Gresham Publishing Co., Ltd., 1910.

Staley, Thomas. "The Emergence of a Form: Style and Consciousness in Jean Rhys's *Quartet.*" *Twentieth Century Literature*, 24(Summer, 1978) pp. 203-24.

_____. *Jean Rhys: A Critical Study*. Austin, Texas: University of Texas Press, 1979. (Contains Selected Bibliography.)

Thurman, Judith. "The Mistress and the Mask: Jean Rhys's Fiction." *Ms.*, Vol 4, #7 (January, 1976), pp. 50-3, 81.

Vicinus, Martha. ed. *Suffer and Be Still: Women in the Victorian Age*. Bloomington, Indiana: Indiana University Press, 1972.

Wyndham, Francis, "Introduction." *Wide Sargasso Sea*. New York: Popular Library, 1966.

General Background

Chase, Richard. *Quest for Myth*. Baton Rouge: Louisiana State University Press, 1946.

Cirlot, J.E. *A Dictionary of Symbols*. Tr. by Jack Sage, Foreword by Herbert Read. New York: Philosophical Library, 1974.

Fiedler, Leslie. "Archetype and Signature." *Sewanee Review*, LX 2(Spring 1952).

Frazer, Sir James G. *The Golden Bough*. London: Macmillan, 1907-15.
_____. *Adonis, Attis, Osiris*. London: 1907.

Freud, Sigmund. *A General Introduction to Psychoanalysis*. Tr. by Joan Riviere. New York: Perma Books, 1953.

Frye, Northrup. *Anatomy of Criticism*. Princeton: Princeton University Press, 1957.

Gayley, Charles Mills. *Classic Myths*. New York: Ginn and Co., 1939.

Grigson, Geoffrey. *The Goddess of Love*. New York: Stein and Day, 1976.

Guyot, Charles. *La legende de la ville d'Ys, d'apres les anciens texte*. Paris: H. Piazza, 1926.

Hays, H.R. *The Dangerous Sex: The Myth of Feminine Evil*. New York: Putnam, 1964.

Heilbrun, Carolyn G. *Toward a Recognition of Androgyny*. New York: Harper and Row, 1973.

Homer. *The Odyssey*. Tr. by Robert Fitzgerald. New York: Doubleday and Co., Inc. An Anchor Book edition, 1963.

Houghton, Walter E. *The Victorian Frame of Mind, 1830-1870*. New Haven: Yale University Press, 1957.

Hunt, Morton M. *the Natural History of Love*. New York: Alfred Knopf, 1959.

James, E.O. *The Cult of the Mother Goddess*. London: Thames and Hudson, 1959.

_____. *The Ancient Gods*. New York: Putnam, 1964.

Jung, Carl G. *The Archetypes and the Collective Unconscious*. Tr. by R.F.C. Hull. Princeton University Press, 1975.

Kerényi, Károly. *Zeus and Hera: Archetypal Image of Father, Husband, and Wife*. Translated by Christopher Holme. Princeton (Bollingen Series LXV .5) and London, 1975.

Mabiogion, The. Tr. by Lady Charlotte Guest. New York: E.P. Dutton and Co., 1913.

Man and His Symbols. Eds. Carl G. Jung and M.L. von Franz. New York: Dell Publishing Co., 1964.

Markale, Jean. *Women of the Celts*. Tr. by A. Mygind, C. Hauck and P. Henry. London: Gordon Cremonesi Publishers, 1975.

Rhys, John. "The Hibbert Lectures for 1886." Lectures on the Origin and Growth of Religion as Illustrated by Celtic Heatnendom. London: 1898.

_____. Studies in Arthurian Legend. Oxford, 1901.

Wingfield-Stratford. *Those Earnest Victorians*. New York: Wm. Morrow & Co., 1930.

Selected Biographical Sources

Contemporary Authors, ed. Carolyn Riley, Vol. 25-28. (Detroit: Gale Research Co., 1971), p. 608.

Contemporary Novelists, ed. James Vinson. 2d ed. (London: St. James Press, c. 1976), pp. 1162-5.

Current Biography Yearbook, 1972, ed. Charles Moritz (New York: H.W. Wilson, 1972-3), pp. 364-7.

International Authors and Writers Who's Who, ed. Ernest Kay, 7th ed. (Cambridge, England: Melrose Press, 1976), p. 500.

Jones, Joseph and Johanna Jones. *Authors and Areas of the West Indies.* No. 2 in series: *People and Places in World-English Literature.* (Austin, Tex: Steck-Vaughn Company, c. 1970), pp. 54-5.

Murray, B.J. and Reynolds, R.C. "A Bibliography of Jean Rhys," *Bulletin of Bibliography,* XXXVI (Oct-Dec 1979), pp. 177-84.

Who's Who 1978 (London: Adam and Charles Black), p. 2056.

The Writers Directory 1976-78. ed. Nancy E. Duin. London: St. James Press; New York: St. Martin's Press, c. 1976, p. 891.

INDEX

(For references to characters, see individual novels, alphabetized.)

ABOUT THE AUTHOR

Helen Nebeker

Helen E. Nebeker is Professor of English and assistant departmental chair at Arizona State University, Tempe. Specializing in contemporary British and American literature, Professor Nebeker has published articles on the works of James Joyce, Katherine Mansfield, Shirley Jackson, Jean Rhys, William Faulkner, as well as on those of nineteenth-century Matthew Arnold and Mark Twain. Her studies have appeared in numerous journals, including *American Literature, Studies in Short Fiction, Modern Fiction Studies, Renascence,* and the *International Journal of Women's Studies.* Professor Nebeker and her husband live in Phoenix, near their family of a son and a daughter, three grandsons, and a granddaughter, Sabrina, to whom this book is dedicated.